Mastering Parallel Programming with R

Master the robust features of R parallel programming to accelerate your data science computations

Simon R. Chapple
Eilidh Troup
Thorsten Forster
Terence Sloan

BIRMINGHAM - MUMBAI

Mastering Parallel Programming with R

First published: May 2016

Production reference: 1240516

Published by Packt Publishing Ltd.
Livery Place
35 Livery Street
Birmingham B3 2PB, UK.

ISBN 978-1-78439-400-4

www.packtpub.com

Credits

Authors
Simon R. Chapple
Eilidh Troup
Thorsten Forster
Terence Sloan

Reviewers
Steven Paul Sanderson II
Joseph McKavanagh
Willem Ligtenberg

Commissioning Editor
Kunal Parikh

Acquisition Editor
Subho Gupta

Content Development Editor
Siddhesh Salvi

Technical Editor
Kunal Chaudhari

Copy Editor
Shruti Iyer

Project Coordinator
Nidhi Joshi

Proofreader
Safis Editing

Indexer
Mariammal Chettiyar

Graphics
Abhinash Sahu

Production Coordinator
Melwyn Dsa

Cover Work
Melwyn Dsa

About the Authors

Simon R. Chapple is a highly experienced solution architect and lead software engineer with more than 25 years of developing innovative solutions and applications in data analysis and healthcare informatics. He is also an expert in supercomputer HPC and big data processing.

Simon is the chief technology officer and a managing partner of Datalytics Technology Ltd, where he leads a team building the next generation of a large scale data analysis platform, based on a customizable set of high performance tools, frameworks, and systems, which enables the entire life cycle of data processing for real-time analytics from capture through analysis to presentation, to be encapsulated for easy deployment into any existing operational IT environment.

Previously, he was director of Product Innovation at Aridhia Informatics, where he built a number of novel systems for healthcare providers in Scotland, including a unified patient pathway tracking system that utilized ten separate data system integrations for both 18-weeks Referral To Treatment and cancer patient management (enabling the provider to deliver best performance on patient waiting times in Scotland). He also built a unique real-time chemotherapy patient mobile-based public cloud-hosted monitoring system undergoing clinical trial in Australia, which is highly praised by nurses and patients, "its like having a nurse in your living room… hopefully all chemo patients will one day know the security and comfort of having an around-the-clock angel of their own."

Simon is also a coauthor of the `ROpenCL` open source package—enabling statistics programs written in R to exploit the parallel computation within graphics accelerator chips.

I would particularly like to thank my fellow authors at Edinburgh Parallel Computing Centre for the SPRINT chapter, and the book reviewers, Willem Ligtenberg, Joe McKavanagh, and Steven Sanderson, for their diligent feedback in the preparation of this book. I would also like to thank the editorial team at Packt for their unending patience in getting this book over the finish line, and my wife and son for their understanding in allowing me to steal precious time away from them to be an author - it is to my loved ones, Heather and Adam, that I dedicate this book.

Eilidh Troup is an Applications Consultant employed by EPCC at the University of Edinburgh. She has a degree in Genetics from the University of Glasgow and she now focuses on making high-performance computing accessible to a wider range of users, in particular biologists. Eilidh works on a variety of software projects, including the Simple Parallel R INTerface (SPRINT) and the SEEK for Science web-based data repository.

Thorsten Forster is a data science researcher at University of Edinburgh. With a background in statistics and computer science, he has obtained a PhD in biomedical sciences and has over 10 years of experience in this interdisciplinary research.

Conducting research on the data analysis approach to biomedical big data rooted in statistics and machine learning (such as microarrays and next-generation sequencing), Thorsten has been a project manager on the SPRINT project, which is targeted at allowing lay users to make use of parallelized analysis solutions for large biological datasets within the R statistical programming language. He is also a co-founder of Fios Genomics Ltd, a university spun-out company providing biomedical big data research with data-analytical services.

Thorsten's current work includes devising a gene transcription classifier for the diagnosis of bacterial infections in newborn babies, transcriptional profiling of interferon gamma activation of macrophages, investigating the role of cholesterol in immune responses to infections, and investigating the genomic factors that cause childhood wheezing to progress to asthma.

Thorsten's complete profile is available at `http://tinyurl.com/ThorstenForster-UEDIN`.

Terence Sloan is a software development group manager at EPCC, the High Performance Computing Centre at the University of Edinburgh. He has more than 25 years of experience in managing and participating in data science and HPC projects with Scottish SMEs, UK corporations, and European and global collaborations.

Terry, was the co-principal investigator on the Wellcome Trust (Award no. 086696/Z/08/Z), the BBSRC (Award no. BB/J019283/1), and the three EPSRC-distributed computational science awards that have helped develop the SPRINT package for R. He has also held awards from the ESRC (Award nos. RES-189-25-0066, RES-149-25-0005) that investigated the use of operational big data for customer behavior analysis.

Terry is a coordinator for the Data Analytics with HPC, Project Preparation, and Dissertation courses on the University of Edinburgh's MSc programme, in HPC with Data Science.

He also plays the drums.

I would like to thank Dr. Alan Simpson, EPCC's technical director and the computational science and engineering director for the ARCHER supercomputer, for supporting the development of SPRINT and its use on UK's national supercomputers.

About the Reviewers

Steven Paul Sanderson II is currently in the last year of his MPH (Masters in Public Health Program) at Stony Brook University School of Medicine's Graduate Program in Public Health. He has a decade of experience in working in an acute care hospital setting. Steven is an active user of the StackExchange sites, and his aim is to self-learn several topics, including SQL, R, VB, and Python.

He is currently employed as a decision support analyst III, supporting both financial and clinical programs.

He has had the privilege to work on other titles from Packt Publishing, including, *Gephi Cookbook* by Devangana Khokhar, *Network Graph Analysis and Visualization with Gephi*, and *Mastering Gephi Network Visualization*, both by Ken Cherven. He has also coauthored a book with former professor Phillip Baldwin, called *The Pleistocene Re-Wilding of Johnny Paycheck*, which can be found as a self-published book at `http://www.lulu.com/shop/phillip-baldwin/the-pleistocene-re-wilding-of-johnny-paycheck/paperback/product-21204148.html`.

I would like to thank my parents for always pushing me to try new things and continue learning. I'd like to thank my wife for being my support system. I would also like to thank Nidhi Joshi at Packt Publishing for continuing to keep me involved in the learning process by keeping me in the review process of new and interesting books.

Willem Ligtenberg first started using R at Eindhoven University of Technology for his master's thesis in biomedical engineering. At this time, he used R from Python through Rpy. Although not a true computer scientist, Willem found himself attracted to distributed computing (the bioinformatics field often requires this) by first using a computer cluster of the Computational Biology group. Reading interesting articles on GPGPU computing, he convinced his professor to buy a high-end graphics card for initial experimentation.

Willem currently works as a bioinformatics/statistics consultant at Open Analytics and has a passion for speed enhancement through either Rcpp or OpenCL. He developed the `ROpenCL` package, which he first presented at UseR! 2011. The RopenCL package will be used later in this book. Willem also teaches parallel computing in R (using both the GPU and CPU). Another interest of his is in how to optimally use databases in workflows, and from this followed another R package (Rango) that he presented at UseR! 2015. Rango allows R users to interact with databases using S4 objects and abstracts differences between various database backends, allowing users to focus on what they want to achieve.

Joseph McKavanagh is a divisional CTO in Kainos and is responsible for technology strategy and leadership. He works with customers in the public and private sectors to deliver and support high-impact digital transformation and managed cloud and big data solutions. Joseph has delivered Digital Transformation projects for central and regional UK governments and spent 18 months as a transformation architect in Government Digital Service, helping to deliver the GDS Exemplar programme. He has an LLB degree in law and accountancy and a master's degree in computer science and applications, both from Queen's University, Belfast.

Table of Contents

Preface

We are in the midst of an information explosion. Everything in our lives is becoming instrumented and connected in real-time with the Internet of Things, from our own biology to the world's environment. By some measures, it is projected that by 2020, world data will have grown by more than a factor of 10 from today to a staggering 44 Zettabytes—just one Zettabyte is the equivalent of 250 billion DVDs. In order to process this volume and velocity of big data, we need to harness a vast amount of compute, memory, and disk resources, and to do this, we need parallelism.

Despite its age, R—the open source statistical programming language, continues to grow in popularity as one of the key cornerstone technologies to analyze data, and is used by an ever-expanding community of, dare I say the currently in-vogue designation of, "data scientists".

There are of course many other tools that a data scientist may deploy in taming the beast of big data. You may also be a Python, SAS, SPSS, or MATLAB guru. However, R, with its long open source heritage since 1997, remains pervasive, and with the extraordinarily wide variety of additional CRAN-hosted plug-in library packages that were developed over the intervening 20 years, it is highly capable of almost all forms of data analysis, from small numeric matrices to very large symbolic datasets, such as bio-molecular DNA. Indeed, I am tempted to go as far as to suggest that R is becoming the *de facto* data science scripting language, which is capable of orchestrating highly complex analytics pipelines that involve many different types of data.

R, in itself, has always been a single-threaded implementation, and it is not designed to exploit parallelism within its own language primitives. Instead, it relies on specifically implemented external package libraries to achieve this for certain accelerated functions and to enable the use of parallel processing frameworks. We will focus on a select number of these that represent the best implementations that are available today to develop parallel algorithms across a range of technologies.

In this book, we will cover many different aspects of parallelism, from Single Program Multiple Data (SPMD) to Single Instruction Multiple Data (SIMD) vector processing, including utilizing R's built-in multicore capabilities with its `parallel` package, message passing using the Message Passing Interface (MPI) standard, and General Purpose GPU (GPGPU)-based parallelism with OpenCL. We will also explore different framework approaches to parallelism, from load balancing through task farming to spatial processing with grids. We will touch on more general purpose batch-data processing in the cloud with Hadoop and (as a bonus) the hot new tech in cluster computing, Apache Spark, which is much better suited to real-time data processing at scale.

We will even explore how to use a real bona fide multi-million pound supercomputer. Yes, I know that you may not own one of these, but in this book, we'll show you what its like to use one and how much performance parallelism can achieve. Who knows, with your new found knowledge, maybe you can rock up at your local Supercomputer Center and convince them to let you spin up some massively parallel computing!

All of the coding examples that are presented in this book are original work and have been chosen partly so as not to duplicate the kind of example you might otherwise encounter in other books of this nature. They are also chosen to hopefully engage you, dear reader, with something a little bit different to the run-of-the-mill. We, the authors, very much hope you enjoy the journey that you are about to undertake through *Mastering Parallel Programming in R*.

What this book covers

Chapter 1, Simple Parallelism with R, starts our journey by quickly showing you how to exploit the multicore processing capability of your own laptop using core R's parallelized versions of `lapply()`. We also briefly reach out and touch the immense computing capacity of the cloud through Amazon Web Services.

Chapter 2, Introduction to Message Passing, covers the standard Message Passing Interface (MPI), which is a key technology that implements advanced parallel algorithms. In this chapter, you will learn how to use two different R MPI packages, `Rmpi` and `pbdMPI`, together with the OpenMPI implementation of the underlying communications subsystem.

Chapter 3, Advanced Message Passing, will complete our tour of MPI by developing a detailed `Rmpi` worked example, illustrating the use of nonblocking communications and localized patterns of interprocess message exchange, which is required to implement spatial Grid parallelism.

Chapter 4, Developing SPRINT, an MPI-based R Package for Supercomputers, introduces you to the experience of running parallel code on a real supercomputer. This chapter also provides a detailed exposition of developing `SPRINT`, an R package written in C for parallel computation that can run on laptops, as well as supercomputers. We'll also show you how you can extend this package with your own natively-coded high performance parallel algorithms and make them accessible to R.

Chapter 5, The Supercomputer in Your Laptop, will show how to unlock the massive parallel and vector processing capability of the Graphics Processing Unit (GPU) inside your very own laptop direct from R using the `ROpenCL` package, an R wrapper for the Open Computing Language (OpenCL).

Chapter 6, The Art of Parallel Programming, concludes this book by providing the basic science behind parallel programming and its performance, the art of best practice by highlighting a number of potential pitfalls you'll want to avoid, and taking a glimpse into the future of parallel computing systems.

Online Chapter, Apache Spa-R-k, is an introduction to Apache Spark, which now succeeds Hadoop as the most popular distributed memory big data parallel computing environment. You will learn how to setup and install a Spark cluster and how to utilize Spark's own DataFrame abstraction direct from R. This chapter can be downloaded from Packt's website at `https://www.packtpub.com/sites/default/files/downloads/B03974_BonusChapter.pdf`

You don't need to read this book in order from beginning to end, although you will find this easiest with respect to the introduction of concepts, and the increasing technical depth of programming knowledge applied. For the most part, each chapter has been written to be understandable when read on it's own.

What you need for this book

To run the code in this book, you will require a multicore modern specification laptop or desktop computer. You will also require a decent bandwidth Internet connection to download R and the various R code libraries from CRAN, the main online repository for R packages.

The examples in this book have largely been developed using RStudio version 0.98.1062, with the 64-bit R version 3.1.0 (CRAN distribution), running on a mid-2014 generation Apple MacBook Pro OS X 10.9.4, with a 2.6 GHz Intel Core i5 processor and 16 GB of memory. However, all of these examples should also work with the latest version of R.

Some of the examples in this book will not be able to run with Microsoft Windows, but they should run without problem on variants of Linux. Each chapter will detail any required additional external libraries or runtime system requirements, and provide you with information on how to access and install them. This book's errata section will highlight any issues discovered post publication.

Who this book is for

This book is for the intermediate to advanced-level R developer who wants to understand how to harness the power of parallel computing to perform long running computations and analyze large quantities of data. You will require a reasonable knowledge and understanding of R programming. You should be a sufficiently capable programmer so that you can read and understand lower-level languages, such as C/C++, and be familiar with the process of code compilation. You may consider yourself to be the new breed of data scientist—a skilled programmer as well as a mathematician.

Conventions

In this book, you will find a number of text styles that distinguish between different kinds of information. Here are some examples of these styles and an explanation of their meaning.

Code words in text, database table names, folder names, filenames, file extensions, pathnames, dummy URLs, user input, and Twitter handles are shown as follows: "You'll note the use of `mpi.cart.create()`, which constructs a Cartesian rank/grid mapping from a group of existing MPI processes."

A block of code is set as follows:

```
Worker_makeSquareGrid <- function(comm,dim) {
  grid <- 1000 + dim    # assign comm handle for this size grid
  dims <- c(dim,dim)    # dimensions are 2D, size: dim X dim
  periods <- c(FALSE,FALSE)  # no wraparound at outermost edges
  if (mpi.cart.create(commold=comm,dims,periods,commcart=grid))
  {
    return(grid)
  }
  return(-1) # An MPI error occurred
}
```

When we wish to draw your attention to a particular part of a code block, the relevant lines or items are set in bold:

```
# Namespace file for sprint

useDynLib(sprint)

export(phello)
export(ptest)
export(pcor)
```

Any command-line input or output is written as follows:

```
$ mpicc -o mpihello.o mpihello.c
$ mpiexec -n 4 ./mpihello.o
```

New terms and **important words** are shown in bold.

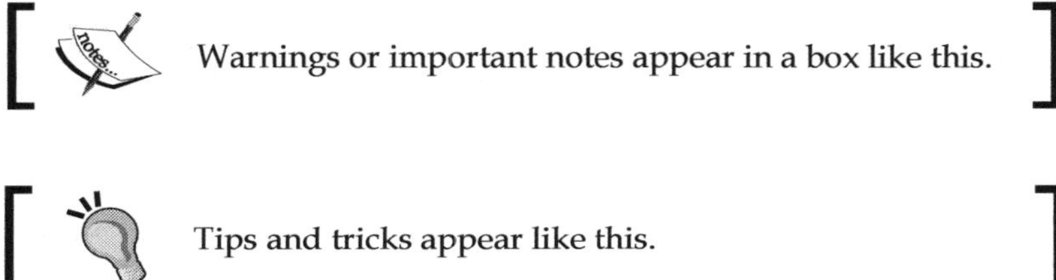

Warnings or important notes appear in a box like this.
Tips and tricks appear like this.

Reader feedback

Feedback from our readers is always welcome. Let us know what you think about this book—what you liked or disliked. Reader feedback is important for us as it helps us develop titles that you will really get the most out of.

To send us general feedback, simply e-mail `feedback@packtpub.com`, and mention the book's title in the subject of your message.

If there is a topic that you have expertise in and you are interested in either writing or contributing to a book, see our author guide at `www.packtpub.com/authors`.

Customer support

Now that you are the proud owner of a Packt book, we have a number of things to help you to get the most from your purchase.

Downloading the example code

You can download the example code files for this book from your account at `http://www.packtpub.com`. If you purchased this book elsewhere, you can visit `http://www.packtpub.com/support` and register to have the files e-mailed directly to you.

You can download the code files by following these steps:

1. Log in or register to our website using your e-mail address and password.
2. Hover the mouse pointer on the **SUPPORT** tab at the top.
3. Click on **Code Downloads & Errata**.
4. Enter the name of the book in the **Search** box.
5. Select the book for which you're looking to download the code files.
6. Choose from the drop-down menu where you purchased this book from.
7. Click on **Code Download**.

You can also download the code files by clicking on the **Code Files** button on the book's webpage at the Packt Publishing website. This page can be accessed by entering the book's name in the **Search** box. Please note that you need to be logged in to your Packt account.

Once the file is downloaded, please make sure that you unzip or extract the folder using the latest version of:

- WinRAR / 7-Zip for Windows
- Zipeg / iZip / UnRarX for Mac
- 7-Zip / PeaZip for Linux

The code bundle for the book is also hosted on GitHub at `https://github.com/PacktPublishing/repository-name`. We also have other code bundles from our rich catalog of books and videos available at `https://github.com/PacktPublishing/`. Check them out!

Downloading the color images of this book

We also provide you with a PDF file that has color images of the screenshots/diagrams used in this book. The color images will help you better understand the changes in the output. You can download this file from `http://www.packtpub.com/sites/default/files/downloads/MasteringParallelProgrammingwithR_ColorImages.pdf`.

Errata

Although we have taken every care to ensure the accuracy of our content, mistakes do happen. If you find a mistake in one of our books—maybe a mistake in the text or the code—we would be grateful if you could report this to us. By doing so, you can save other readers from frustration and help us improve subsequent versions of this book. If you find any errata, please report them by visiting `http://www.packtpub.com/submit-errata`, selecting your book, clicking on the **Errata Submission Form** link, and entering the details of your errata. Once your errata are verified, your submission will be accepted and the errata will be uploaded to our website or added to any list of existing errata under the Errata section of that title.

To view the previously submitted errata, go to `https://www.packtpub.com/books/content/support` and enter the name of the book in the search field. The required information will appear under the **Errata** section.

Piracy

Piracy of copyrighted material on the Internet is an ongoing problem across all media. At Packt, we take the protection of our copyright and licenses very seriously. If you come across any illegal copies of our works in any form on the Internet, please provide us with the location address or website name immediately so that we can pursue a remedy.

Please contact us at `copyright@packtpub.com` with a link to the suspected pirated material.

We appreciate your help in protecting our authors and our ability to bring you valuable content.

Questions

If you have a problem with any aspect of this book, you can contact us at `questions@packtpub.com`, and we will do our best to address the problem.

1
Simple Parallelism with R

In this chapter, you will start your journey toward mastery of parallelism in R by quickly learning to exploit the multicore processing capability of your own laptop and travel onward to our first look at how you can most simply exploit the vast computing capacity of the cloud.

You will learn about `lapply()` and its variations supported by R's core `parallel` package as well as about the `segue` package that enables us to utilize **Amazon Web Services** (**AWS**) and the **Elastic Map Reduce** (**EMR**) service. For the latter, you will need to have an account set up with AWS.

Our worked example throughout this chapter will be an iterative solver for an ancient puzzle known as Aristotle's Number Puzzle. Hopefully, this will be something new to you and pique your interest. It has been specifically chosen to demonstrate an important issue that can arise when running code in parallel, namely imbalanced computation. It will also serve to help develop our performance benchmarking skills—an important consideration in parallelism—measuring overall computational effectiveness.

The examples in this chapter are developed using RStudio version 0.98.1062 with the 64-bit R version 3.1.0 (CRAN distribution) running on a mid-2014 generation Apple MacBook Pro OS X 10.9.4 with a 2.6 GHz Intel Core i5 processor and 16 GB memory. Some of the examples in this chapter will not be able to run with Microsoft Windows, but should run without problem on all variants of Linux.

Aristotle's Number Puzzle

The puzzle we will solve is known as Aristotle's Number Puzzle, and this is a magic hexagon. The puzzle requires us to place 19 tiles, numbered 1 to 19, on a hexagonal grid such that each horizontal row and each diagonal across the board adds up to 38 when summing each of the numbers on each of the tiles in the corresponding line. The following, on the left-hand side, is a pictorial representation of the unsolved puzzle showing the hexagonal grid layout of the board with the tiles placed in order from the upper-left to the lower-right. Next to this, a partial solution to the puzzle is shown, where the two rows (starting with the tiles 16 and 11) and the four diagonals all add up to 38, with empty board cells in the positions 1, 3, 8, 10, 12, 17, and 19 and seven remaining unplaced tiles, 2, 8, 9, 12, 13, 15, and 17:

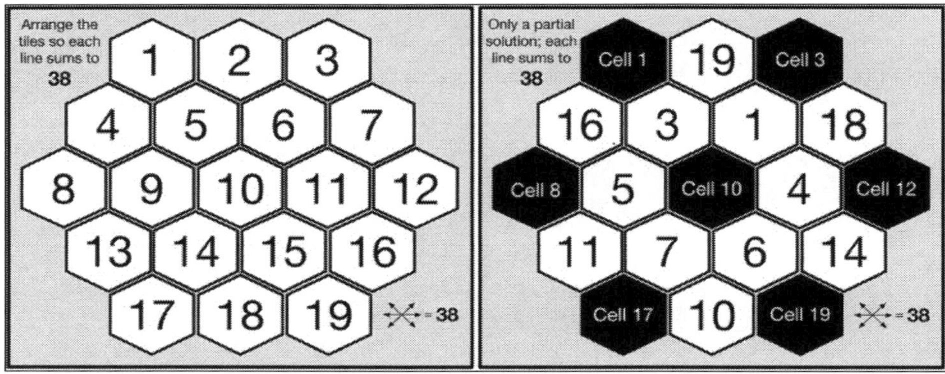

The mathematically minded among you will already have noticed that the number of possible tile layouts is the factorial 19; that is, there is a total of 121,645,100,408,832,000 unique combinations (ignoring rotational and mirror symmetry). Even when utilizing a modern microprocessor, it will clearly take a considerable period of time to find which of these 121 quadrillion combinations constitute a valid solution.

The algorithm we will use to solve the puzzle is a depth-first iterative search, allowing us to trade off limited memory for compute cycles; we could not feasibly store every possible board configuration without incurring huge expense.

Solver implementation

Let's start our implementation by considering how to represent the board. The simplest way is to use a one-dimensional R vector of length 19, where the index i of the vector represents the corresponding i^{th} cell on the board. Where a tile is not yet placed, the value of the board vector's "cell" will be the numeric 0.

```
empty_board   <- c(0,0,0,0,0,0,0,0,0,0,0,0,0,0,0,0,0,0,0)
partial_board <- c(0,19,0,16,3,1,18,0,5,0,4,0,11,7,6,14,0,10,0)
```

Next, let's define a function to evaluate whether the layout of tiles on the board represents a valid solution. As part of this, we need to specify the various combinations of board cells or "lines" that must add up to the target value `38`, as follows:

```
all_lines <- list(
  c(1,2,3),          c(1,4,8),          c(1,5,10,15,19),
  c(2,5,9,13),       c(2,6,11,16),      c(3,7,12),
  c(3,6,10,14,17), c(4,5,6,7),         c(4,9,14,18),
  c(7,11,15,18),     c(8,9,10,11,12), c(8,13,17),
  c(12,16,19),       c(13,14,15,16),  c(17,18,19)
)
evaluateBoard <- function(board)
{
  for (line in all_lines) {
    total <- 0
    for (cell in line) {
      total <- total + board[cell]
    }
    if (total != 38) return(FALSE)
  }
  return(TRUE) # We have a winner!
}
```

In order to implement the depth-first solver, we need to manage the list of remaining tiles for the next tile placement. For this, we will utilize a variation on a simple stack by providing push and pop functions for both the first and last item within a vector. To make this distinct, we will implement it as a class and call it `sequence`.

Here is a simple S3-style class sequence that implements a double-ended head/tail stack by internally maintaining the stack's state within a vector:

```
sequence <- function()
{
  sequence <- new.env()      # Shared state for class instance
  sequence$.vec <- vector()  # Internal state of the stack
  sequence$getVector <- function() return (.vec)
  sequence$pushHead <- function(val) .vec <<- c(val, .vec)
  sequence$pushTail <- function(val) .vec <<- c(.vec, val)
  sequence$popHead <- function() {
    val <- .vec[1]
    .vec <<- .vec[-1]        # Update must apply to shared state
    return(val)
```

```
    }
    sequence$popTail <- function() {
      val <- .vec[length(.vec)]
      .vec <<- .vec[-length(.vec)]
      return(val)
    }
    sequence$size <- function() return( length(.vec) )
    # Each sequence method needs to use the shared state of the
    # class instance, rather than its own function environment
    environment(sequence$size)      <- as.environment(sequence)
    environment(sequence$popHead)   <- as.environment(sequence)
    environment(sequence$popTail)   <- as.environment(sequence)
    environment(sequence$pushHead)  <- as.environment(sequence)
    environment(sequence$pushTail)  <- as.environment(sequence)
    environment(sequence$getVector) <- as.environment(sequence)
    class(sequence) <- "sequence"
    return(sequence)
  }
```

The implementation of the sequence should be easy to understand from some example usage, as in the following:

```
> s <- sequence()      ## Create an instance s of sequence
> s$pushHead(c(1:5))   ## Initialize s with numbers 1 to 5
> s$getVector()
[1] 1 2 3 4 5
> s$popHead()          ## Take the first element from s
[1] 1
> s$getVector()        ## The number 1 has been removed from s
[1] 2 3 4 5
> s$pushTail(1)        ## Add number 1 as the last element in s
> s$getVector()
[1] 2 3 4 5 1
```

We are almost there. Here is the implementation of the `placeTiles()` function to perform the depth-first search:

```
placeTiles <- function(cells,board,tilesRemaining)
{
 for (cell in cells) {
   if (board[cell] != 0) next # Skip cell if not empty
   maxTries <- tilesRemaining$size()
   for (t in 1:maxTries) {
```

```
07      board[cell] = tilesRemaining$popHead()
08      retval <- placeTiles(cells,board,tilesRemaining)
09      if (retval$Success) return(retval)
10      tilesRemaining$pushTail(board[cell])
11    }
12    board[cell] = 0 # Mark this cell as empty
13    # All available tiles for this cell tried without success
14    return( list(Success = FALSE, Board = board) )
15  }
16  success <- evaluateBoard(board)
17  return( list(Success = success, Board = board) )
18 }
```

The function exploits recursion to place each subsequent tile on the next available cell. As there are a maximum of 19 tiles to place, recursion will descend to a maximum of 19 levels (Line 08). The recursion will bottom out when no tiles remain to be placed on the board, and the board will then be evaluated (Line 16). A successful evaluation will immediately unroll the recursion stack (Line 09), propagating the final completed state of the board to the caller (Line 17). An unsuccessful evaluation will recurse one step back up the calling stack and cause the next remaining tile to be tried instead. Once all the tiles are exhausted for a given cell, the recursion will unroll to the previous cell, the next tile in the sequence will be tried, the recursion will progress again, and so on.

Usefully, the `placeTiles()` function enables us to test a partial solution, so let's try out the partial tile placement from the beginning of this chapter. Execute the following code:

```
> board <- c(0,19,0,16,3,1,18,0,5,0,4,0,11,7,6,14,0,10,0)
> tiles <- sequence()
> tiles$pushHead(c(2,8,9,12,13,15,17))
> cells <- c(1,3,8,10,12,17,19)
> placeTiles(cells,board,tiles)
$Success
[1] FALSE
$Board
[1]  0 19  0 16  3  1 18  0  5  0  4  0 11  7  6 14  0 10  0
```

Downloading the example code

You can download the example code files for this book from your account at `http://www.packtpub.com`. If you purchased this book elsewhere, you can visit `http://www.packtpub.com/support` and register to have the files e-mailed directly to you.

You can download the code files by following these steps:

- Log in or register to our website using your e-mail address and password.
- Hover the mouse pointer on the **SUPPORT** tab at the top.
- Click on **Code Downloads & Errata**.
- Enter the name of the book in the **Search** box.
- Select the book for which you're looking to download the code files.

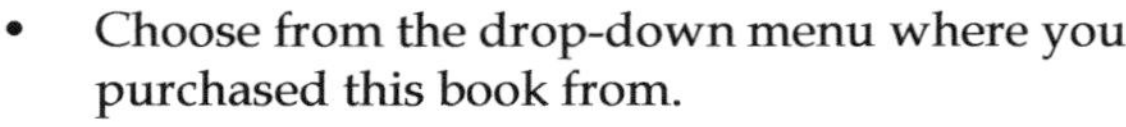

- Choose from the drop-down menu where you purchased this book from.

- Click on **Code Download**.

You can also download the code files by clicking on the **Code Files** button on the book's webpage at the Packt Publishing website. This page can be accessed by entering the book's name in the **Search** box. Please note that you need to be logged in to your Packt account.

Once the file is downloaded, please make sure that you unzip or extract the folder using the latest version of:

- WinRAR / 7-Zip for Windows
- Zipeg / iZip / UnRarX for Mac
- 7-Zip / PeaZip for Linux

The code bundle for the book is also hosted on GitHub at `https://github.com/PacktPublishing/repository-name`. We also have other code bundles from our rich catalog of books and videos available at `https://github.com/PacktPublishing/`. Check them out!

Unfortunately, our partial solution does not yield a complete solution.

We'll clearly have to try a lot harder.

Refining the solver

Before we jump into parallelizing our solver, let's first examine the efficiency of our current serial implementation. With the existing `placeTiles()` implementation, the tiles are laid until the board is complete, and then it is evaluated. The partial solution we tested previously, with seven cells unassigned, required *7! = 5,040* calls to `evaluateBoard()` and a total of 13,699 tile placements.

The most obvious refinement we can make is to test each tile as we place it and check whether the partial solution up to this point is correct rather than waiting until all the tiles are placed. Intuitively, this should significantly reduce the number of tile layouts that we have to explore. Let's implement this change and then compare the difference in performance so that we understand the real benefit from doing this extra implementation work:

```
  cell_lines <- list(
    list( c(1,2,3),    c(1,4,8),    c(1,5,10,15,19) ), #Cell 1
.. # Cell lines 2 to 18 removed for brevity
    list( c(12,16,19), c(17,18,19), c(1,5,10,15,19) )  #Cell 19
  )
  evaluateCell <- function(board,cellplaced)
  {
    for (lines in cell_lines[cellplaced]) {
      for (line in lines) {
        total <- 0
        checkExact <- TRUE
        for (cell in line) {
          if (board[cell] == 0) checkExact <- FALSE
          else total <- total + board[cell]
        }
        if ((checkExact && (total != 38)) || total > 38)
          return(FALSE)
      }
    }
    return(TRUE)
  }
```

For efficiency, the `evaluateCell()` function determines which lines need to be checked based on the cell that is just placed by performing direct lookup against `cell_lines`. The `cell_lines` data structure is easily compiled from `all_lines` (you could even write some simple code to generate this). Each cell on the board requires three specific lines to be tested. As any given line being tested may not be filled with tiles, `evaluateCell()` includes a check to ensure that it only applies the 38 sum test when a line is complete. For a partial line, a check is made to ensure that the sum does not exceed 38.

We can now augment `placeTiles()` to call `evaluateCell()` as follows:

```
placeTiles <- function(cells,board,tilesRemaining)
..
   for (t in 1:maxTries) {
     board[cell] = tilesRemaining$popHead()
     if (evaluateCell(board,cell)) {
       retval <- placeTiles(cells,board,tilesRemaining)
       if (retval$Success) return(retval)
     }
     tilesRemaining$pushTail(board[cell])
   }
..
```

Measuring the execution time

Before we apply this change, we need to first benchmark the current `placeTiles()` function so that we can determine the resulting performance improvement. To do this, we'll introduce a simple timing function, `teval()`, that will enable us to measure accurately how much work the processor does when executing a given R function. Take a look at the following:

```
teval <- function(...) {
  gc(); # Perform a garbage collection before timing R function
  start <- proc.time()
  result <- eval(...)
  finish <- proc.time()
  return ( list(Duration=finish-start, Result=result) )
}
```

The `teval()` function makes use of an internal system function, `proc.time()`, to record the current consumed user and system cycles as well as the wall clock time for the R process [unfortunately, this information is not available when R is running on Windows]. It captures this state both before and after the R expression being measured is evaluated and computes the overall duration. To help ensure that there is a level of consistency in timing, a preemptive garbage collection is invoked, though it should be noted that this does not preclude R from performing a garbage collection at any further point during the timing period.

So, let's run `teval()` on the existing `placeTiles()` as follows:

```
> teval(placeTiles(cells,board,tiles))
$Duration
   user  system elapsed
  0.421   0.005   0.519
$Result
..
```

Now, let's make the changes in `placeTiles()` to call `evaluateCell()` and run it again via the following code:

```
> teval(placeTiles(cells,board,tiles))
$Duration
   user  system elapsed
  0.002   0.000   0.002
$Result
..
```

This is a nice result! This one change has significantly reduced our execution time by a factor of 200. Obviously, your own absolute timings may vary based on the machine you use.

Benchmarking code

For true comparative benchmarking, we should run tests multiple times and from a full system startup for each run to ensure there are no caching effects or system resource contention issues taking place that might skew our results. For our specific simple example code, which does not perform file I/O or network communications, handle user input, or use large amounts of memory, we should not encounter these issues. Such issues will typically be indicated by significant variation in time taken over multiple runs, a high percentage of `system` time or the `elapsed` time being substantively greater than the `user` + `system` time.

This kind of performance profiling and enhancement is important as later in this chapter, we will pay directly for our CPU cycles in the cloud; therefore, we want our code to be as cost effective as possible.

Instrumenting code

For a little deeper understanding of the behavior of our code, such as how many times a function is called during program execution, we either need to add explicit instrumentation, such as counters and `print` statements, or use external tools such as Rprof. For now, though, we will take a quick look at how we can apply the base R function `trace()` to provide a generic mechanism to profile the number of times a function is called, as follows:

```
profileFn <- function(fn)       ## Turn on tracing for "fn"
{
  assign("profile.counter",0,envir=globalenv())
  trace(fn,quote(assign("profile.counter",
```

```
                    get("profile.counter",envir=globalenv()) + 1,
                   envir=globalenv())), print=FALSE)
    }
    profileFnStats <- function(fn)  ## Get collected stats
    {
      count <- get("profile.counter",envir=globalenv())
      return( list(Function=fn,Count=count) )
    }
    unprofileFn <- function(fn)     ## Turn off tracing and tidy up
    {
      remove(list="profile.counter",envir=globalenv())
      untrace(fn)
    }
```

The `trace()` function enables us to execute a piece of code each time the function being traced is called. We will exploit this to update a specific counter we create (`profile.counter`) in the global environment to track each invocation.

> `trace()`
>
> This function is only available when the tracing is explicitly compiled into R itself. If you are using the CRAN distribution of R for either Mac OS X or Microsoft Windows, then this facility will be turned on. Tracing introduces a modicum of overhead even when not being used directly within code and therefore tends not to be compiled into R production environments.

We can demonstrate `profileFn()` working in our running example as follows:

```
> profile.counter
Error: object 'profile.counter' not found
> profileFn("evaluateCell")
[1] "evaluateCell"
> profile.counter
[1] 0
> placeTiles(cells,board,tiles)
..
> profileFnStats("evaluateCell")
$Function
[1] "evaluateCell"
$Count
```

```
[1] 59
> unprofileFn("evaluateCell")
> profile.counter
Error: object 'profile.counter' not found
```

What this result shows is that `evaluateCell()` is called `59` times as compared to our previous `evaluateBoard()` function, which was called 5,096 times. This accounts for the significantly reduced runtime and combinatorial search space that must be explored.

Splitting the problem into multiple tasks

Parallelism relies on being able to split a problem into separate units of work. Trivial—or as it is sometimes referred to, naïve parallelism—treats each separate unit of work as entirely independent of one another. Under this scheme, while a unit of work, or task, is being processed, there is no requirement for the computation to interact with or share information with other tasks being computed, either now, previously, or subsequently.

For our number puzzle, an obvious approach would be to split the problem into 19 separate tasks, where each task is a different-numbered tile placed at cell 1 on the board, and the task is to explore the search space to find a solution stemming from the single tile starting position. However, this only gives us a maximum parallelism of 19, meaning we can explore our search space a maximum of 19 times faster than in serial. We also need to consider our overall efficiency. Does each of the starting positions result in the same amount of required computation? In short, no; as we will use a depth-first algorithm in which a correct solution found will immediately end the task in contrast to an incorrect starting position that will likely result in a much larger, variable, and inevitably fruitless search space being explored. Our tasks are therefore not balanced and will require differing amounts of computational effort to complete. We also cannot predict which of the tasks will take longer to compute as we do not know which starting position will lead to the correct solution a priori.

Imbalanced computation

This type of scenario is typical of a whole host of real-world problems where we search for an optimal or near-optimal solution in a complex search space—for example, finding the most efficient route and means of travel around a set of destinations or planning the most efficient use of human and building resources when timetabling a set of activities. Imbalanced computation can be a significant problem where we have a fully committed compute resource and are effectively waiting for the slowest task to be performed before the overall computation can complete. This reduces our parallel speed-up in comparison to running in serial, and it may also mean that the compute resource we are paying for spends a significant period of time idle rather than doing useful work.

To increase our overall efficiency and opportunity for parallelism, we will split the problem into a larger number of smaller computational tasks, and we will exploit a particular feature of the puzzle to significantly reduce our overall search space.

We will generate the starting triple of tiles for the first (top) line of the board, cells 1 to 3. We might expect that this will give us *19x18x17 = 5,814* tile combinations. However, only a subset of these tile combinations will sum to 38; *1+2+3* and *17+18+19* clearly are not valid. We can also filter out combinations that are a mirror image; for example, for the first line of the board, *1+18+19* will yield an equivalent search space to *19+18+1*, so we only need to explore one of them.

Here is the code for `generateTriples()`. You will notice that we are making use of a 6-character string representation of a tile-triple to simplify the mirror image test, and it also happens to be a reasonably compact and efficient implementation:

```
generateTriples <- function()
{
  triples <- list()
  for (x in 1:19) {
    for (y in 1:19) {
      if (y == x) next
      for (z in 1:19) {
        if (z == x || z == y || x+y+z != 38) next
        mirror <- FALSE
        reversed <- sprintf("%02d%02d%02d",z,y,x)
        for (t in triples) {
          if (reversed == t) {
            mirror <- TRUE
            break
          }
        }
```

```
            if (!mirror) {
              triples[length(triples)+1] <-
                        sprintf("%02d%02d%02d",x,y,z)
            }
          }
        }
      }
      return (triples)
    }
```

If we run this, we will generate just 90 unique triples, a significant saving over 5,814 starting positions:

```
> teval(generateTriples())
$Duration
   user  system elapsed
  0.025   0.001   0.105
$Result[[1]]
[1] "011819"
  ..
$Result[[90]]
[1] "180119"
```

Executing multiple tasks with lapply()

Now that we have an efficiently defined set of board starting positions, we can look at how we can manage the set of tasks for distributed computation. Our starting point will be `lapply()` as this enables us to test out our task execution and formulate it into a program structure, for which we can do a simple drop-in replacement to run in parallel.

The `lapply()` function takes two arguments, the first is a list of objects that act as input to a user-defined function, and the second is the user-defined function to be called, once for each separate input object; it will return the collection of results from each function invocation as a single list. We will repackage our solver implementation to make it simpler to use with `lapply()` by wrapping up the various functions and data structures we developed thus far in an overall `solver()` function, as follows (the complete source code for the solver is available on the book's website):

```
solver <- function(triple)
{
  all_lines <- list(..
  cell_lines <- list(..
```

```
    sequence <- function(..
    evaluateBoard <- function(..
    evaluateCell <- function(..
    placeTiles <- function(..
    teval <- function(..

    ## The main body of the solver
    tile1 <- as.integer(substr(triple,1,2))
    tile2 <- as.integer(substr(triple,3,4))
    tile3 <- as.integer(substr(triple,5,6))
    board <- c(tile1,tile2,tile3,0,0,0,0,0,0,0,0,0,0,0,0,0,0,0,0)
    cells <- c(4,5,6,7,8,9,10,11,12,13,14,15,16,17,18,19)
    tiles <- sequence()
    for (t in 1:19) {
      if (t == tile1 || t == tile2 || t == tile3) next
      tiles$pushHead(t)
    }
    result <- teval(placeTiles(cells,board,tiles))
    return( list(Triple = triple, Result = result$Result,
                 Duration= result$Duration) )
  }
```

Let's run our solver with a selection of four of the tile-triples:

```
> tri <- generateTriples()
> tasks <- list(tri[[1]],tri[[21]],tri[[41]],tri[[61]])
> teval(lapply(tasks,solver))
$Duration                ## Overall
   user  system elapsed
171.934   0.216 172.257
$Result[[1]]$Duration    ## Triple "011819"
   user  system elapsed
  1.113   0.001   1.114
$Result[[2]]$Duration    ## Triple "061517"
   user  system elapsed
 39.536   0.054  39.615
$Result[[3]]$Duration    ## Triple "091019"
   user  system elapsed
 65.541   0.089  65.689
$Result[[4]]$Duration    ## Triple "111215"
   user  system elapsed
 65.609   0.072  65.704
```

The preceding output has been trimmed and commented for brevity and clarity. The key thing to note is that there is significant variation in the time (the `elapsed` time) it takes on my laptop to run through the search space for each of the four starting tile-triples, none of which happen to result in a solution to the puzzle. We can (perhaps) project from this that it will take at least 90 minutes to run through the complete set of triples if running in serial. However, we can solve the puzzle much faster if we run our code in parallel; so, without further ado....

The R parallel package

The R `parallel` package is now part of the core distribution of R. It includes a number of different mechanisms to enable you to exploit parallelism utilizing the multiple cores in your processor(s) as well as compute the resources distributed across a network as a cluster of machines. However, as our theme in this chapter is one of simplicity, we will stick to making the most of the resources available on the machine on which you are running R.

The first thing you need to do is to enable the parallelism package. You can either just use R's `library()` function to load it, or if you are using RStudio, you can just tick the corresponding entry in the **User Library** list in the **Packages** tab. The second thing we need to do is determine just how much parallelism we can utilize by calling the parallel package function `detectCores()`, as follows:

```
> library("parallel")
> detectCores()
[1] 4
```

As we can immediately note, on my MacBook device, I have four cores available across which I can run R programs in parallel. It's easy to verify this using Mac's **Activity Monitor** app and selecting the **CPU History** option from the **Window** menu. You should see something similar to the following, with one timeline graph per core:

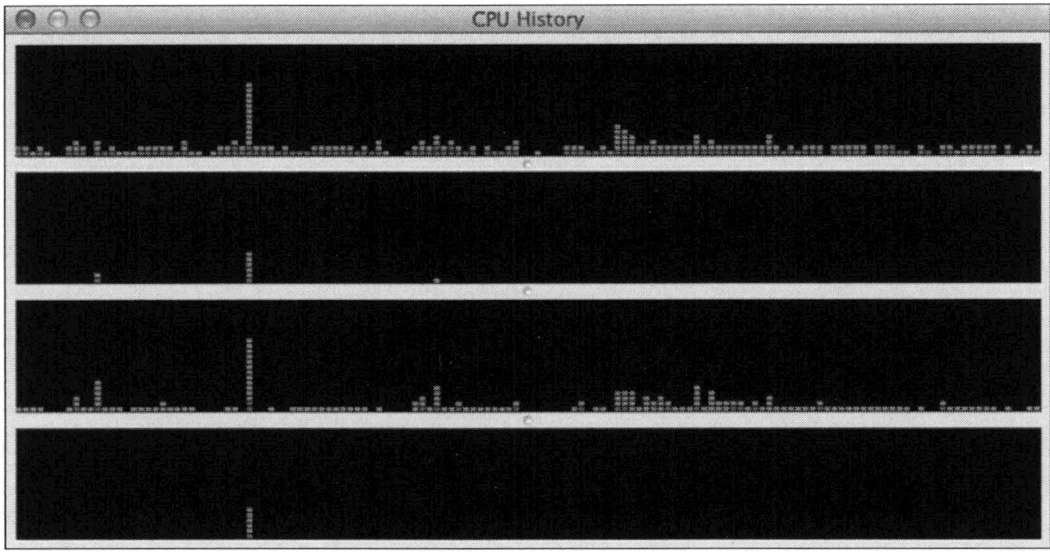

The green elements of the plotted bars indicate the proportion of CPU spent in user code, and the red elements indicate the proportion of time spent in system code. You can vary the frequency of graph update to a maximum of once a second. A similar multicore CPU history is available in Microsoft Windows. It is useful to have this type of view open when running code in parallel as you can immediately see when your code is utilizing multiple cores. You can also see what other activity is taking place on your machine that might impact your R code running in parallel.

Using mclapply()

The simplest mechanism to achieve parallelism in R is to use parallel's multicore variant of `lapply()` called (logically) `mclapply()`.

The mclapply() function is Unix-only

The `mclapply()` function is only available when you are running R on Mac OS X or Linux or other variants of Unix. It is implemented with the Unix `fork()` system call and therefore cannot be used on Microsoft Windows; rest assured, we will come to a Microsoft Windows compatible solution shortly. The Unix `fork()` system call operates by replicating the currently running process (including its entire memory state, open file descriptors, and other process resources, and importantly, from an R perspective, any currently loaded libraries) as a set of independent child processes that will each continue separate execution until they make the `exit()` system call, at which point the parent process will collect their exit state. Once all children terminate, the fork will be completed. All of this behavior is wrapped up inside the call to `mclapply()`. If you view your running processes in **Activity Monitor** on Mac OS X, you will see `mc.cores` number of spawned rsession processes with high CPU utilization when `mclapply()` is called.

Activity Monitor (All Processes)

CPU | Memory | Energy | Disk | Network

Process Name	% CPU	CPU Time	Threads	Idle Wake Ups	PID	User
rsession	95.6	26:37.97	1	0	38883	simon
rsession	95.6	26:38.67	1	0	38881	simon
rsession	95.5	26:38.02	1	0	38884	simon
rsession	94.2	26:38.29	1	0	38882	simon
Activity Monitor	4.1	46:30.57	4	3	7694	simon

Similar to `lapply()`, the first argument is the list of function inputs corresponding to independent tasks, and the second argument is the function to be executed for each task. An optional argument, `mc.cores`, allows us to specify how many cores we want to make use of—that is, the degree of parallelism we want to use. If when you ran `detectCores()` and the result was `1`, then `mclapply()` will resort to just calling `lapply()` internally—that is, the computation will just run serially.

Let's initially run `mclapply()` through a small subset of the triple tile board starting positions using the same set we tried previously with `lapply()` for comparison, as follows:

```
> tri <- generateTriples()
> tasks <- list(tri[[1]],tri[[21]],tri[[41]],tri[[61]])
> teval(mclapply(tasks,solver,mc.cores=detectCores()))
$Duration                 ## Overall
   user  system elapsed
146.412   0.433  87.621
$Result[[1]]$Duration     ## Triple "011819"
   user  system elapsed
```

```
  2.182    0.010    2.274
$Result[[2]]$Duration    ## Triple "061517"
   user  system elapsed
 58.686    0.108   59.391
$Result[[3]]$Duration    ## Triple "091019"
   user  system elapsed
 85.353    0.147   86.198
$Result[[4]]$Duration    ## Triple "111215"
   user  system elapsed
 86.604    0.152   87.498
```

The preceding output is again trimmed and commented for brevity and clarity. What you should immediately notice is that the overall elapsed time for executing all of the tasks is no greater than the length of time it took to compute the longest running of the four tasks. Voila! We have managed to significantly reduce our running time from 178 seconds running in serial to just 87 seconds by making simultaneous use of all the four cores available. However, 87 seconds is only half of 178 seconds, and you may have expected that we would have seen a four-times speedup over running in serial. You may also notice that our individual runtime increased for each individual task compared to running in serial—for example, for tile-triple `111215` from 65 seconds to 87 seconds. Part of this difference is due to the overhead from the forking mechanism and the time it takes to spin up a new child process, apportion it tasks, collect its results, and tear it down. The good news is that this overhead can be amortized by having each parallel process compute a large number of tasks.

Another consideration is that my particular MacBook laptop uses an Intel Core i5 processor, which, in practice, is more the equivalent of 2 x 1.5 cores as it exploits hyperthreading across two full processor cores to increase performance and has certain limitations but is still treated by the operating system as four fully independent cores. If I run the preceding example on two of my laptop cores, then the overall runtime is just 107 seconds. Two times hyperthreading, therefore, gains me an extra 20% on performance, which although good, is still much less than the desired 50% performance improvement.

I'm sure at this point, if you haven't already done so, then you will have the urge to run the solver in parallel across all 90 of the starting tile-triples and find the solution to Aristotle's Number Puzzle, though you might want to take a long coffee break or have lunch while it runs....

Options for mclapply()

The `mclapply()` function has more capability than we have so far touched upon. The following table summarizes these extended capabilities and briefly discusses when they are most appropriately applied:

```
mclapply(X, FUN, ..., mc.preschedule=TRUE, mc.set.seed=TRUE,
         mc.silent=FALSE, mc.cores=getOption("mc.cores",2L),
         mc.cleanup=TRUE, mc.allow.recursive=TRUE)
returns: list of FUN results, where length(returns)=length(X)
```

Option [default=value]	**Description**
`X`	This is the list (or vector) of items that represent tasks to be computed by the user-defined `FUN` function.
`FUN`	This is the user-defined function to execute on each task. `FUN` will be called multiple times: `FUN(x,...)`, where `x` is one of the remaining task items in `X` to be computed on and ... matches the extra arguments passed into `mclapply()`.
...	Any extra non-mclapply arguments are passed directly into `FUN` on each task execution.
`mc.preschedule` [default=`TRUE`]	If this is `TRUE`, then one child process is forked for each core requested, the tasks are split as evenly as possible between cores in the "round-robin" order, and each child executes its allotted set of tasks. For most parallel workloads, this is normally the best choice. If this is `FALSE`, then a new child process is forked afresh for each task executed. This option is useful where tasks are relatively long running but have significant variance in compute time as it enables a level of adaptive load balancing to be employed at the cost of increased overhead of a fork per task, as opposed to a fork per core. In either case, there will be a maximum of `mc.cores` child processes running at any given time while `mcapply()` is executed.
`mc.set.seed` [default=`TRUE`]	The behavior of this option is governed by the type of **random number generator (RNG)** in use for the current R session. If this is `TRUE` and an appropriate RNG is selected, then the child process will be launched with a specific RNG sequence selected, such that a subsequent invocation of `mclapply()` with the same arguments set will produce the same result (assuming the computation makes use of the specific RNG). Otherwise, the behavior is as for `FALSE`. If this is `FALSE`, then the child process inherits the random number state at the start of its execution from the parent R session, and it is likely that it will be difficult to generate reproducible results. Having consistent random number generation for parallel code is a topic we will cover in the online chapter.
`mc.silent` [default=`FALSE`]	If this is `TRUE`, then any output generated to the standard output stream will be suppressed (such as the `print` statement output). If this is `FALSE`, then standard output is unaffected. However, also refer to the tip following this table. In either case, the output to the standard error stream is unaffected.

Option [default=value]	Description
`mc.cores` [default=2 or if defined `getOption("mc.cores")`]	This option sets the degree of parallelism to use and is arguably misnamed as it actually controls the number of simultaneous processes running that execute tasks, and this can well exceed the number of physical processor cores should you so desire. For some types of parallel workload, such as a small number of long-running but variable compute tasks where intermediate results can be generated (such as to the filesystem or by messaging). This may even be helpful as it enables the operating system time slicing of processes to ensure fair progress on a set of tasks. Of course, the downside is increased overhead of constant switching between running processes. Constraints on the upper bound for this are dependent on the operating system and machine resource, but in general, it will be in the 100s as opposed to 1000s.
`mc.cleanup` [default=`TRUE`]	If this is `TRUE`, then the child processes will forcibly be terminated by the parent. If this is `FALSE`, then child processes may be left running after they complete the `mclapply()` operation. The latter is potentially useful for post-compute debugging by attaching to the still-running process. In either case, `mclapply()` waits until all the children complete their tasks and then returns the combined set of computed results.
`mc.allow.recursive` [default=`TRUE`]	If this is `TRUE`, then `FUN` can itself make calls to `mclapply()` or call code that also invokes `mclapply()`. On the whole, such recursion is only used in exotic forms of parallel programming. If this is `FALSE`, then a recursive attempt to call `mclapply()` will simply result in an internal call to `lapply()`, enforcing serial execution within the child process.

Lets have a look at a tip:

The print() function in parallel

In Rstudio, the output is not directed to the screen when running in parallel with `mclapply()`. If you wish to generate print messages or other console output, you should run your program directly from the command shell rather than from within RStudio. In general, the authors of `mclapply()` do not recommend running parallel R code from a GUI console editor because it can cause a number of complications, with multiple processes attempting to interact with the GUI. It is not suitable, for example, to attempt to plot to the GUI's graphics display when running in parallel. With our solver code, though, you should not experience any specific issue. It's also worth noting that having multiple processes writing messages to the same shared output stream can become very confusing as messages can potentially be interleaved and unreadable, depending on how the output stream buffers I/O. We will come back to the topic of parallel I/O in a later chapter.

Using parLapply()

The `mclapply()` function is closely related to the more generic `parallel` package function `parLapply()`. The key difference is that we separately create a cluster of parallel R processes using `makeCluster()`, and `parLapply()` then utilizes this cluster when executing a function in parallel. There are two key advantages to this approach. Firstly, with `makeCluster()`, we can create different underlying implementations of a parallel processing pool, including a forked process cluster (FORK) similar to that used internally within `mclapply()`, a socket-based cluster (PSOCK) that will operate on Microsoft Windows as well as OS X and Linux, and a message-passing-based cluster (MPI), whichever is best suited to our circumstances. Secondly, the overhead of creating and configuring the cluster (we will visit the R configuration of the cluster in a later chapter) is amortized as it can be continually reused within our session.

The PSOCK and MPI types of cluster also enable R to utilize multiple machines within a network and perform true distributed computing (the machines may also be running different operating systems). However, for now, we will focus on the PSOCK cluster type and how this can be utilized within a single machine context. We will explore MPI in detail in *Chapter 2, Introduction to MessagePassing, Chapter 3, Advanced Message Passing, Chapter 4, Developing SPRINT an MPI-based Package for Supercomputers.*

Let's jump right in; run the following:

```
> cluster <- makeCluster(detectCores(),"PSOCK")


> tri <- generateTriples()
> tasks <- list(tri[[1]],tri[[21]],tri[[41]],tri[[61]])
> teval(parLapply(cluster,tasks,solver))
$Duration                ## Overall
   user  system elapsed
  0.119   0.148  83.820
$Result[[1]]$Duration    ## Triple "011819"
   user  system elapsed
  2.055   0.008   2.118
$Result[[2]]$Duration    ## Triple "061517"
   user  system elapsed
 55.603   0.156  56.749
$Result[[3]]$Duration    ## Triple "091019"
   user  system elapsed
```

```
 81.949    0.208  83.195
$Result[[4]]$Duration    ## Triple "111215"
   user  system elapsed
 82.591    0.196  83.788

> stopCluster(cluster)   ## Shutdown the cluster (reap processes)
```

What you may immediately notice from the timing results generated before is that the overall user time is recorded as negligible. This is because in the launching process, your main R session (referred to as the master) does not perform any of the computation, and all of the computation is carried out by the cluster. The master merely has to send out the tasks to the cluster and wait for the results to return.

What's also particularly apparent when running a cluster in this mode is the imbalance in computation across the processes in the cluster (referred to as workers). As the following image demonstrates very clearly, each R worker process in the cluster computed a single task in variable time, and the **PID 41527** process sat idle after just two seconds while the **PID 41551** process was busy still computing its task for a further 1m 20s:

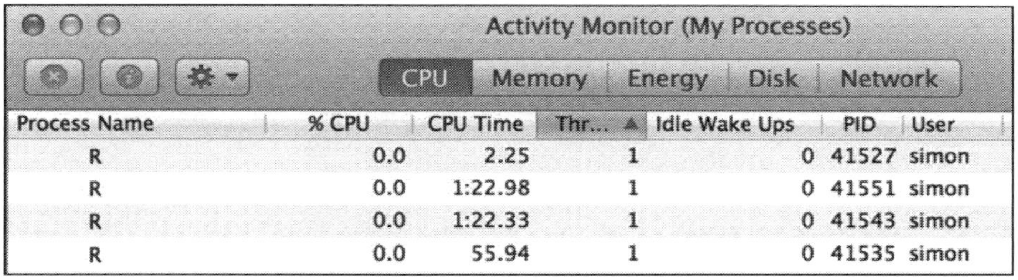

Activity Monitor (My Processes)

CPU | Memory | Energy | Disk | Network

Process Name	% CPU	CPU Time	Thr...	Idle Wake Ups	PID	User
R	0.0	2.25	1	0	41527	simon
R	0.0	1:22.98	1	0	41551	simon
R	0.0	1:22.33	1	0	41543	simon
R	0.0	55.94	1	0	41535	simon

While increasing the number of tasks for the cluster to perform and assuming a random assignment of tasks to workers should increase efficiency, we still could end up with a less-than optimal overall utilization of resource. What we need is something more adaptive that hands out tasks dynamically to worker processes whenever they are next free to do more work. Luckily for us, there is a variation on `parLapply()` that does just this....

Other parApply functions

There is a whole family of cluster functions to suit different types of workload, such as processing R matrices in parallel. These are summarized briefly here:

- `parSapply()`: This is the parallel variant of `sapply()` that simplifies the return type (if possible) to a choice of vector, matrix, or array.
- `parCapply()`, `parRapply()`: These are the parallel operations that respectively apply to the columns and rows of a matrix.
- `parLapplyLB()`, `parSapplyLB()`: These are the load-balancing versions of their similarly named cousins. Load balancing is discussed in the next section.
- `clusterApply()`, `clusterApplyLB()`: These are generic apply and load-balanced apply that are utilized by all the `parApply` functions. These are discussed in the next section.
- `clusterMap()`: This is a parallel variant of `mapply()`/`map()` enabling a function to be invoked with separate parameter values for each task, with an optional simplification of the return type (such as `sapply()`).

More information is available by typing `help(clusterApply)` in R. Our focus in this chapter will remain on processing a list of tasks.

Parallel load balancing

The `parLapplyLB()` function is a load-balancing variant of `parLapply()`. Both these functions are essentially lightweight wrappers that internally make use of the directly callable `parallel` package functions `clusterApplyLB()` and `clusterApply()`, respectively. However, it is important to understand that the `parLapply` functions split the list of tasks into a number of equal-sized subsets matching the number of workers in the cluster before invoking the associated `clusterApply` function.

If you call `clusterApply()` directly, it will simply process the list of tasks presented in blocks of cluster size—that is, the number of workers in the cluster. It does this in a sequential order, so assuming there are four workers, then task 1 will go to worker 1, task 2 to worker 2, task 3 to worker 3, and task 4 to worker 4 and then 5 will go to worker 1, task 6 to worker 2, and so on. However, it is worth noting that `clusterApply()` also waits between each block of tasks for all the tasks in this block to complete before moving on to the next block.

This has important performance implications, as we can note in the following code snippet. In this example, we will use a particular subset (16) of the 90 tile-triples to demonstrate the point:

```
> cluster <- makeCluster(4,"PSOCK")
> tri <- generateTriples()
> triples <- list(tri[[1]],tri[[20]],tri[[70]],tri[[85]],
                  tri[[2]],tri[[21]],tri[[71]],tri[[86]],
                  tri[[3]],tri[[22]],tri[[72]],tri[[87]],
                  tri[[4]],tri[[23]],tri[[73]],tri[[88]])
> teval(clusterApply(cluster,triples,solver))
$Duration
   user  system elapsed
  0.613   0.778 449.873
> stopCluster(cluster)
```

Process Name	% CPU	CPU Time	Thr... ▲	Idle Wake Ups	PID	User
R	0.0	6:34.15	1	0	42720	simon
R	0.0	3:34.99	1	0	42712	simon
R	0.0	8.36	1	0	42704	simon
R	0.0	7:26.65	1	0	42728	simon

What the preceding results illustrate is that because of the variation in compute time per task, workers are left waiting for the longest task in a block to complete before they are all assigned their next task to compute. If you watch the process utilization during execution, you will see this behavior as the lightest loaded process, in particular, briefly bursts into life at the start of each of the four blocks. This scenario is particularly inefficient and can lead to significantly extended runtimes and, in the worst case, potentially no particular advantage running in parallel compared to running in serial. Notably, `parLapply()` avoids invoking this behavior because it first splits the available tasks into exactly cluster-sized `lapply()` metatasks, and `clusterApply()` only operates on a single block of tasks then. However, a poor balance of work across this initial split will still affect the `parLapply` function's overall performance.

By comparison, `clusterApplyLB()` distributes one task at a time per worker, and whenever a worker completes its task, it immediately hands out the next task to the first available worker. There is some extra overhead to manage this procedure due to increased communication and workers still potentially queuing to wait on their next task to be assigned if they collectively finish their previous task at the same point in time. It is only, therefore, appropriate where there is considerable variation in computation for each task, and most of the tasks take some nontrivial period of time to compute.

Using `clusterApplyLB()` in our running example leads to an improvement in overall runtime (around 10%), with significantly improved utilization across all worker processes, as follows:

```
> cluster <- makeCluster(4,"PSOCK")
> teval(clusterApplyLB(cluster,triples,solver))
$Duration
   user  system elapsed
  0.586   0.841 421.859
> stopCluster(cluster)
```

Process Name	% CPU	CPU Time	Thr... ▲	Idle Wake Ups	PID	User
R	0.0	6:51.47	1	0	43092	simon
R	0.0	6:14.22	1	0	43084	simon
R	0.0	6:12.69	1	0	43076	simon
R	0.0	5:14.08	1	0	43100	simon

The final point to highlight here is that the a priori balancing of a distributed workload is the most efficient option when it is possible to do so. For our running example, executing the selected 16 triples in the order they are listed in with `parLapply()` results in the shortest overall runtime, beating `clusterApplyLB()` by 10 seconds and indicating that the load balancing equates to around a 3% overhead. The order of the selected triples happens to align perfectly with the `parLapply` function's packaging of tasks across the four-worker cluster. However, this is an artificially constructed scenario, and for the full tile-triple variable task workload, employing dynamic load balancing is the best option.

The segue package

Up until now, we looked at how we can employ parallelism in the context of our own computer running R. However, our own machine can only take us so far in terms of its resources. To access the essentially unlimited compute, we need to look further afield, and to those of us mere mortals who don't have our own private data center available, we need to look to the cloud. The market leader in providing cloud services is Amazon with their AWS offering and of particular interest is their EMR service based on Hadoop that provides reliable and scalable parallel compute.

Luckily for us, there is a specific R package, `segue`, written by James "JD" Long and designed to simplify the whole experience of setting up an AWS EMR Hadoop cluster and utilizing it directly from an R session running on our own computer. The `segue` package is most applicable to run large-scale simulations or optimization problems—that is, problems that require large amounts of compute but only small amounts of data—and hence is suitable for our puzzle solver.

Before we can start to make use of `segue`, there are a couple of prerequisites we need to deal with: firstly, installing the `segue` package and its dependencies, and secondly, ensuring that we have an appropriately set-up AWS account.

Warning: credit card required!

As we work through the `segue` example, it is important to note that we will incur expenses. AWS is a paid service, and while there may be some free AWS service offerings that you are entitled to and the example we will run will only cost a few dollars, you need to be very aware of any ongoing billing charges you may be incurring for the various aspects of AWS that you use. It is critical that you are familiar with the AWS console and how to navigate your way around your account settings, your monthly billing statements, and, in particular, EMR, **Elastic Compute Cloud** (**EC2**), and **Simple Storage Service** (**S3**) (these are elements as they will all be invoked when running the `segue` example in this chapter. For introductory information about these services, refer to the following links:

`http://docs.aws.amazon.com/awsconsolehelpdocs/latest/gsg/getting-started.html`

`https://aws.amazon.com/elasticmapreduce/`

So, with our bank manager duly alerted, let's get started.

Installing segue

The `segue` package is not currently available as a CRAN package; you need to download it from the following location: `https://code.google.com/p/segue/downloads/detail?name=segue_0.05.tar.gz&can=2&q=`

The `segue` package depends on two other packages: `rJava` and `caTools`. If these are not already available within your R environment, you can install them directly from CRAN. In RStudio, this can simply be done from the **Packages** tab by clicking on the **Install** button. This will present you with a popup into which you can type the names `rJava` and `caTools` to install.

Once you download `segue`, you can install it in a similar manner in RStudio; the **Install Packages** popup has an option by which you can switch from **Repository (CRAN, CRANextra)** to **Package Archive File** and can then browse to the location of your downloaded `segue` package and install it. Simply loading the `segue` library in R will then load its dependencies as follows:

```
> library(segue)

Loading required package: rJava

Loading required package: caTools

Segue did not find your AWS credentials. Please run the
setCredentials() function.
```

The segue package interacts with AWS via its secure API, and this, in turn, is only accessible through your own unique AWS credentials—that is, your AWS Access Key ID and Secret Access Key. This pair of keys must be supplied to `segue` through its `setCredentials()` function. In the next section, we will take a look at how to set up your AWS account in order to obtain your root API keys.

Setting up your AWS account

Our assumption at this point is that you have successfully signed up for an AWS account at `http://aws.amazon.com`, having provided your credit card details and so on and gone through the e-mail verification procedure. If so, then the next step is to obtain your AWS security credentials. When you are logged into the AWS console, click on your name (in the upper-right corner of the screen) and select **Security Credentials** from the drop-down menu.

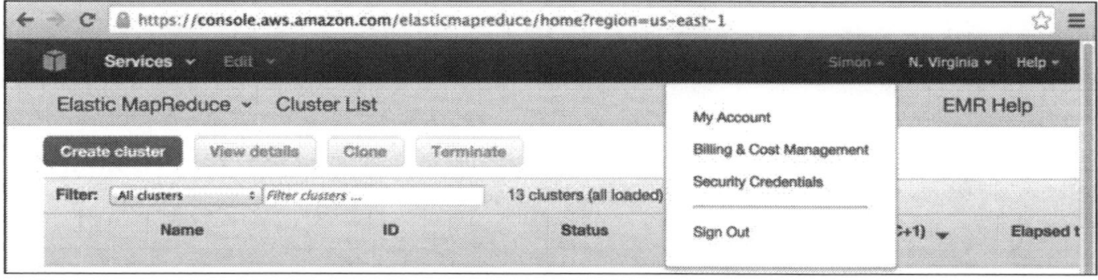

In the preceding screenshot, you can note that I have logged into the AWS console (accessible at the web URL `https://console.aws.amazon.com`) and have previously browsed to my EMR clusters (accessed via the **Services** drop-down menu to the upper-left) within the Amazon US-East-1 region in North Virginia.

This is the Amazon data center region used by `segue` to launch its EMR clusters. Having selected **Security Credentials** from your account name's drop-down menu, you will be taken to the following page:

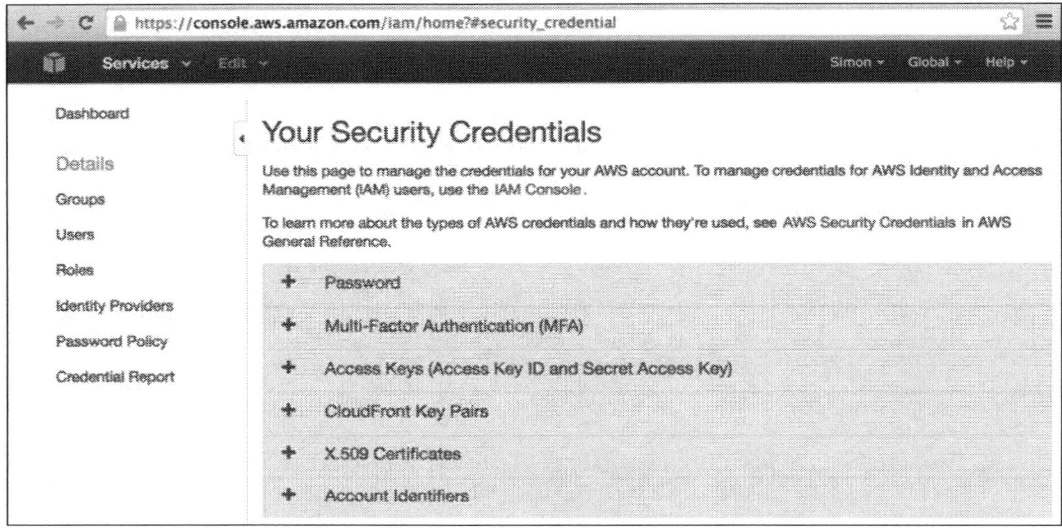

On this page, simply expand the **Access Keys** tab (click on **+**) and then click on the revealed **Create New Access Key** button (note that this button will not be enabled if you already have two existing sets of security keys still active). This will present you with the following popup with new keys created, which you should immediately download and keep safe:

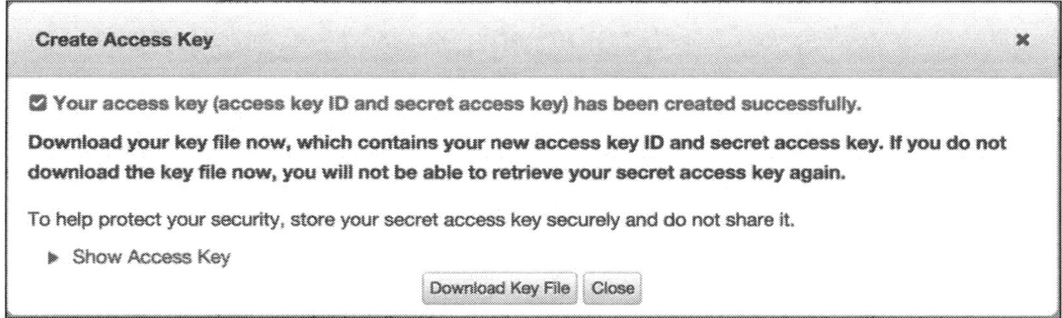

Let's have a look at a tip:

> **Warning: Keep your credentials secure at all times!**
>
> You must keep your AWS access keys secure at all times. If at any point you think that these keys may have become known to someone, you should immediately log in to your AWS account, access this page, and disable your keys. It is a simple process to create a new key pair, and in any case, Amazon's recommended security practice is to periodically reset your keys. It hopefully goes without saying that you should keep the R script where you make a call to the `segue` package `setCredentials()` particularly secure within your own computer.

Running segue

The basic operation of `segue` follows a similar pattern and has similar names to the `parallel` package's cluster functions we looked at in the previous section, namely:

```
> setCredentials("<Access Key ID>","<Secret Access Key>")
> cluster <- createCluster(numInstances=<number of EC2 nodes>)
> results <- emrlapply(cluster, tasks, FUN,
taskTimeout=<10 mins default>)
> stopCluster(cluster) ## Remember to save your bank balance!
```

A key thing to note is that as soon as the cluster is created, Amazon will charge you in dollars until you successfully call `stopCluster()`, even if you never actually invoke the `emrlapply()` parallel compute function.

The `createCluster()` function has a large number of options (detailed in the following table), but our main focus is the `numInstances` option as this determines the degree of parallelism used in the underlying EMR Hadoop cluster—that is, the number of independent EC2 compute nodes employed in the cluster. However, as we are using Hadoop as the cloud cluster framework, one of the instances in the cluster must act as the dedicated master process responsible for assigning tasks to workers and marshaling the results of the parallel MapReduce operation. Therefore, if we want to deploy a 15-way parallelism, then we would need to create a cluster with 16 instances.

Another key thing to note with `emrlapply()` is that you can optionally specify a task timeout option (the default is 10 minutes). The Hadoop master process will consider any task that does not deliver a result (or generate a file I/O) within the timeout period as having failed, the task execution will then be cancelled (and will not be retried by another worker), and a null result will be generated for the task and returned eventually by `emrlapply()`. If you have individual tasks (such as simulation runs) that you know are likely to exceed the default timeout, then you should set the timeout option to an appropriate higher value (the units are minutes). Be aware though that you do want to avoid generating an infinitely running worker process that will rapidly chew through your credit balance.

Options for createCluster()

The `createCluster()` function has a large number of options to select resources for use and to configure the R environment running within AWS EMR Hadoop. The following table summarizes these configuration options. Take a look at the following code:

```
createCluster(numInstances=2,cranPackages=NULL,
  customPackages=NULL, filesOnNodes=NULL,
  rObjectsOnNodes=NULL, enableDebugging=FALSE,
  instancesPerNode=NULL, masterInstanceType="m1.large",
  slaveInstanceType="m1.large", location="us-east-1c",
  ec2KeyName=NULL, copy.image=FALSE, otherBootstrapActions=NULL,
  sourcePackagesToInstall=NULL, masterBidPrice=NULL,
  slaveBidPrice=NULL)
returns: reference object for the remote AWS EMR Hadoop cluster
```

Option [default=value]	Description
`numInstances` [default=2]	This is the degree of parallelism (-1) to employ and equates to 1xMaster and (`numInstances`-1)xWorker EC2 nodes to have in the cluster. The valid range is minimum=2 and (current) maximum=20.
`cranPackages` [default=`NULL`]	This option is a vector of the CRAN package names to be loaded into each node's R session during the cluster startup phase.
`customPackages` [default=`NULL`]	This option is a vector of locally held package filenames to be loaded into each node's R session during the cluster startup phase. The `segue` package will copy these package files from localhost up to the remote AWS cluster using the AWS API.
`filesOnNodes` [default=`NULL`]	This option is a vector of local filenames, typically holding data to be explicitly read in by the parallel function as part of its execution during `emrlapply()`. Segue will copy these files from localhost up to the remote AWS cluster using the AWS API. They will then be located relative to the current working directory of the node and accessible as "`./filename`".

Option [default=value]	Description
rObjectsOnNodes [default=NULL]	This option is a list of named R objects to be attached to the R sessions on each of the worker nodes. Take a look at help(attach) in R for more information.
enableDebugging [default=FALSE]	Turn on/off AWS debugging for this EMR cluster. If set to TRUE, it will enable additional AWS log files to be generated by the nodes, which can help in diagnosing particular problems. You will need to be able to use the AWS console and potentially enable the SSH login to the nodes in order to view the log files and carry out debugging.
instancesPerNode [default=NULL]	This is the number of R session instances running per EC2 compute node. The default is set by AWS. Currently, the default is one R session per worker—that is, one per EC2 compute node.
masterInstanceType [default="m1.large"]	This is the AWS EC2 instance type to be launched for the master node. For segue to operate correctly, this has to be a 64-bit instance type. Valid instance types are described at: link.
slaveInstanceType [default="m1.large"]	This is the AWS EC2 instance type to be launched for the worker node. For segue to operate correctly, this has to be a 64-bit instance type. Valid instance types are described at: link
location [default="us-east-1c"]	This is the AWS region and availability zone in which to run your Hadoop cluster. At the time of writing, this value cannot be changed successfully to launch an EMR cluster in a different AWS region.
ec2KeyName [default=NULL]	This is the EC2 key to be used to log in to the Master node in the EMR cluster. The associated username will be "hadoop."
copy.image [default=FALSE]	If this is TRUE, then the entire current local R session state will be saved, copied, and then loaded into each of the worker's R sessions. Use this with caution.
otherBootstrapActions [default=NULL]	This option is a list of lists of bootstrap actions to be performed on the cluster nodes.
sourcePackagesToInstall [default=NULL]	This option is a vector of full file paths to source the packages to be installed in each worker's R session in the cluster.
masterBidPrice [default=NULL]	This is AWS' desired price to pay for a spot instance master node if available. By default, a standard on-demand EC2 node of the specified masterInstanceType parameter will be deployed and charged for.
slaveBidPrice [default=NULL]	This is AWS' desired price to pay for spot instance worker nodes if available. By default, a standard on-demand EC2 node of the specified slaveInstanceType parameter will be deployed and charged for.

AWS console views

In operation, `segue` has to perform a considerable amount of work to start up a remotely hosted EMR cluster. This includes requesting EC2 resources and utilizing S3 storage areas for the file transfer of the startup configuration and result collection. It's useful to look at the resources that are configured by `segue` using the AWS API through the AWS console that operates in the web browser. Using the AWS console can be critical to sorting out any problems that occur during the provisioning and running of the cluster. Ultimately, the AWS console is the last resort for releasing resources (and therefore limiting further expense) whenever `segue` processes go wrong, and occasionally, this does happen for many different reasons.

The following is the AWS console view of an EMR cluster that was created by `segue`. It just finished the `emrlapply()` parallel compute phase (you can see the step it just carried out , which took 34 minutes, in the center of the screen) and is now in the Waiting state, ready for more tasks to be submitted. You can note, to the lower-left, that it has one master and 15 core workers running as `m1.large` instances. You can also see that `segue` carried out two bootstrap actions on the cluster when it was created, installing the latest version of R and ensuring that all the R packages are up to date. Bootstrap actions obviously create extra overhead in readying the cluster for compute operations:

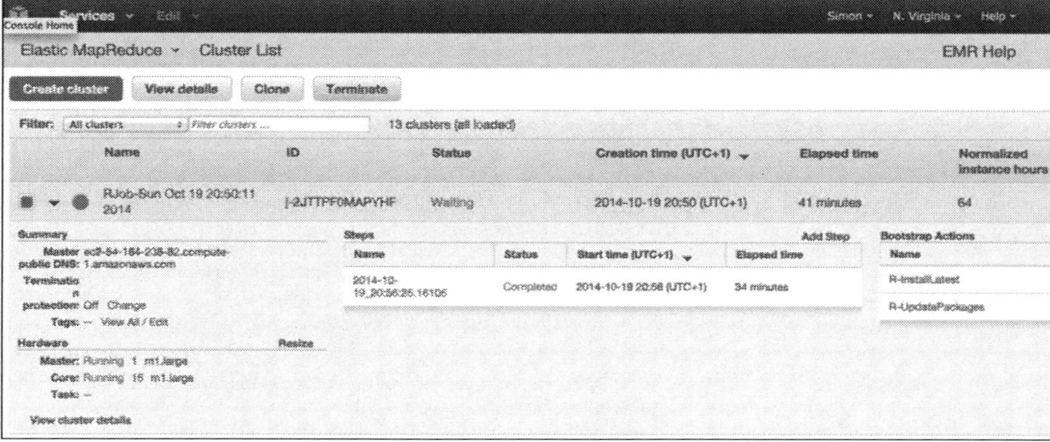

Note that it is from this screen that you can select an individual cluster and terminate it manually, freeing up the resources and preventing further charges, by clicking on the **Terminate** button.

EMR resources are made up of EC2 instances, and the following view shows the equivalent view of "Hardware" in terms of the individual EC2 running instances. They are still running, clocking up AWS chargeable CPU hours, even though they are idling and waiting for more tasks to be assigned. Although EMR makes use of EC2 instances, you should never normally terminate an individual EC2 instance within the EMR cluster from this screen; you should only use the **Terminate** cluster operation from the main EMR **Cluster List** option from the preceding screen.

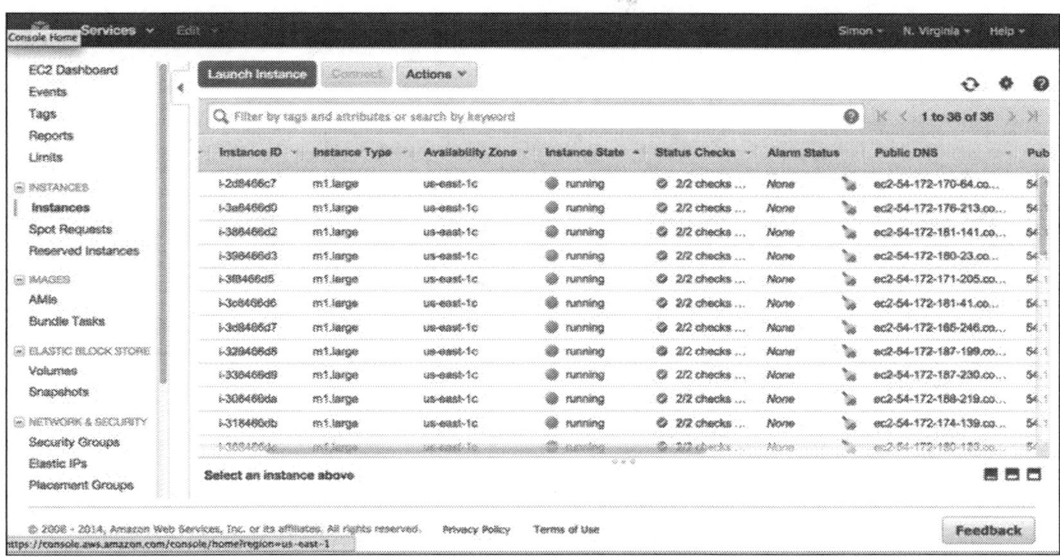

The final AWS console screen worth viewing is the S3 storage screen. The `segue` package creates three separate storage buckets (the name is prefixed with a unique random string), which, to all intents and purposes, can be thought of as three separate top-level directories in which various different types of files are held. These include a cluster-specific log directory (postfix: `segue-logs`), configuration directory (postfix: `segue`), and task results directory (postfix: `segueout`).

The following is a view of the `results` subdirectory within the `segueout` postfix folder associated with the cluster in the previous screens, showing the individual "part-XXXXX" result files being generated by the Hadoop worker nodes as they process the individual tasks:

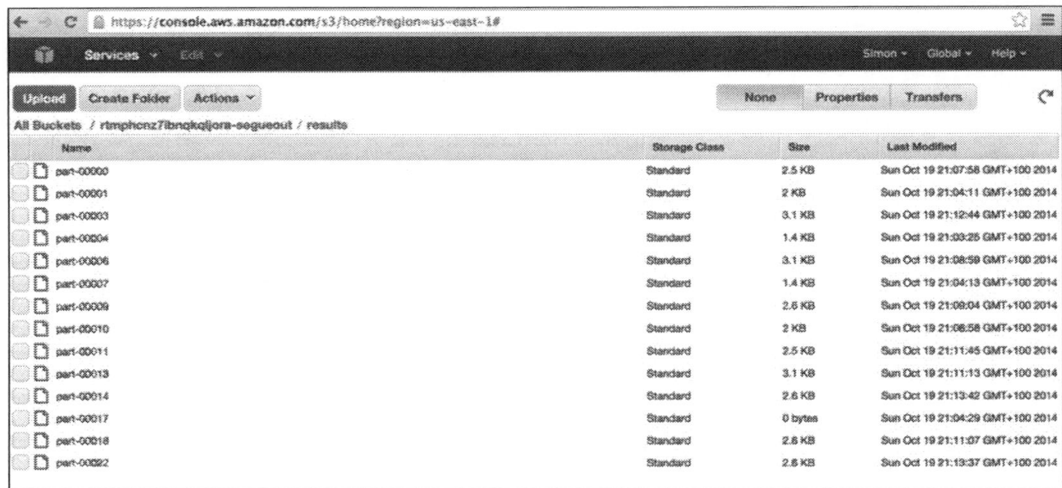

Solving Aristotle's Number Puzzle

At long last, we can now finally run our puzzle solver fully in parallel. Here, we chose to run the EMR cluster with 16 EC2 nodes, equating to one master node and 15 core worker nodes (all `m1.large` instances). It should be noted that there is significant overhead in both starting up the remote AWS EMR Hadoop cluster and in shutting it down again. Run the following code:

```
> setCredentials("<Access Key ID>","<Secret Access Key>")
>
> cluster <- createCluster(numInstances=16)
STARTING - 2014-10-19 19:25:48
## STARTING messages are repeated ~every 30 seconds until
## the cluster enters BOOTSTRAPPING phase.
STARTING - 2014-10-19 19:29:55
BOOTSTRAPPING - 2014-10-19 19:30:26
BOOTSTRAPPING - 2014-10-19 19:30:57
WAITING - 2014-10-19 19:31:28
Your Amazon EMR Hadoop Cluster is ready for action.
Remember to terminate your cluster with stopCluster().
```

```
Amazon is billing you!
## Note that the process of bringing the cluster up is complex
## and can take several minutes depending on size of cluster,
## amount of data/files/packages to be transferred/installed,
## and how busy the EC2/EMR services may be at time of request.

> results <- emrlapply(cluster, tasks, FUN, taskTimeout=10)
RUNNING - 2014-10-19 19:32:45
## RUNNING messages are repeated ~every 30 seconds until the
## cluster has completed all of the tasks.
RUNNING - 2014-10-19 20:06:46
WAITING - 2014-10-19 20:17:16

> stopCluster(cluster) ## Remember to save your bank balance!
## stopCluster does not generate any messages. If you are unable
## to run this successfully then you will need to shut the
## cluster down manually from within the AWS console (EMR).
```

Overall, the `emrlapply()` compute phase took around 34 minutes—not bad! However, the startup and shutdown phases took many minutes to run, making this aspect of overhead considerable. We could, of course, run more node instances (up to a maximum of 20 on AWS EMR currently), and we could use a more powerful instance type rather than just `m1.large` to speed up the compute phase further. However, such further experimentation I will leave to you, dear reader!

The AWS error in emrapply()

Very occasionally, the call to `emrlapply()` may fail with an error message of the following type:

- **Status Code: 404, AWS Service: Amazon S3, AWS Request ID: 5156824C0BE09D70, AWS Error Code: NoSuchBucket, AWS Error Message: The specified bucket does not exist...**

This is a known problem with `segue`. The workaround is to disable your existing AWS credentials and generate a new pair of root security keys, manually terminate the AWS EMR cluster that was created by `segue`, restart your R session afresh, update your AWS keys in the call to `setCredentials()`, and then try again.

Analyzing the results

If we plot the respective elapsed time to compute the potential solution for each of the 90 starting tile-triples using R's built-in `barplot()` function, as can be noted in the following figure, then we will see some interesting features of the problem domain. Correct solutions found are indicated by the dark colored bars, and the rest are all fails.

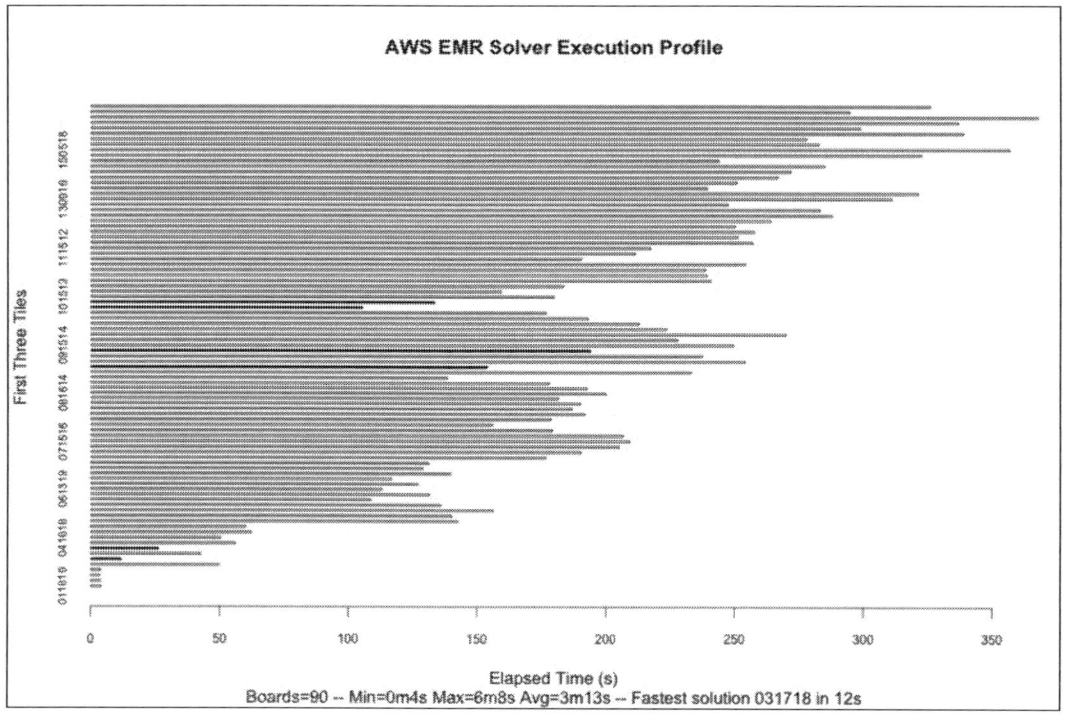

Firstly, we can note that we identified only six board-starting tile-triple configurations that result in a correct solution; I won't spoil the surprise by showing the solution here. Secondly, there is considerable variation in the time taken to explore the search space for each tile-triple with the extremes of 4 seconds and 6 minutes, with the fastest complete solution to the puzzle found in just 12 seconds. The computation is, therefore, very imbalanced, confirming what our earlier sample runs showed. There also appears to be a tendency for the time taken to increase the higher the value of the very first tile placed, something that warrants further investigation if, for example, we were keen to introduce heuristics to improve our solver's ability to choose the next best tile to place.

The cumulative computational time to solve all 90 board configurations was 4 hours and 50 minutes. In interpreting these results, we need to verify that the elapsed time is not adrift of user and system time combined. For the results obtained in this execution, there is a maximum of one percent difference in elapsed time compared to the `user` + `system` time. We would of course expect this as we are paying for dedicated resources in the AWS EMR Hadoop cluster spun up through `segue`.

Summary

In this chapter, you were introduced to three simple yet different techniques of utilizing parallelism in R, operating both FORK and PSOCK implemented clusters with the base R `parallel` package, which exploit the multicore processing capability of your own computer, and using larger-scale AWS EMR Hadoop clusters hosted remotely in the cloud directly from your computer through the `segue` package.

Along the way, you learned how to split a problem efficiently into independent parallelizable tasks and how imbalanced computation can be dealt with through dynamic load-balancing task management. You also saw how to effectively instrument, benchmark, and measure the runtime of your code in order to identify areas for both serial and parallel performance improvement. In fact, as an extra challenge, the current implementation of `evaluateCell()` can itself be improved upon and sped up....

You have also now solved Aristotle's Number Puzzle(!), and if this piqued your interest, then you can find out more about the magic hexagon at `http://en.wikipedia.org/wiki/Magic_hexagon`.

Who knows, you may even be able to apply your new parallel R skills to discover a new magic hexagon solution....

This chapter gave you a significant grounding in the simplest methods of parallelism using R. You should now be able to apply this knowledge directly to your own context and accelerate your own R code. In the remainder of this book, we will look at other forms of parallelism and frameworks that can be used to approach more data-intensive problems on a larger scale. You can either read the book linearly from here to the concluding one, *Chapter 6, The Art of Parallel Programming*, which summarizes the key learning for successful parallel programming, or you can drop into specific chapters for particular technologies, such as *Chapter 2, Introduction to Message Passing*, *Chapter 3, Advanced Message Passing*, and *Chapter 4, Developing SPRINT an MPI-based R package for Supercomputers* for explicit message-passing-based parallelism using MPI and *Chapter 5, The Supercomputer in your Laptop* for GPU-accelerated parallelism using OpenCL.

There is also a bonus chapter that will introduce you to Apache Spark, one of the newest and most popular frameworks implementing distributed parallel computation that supports complex analytics and is arguably the successor to the established, Hadoop-based Map/Reduce, which can also be applied to real-time data analysis.

2
Introduction to Message Passing

In this chapter, we will take our first look at a lower level of parallelism: explicit message passing between multiple communicating R processes. We will utilize the standard **Message Passing Interface** (**MPI**) API available to us in a number of forms on laptops, cloud clusters, and supercomputers.

In this chapter, you will learn about:

- The MPI API and how to use this via the two different R packages, `Rmpi` and `pbdMPI`, together with the OpenMPI implementation of the communications subsystem
- Blocking and non-blocking point-to-point communications
- Group-based collective communications

In the next two chapters, we will explore a more advanced use of MPI, including grid-based parallel processing and running R to scale on a real-life supercomputer; however, for now, we will take an introductory tour of MPI and once again focus on our own Mac computer as the target compute environment; the information required to get you up and running with MPI on Microsoft Windows is also provided.

Setting up your system environment for MPI

In order to use MPI with R, there are a number of prerequisites we need to install. The picture is a little more complicated for setting up MPI as compared to other R packages as we require both an R interface to MPI and an implementation of MPI that it will call into. We also have a number of options available to us, both for the R package and for the underlying MPI subsystem.

Choice of R packages for MPI

There are two MPI-based R-interfacing packages available that we can make use of, namely `Rmpi` and `pbdMPI`:

`Rmpi` is available from CRAN at the following link: `https://cran.r-project.org/web/packages/Rmpi/index.html`

The main `Rmpi` website is `http://www.stats.uwo.ca/faculty/yu/Rmpi/`.

Instructions for installing `Rmpi` on Mac OS X are provided at `http://www.stats.uwo.ca/faculty/yu/Rmpi/mac_os_x.htm`.

Instructions for installing `Rmpi` on Windows are provided at `http://www.stats.uwo.ca/faculty/yu/Rmpi/windows.htm`.

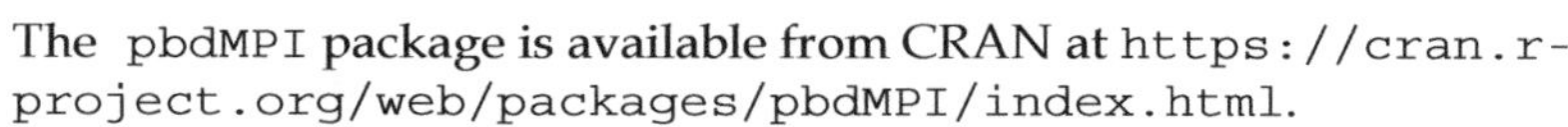

The `pbdMPI` package is available from CRAN at `https://cran.r-project.org/web/packages/pbdMPI/index.html`.

The main **Programming with Big Data (pbd)** website is at `http://r-pbd.org/`.

Detailed instructions for installing `pbdMPI` on Mac OS X with screenshots are provided at `https://rawgit.com/wrathematics/installation-instructions/master/output/with_screenshots/html/index_mac.html`.

Detailed instructions for installing `pbdMPI` on Windows with screenshots are provided at `https://rawgit.com/wrathematics/installation-instructions/master/output/with_screenshots/html/index_windows.html`.

While each of these packages provides an interface for standard MPI implementations, they operate in slightly different ways and provide their own specific additional functionality. One particular difference is that `Rmpi` is able to run directly within an interactive R session, whereas `pbdMPI` must be run through the standard MPI-specific launch program (`mpiexec`) from your computer system's command-line shell.

Choice of MPI subsystems

We also have the option of selecting from a number of underlying MPI subsystems to use with either of these R packages. In this chapter, we will use the most popular open source MPI implementation compatible with Mac OS X, namely OpenMPI, although alternatives do exist, including MPICH and MS-MPI, all of which are compatible with version 3.0 of the MPI standard.

- **OpenMPI**: OpenMPI started in 2004 with the goal of building a modular and portable high-performance implementation. OpenMPI is supported across a range of platforms and used to be shipped built-in with Mac OS X prior to 10.7 (Lion). For more information, refer to `http://www.open-mpi.org/`.
- **MPICH**: MPICH (MPI over Chameleon) originated as the reference implementation for MPI when the standard was first formed in 1992. Since then, it has seen wide adoption among the supercomputer community. For more information, refer to `http://www.mpich.org/`. We will use MPICH on the UK's ARCHER supercomputer in a following chapter.
- **MS-MPI**: While it is technically possible to build OpenMPI and MPICH for Windows, ongoing development and support for both has recently been discontinued for the Windows platform. However, all is not lost! Take a look at the following link for information about Microsoft's own distribution of MPI for Windows (MS-MPI), including downloadable and installable libraries that can be used with both `Rmpi` and `pbdMPI`: `https://msdn.microsoft.com/en-us/library/bb524831(v=vs.85).aspx`.

Installing OpenMPI

The basic installation of OpenMPI on OS X is straightforward if using the excellent Homebrew installer. Run the following command:

```
mac:~ brew install openmpi
```

Homebrew

The `brew` command is a package manager for OS X, itself written in Ruby, and is widely used by the OS X development community. Refer to `http://brew.sh/` and `https://github.com/Homebrew/homebrew/tree/master/share/doc/homebrew#readme` for the latest information and instructions on how to install.

This will take a little while to run and pull in a number of dependencies, including **Gnu C Compiler** (GCC). You can then type the following sequence of shell commands in your terminal window to check whether the install is successful:

```
mac:~ simon$ which mpiexec
/usr/local/bin/mpiexec
mac:~ simon$ ls -la /usr/local/bin/mpiexec
lrwxr-xr-x  1 simon  admin  37  7 Sep 15:54 /usr/local/bin/mpiexec -> ../
Cellar/open-mpi/1.10.0/bin/mpiexec
mac:~ simon$ mpiexec --version
mpiexec (OpenRTE) 1.10.0
Report bugs to http://www.open-mpi.org/community/help/
```

This shows that I have version 1.10 of OpenMPI installed and placed in the standard system directory on 'nixes—that is, symbolically linked from homebrew's default "`Cellar`" location to `/usr/local`.

The MPI standard

You can view the complete version 3.0 MPI standard, which runs to a desk-walloping 822 pages in the form of a PDF Report at (MPI Ref) `http://www.mpi-forum.org/docs/mpi-3.0/mpi30-report.pdf`.

At the time of writing, version 3.1 of the MPI standard is published (June 2015). Although we will be focusing on the previous version, that is 3.0, the differences are not material for our purposes. MPI version 3.0 is both mature and comprehensive.

Due to some of the limitations of R and, in particular, its inherent single-threaded nature, only a subset of the MPI standard is implemented in either `Rmpi` or `pbdMPI`. However, all the basics for point-to-point and collective group communications are available, and we shall explore these through the remainder of this chapter. To begin, we need to understand some basic concepts that apply to the world of MPI.

The MPI universe

MPI considers each separate thread of computation to be a process, and each process is assigned a unique rank, which is a number from 0 to *N-1* where *N* is the total number of independent processes that we create in the MPI universe. A communicator defines the scope for communications between processes in the universe. A process can send a message to another process or a group of processes to receive within the context of a specific communicator. MPI provides options for whether the sending and/or receiving process should wait for a communication to/from them to be completed or can proceed with other activities and check later for its completion. An MPI program may utilize multiple communicators in order to separate out patterns of communication between processes so that they are not confused. Consider, for example, a library function that utilizes MPI internally for its parallel implementation. It's important that its communications are kept completely separate from any other MPI-enabled code within your program.

In essence, the preceding paragraph described the basic capabilities of MPI; everything else provides additional programming convenience or follows as a necessary consequence of managing parallelism based on message passing. Of course, in reality, we also need to add a healthy pinch of salt to this declaration.

Without further ado, having installed OpenMPI, let's jump in and get both `Rmpi` and `pbdMPI` up and running...

Installing Rmpi

From your R session, type the following to download and build the current `Rmpi` package from a CRAN mirror of your choice:

```
> install.packages(""Rmpi"", type=""source"")
```

Then, load the built library into your active R session:

```
> library(Rmpi)
```

To test whether everything is working correctly, we will start up the `Rmpi` package's default configuration of master/workers, execute a simple print statement, and immediately shut the workers down. You should see output similar to the following:

```
> mpi.spawn.Rslaves() # Set up Workers
4 slaves are spawned successfully. 0 failed.
master (rank 0, comm 1) of size 5 is running on: Simons-Mac-mini
slave1 (rank 1, comm 1) of size 5 is running on: Simons-Mac-mini
```

```
slave2 (rank 2, comm 1) of size 5 is running on: Simons-Mac-mini
slave3 (rank 3, comm 1) of size 5 is running on: Simons-Mac-mini
slave4 (rank 4, comm 1) of size 5 is running on: Simons-Mac-mini
> mpi.remote.exec(paste(""Worker"", mpi.comm.rank(),""of"", mpi.comm.
size()))
$slave1
[1] ""Worker 1 of 5""
$slave2
[1] ""Worker 2 of 5""
$slave3
[1] ""Worker 3 of 5""
$slave4
[1] ""Worker 4 of 5""
> mpi.close.Rslaves() # Tear down Workers
```

You will note that on my system, which has four cores, five MPI processes were created, one master and four workers, with MPI ranks assigned 0 through 4 and a default communicator context identifiable through the API calls as the number `1`. The master is the interactive session, while the four workers are launched as additional external R processes, as you can note from the following screenshot of **Activity Monitor** (after `mpi.spawn.Rslaves()` and before `mpi.close.Rslaves()`):

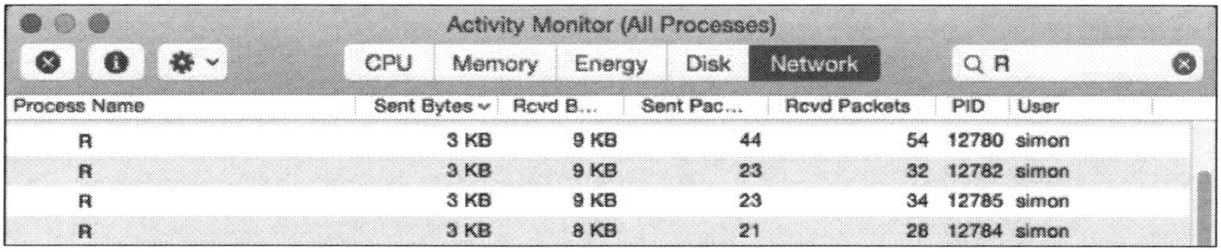

Activity Monitor (All Processes)

CPU | Memory | Energy | Disk | Network

Process Name	Sent Bytes	Rcvd B...	Sent Pac...	Rcvd Packets	PID	User
R	3 KB	9 KB	44	54	12780	simon
R	3 KB	9 KB	23	32	12782	simon
R	3 KB	9 KB	23	34	12785	simon
R	3 KB	8 KB	21	28	12784	simon

Figure 1: Activity Monitor view of the R Worker MPI processes launched by Rmpi.

You may notice as you watch the **Network** tab on **Activity Monitor** that the number of Rcvd packets increases even though you may not be executing any parallel code; this is just the internal background OpenMPI "heartbeat" system communications making sure all MPI processes are still running correctly.

Installing pbdMPI

Installing `pbdMPI` is also straightforward. However, I would recommend installing from the system shell command line rather than an interactive R session because at the time of writing, you may run into a dynamic library issue on OS X that requires a slight tweak (refer to the following "Yosemite" breakout box for a workaround).

Download the latest `pbdMPI` package source from `https://cran.r-project.org/web/packages/pbdMPI/index.html`.

Open a terminal window, change to the directory with the downloaded package (in this case, I downloaded `pbdMPI_0.2-5.tar.gz` and pre-extracted it to expose all the files within) and type the following:

```
mac:~ simon$ R CMD INSTALL pbdMPI --configure-args=''--with-mpi-
type=OPENMPI''
```

This will compile `pbdMPI` to use OpenMPI, which we installed previously. Assuming this step is successful, I recommend running one of the package's demo test programs to confirm that all is well.

For `pbdMPI`, we always need to run our R code using a special command, `mpiexec`, which comes as part of the OpenMPI installation, as follows:

```
mac:~ simon$ cd pbdMPI/inst/examples/test_spmd
mac:~ simon$ mpiexec -np 2 Rscript --vanilla allgather.r
...
COMM.RANK = 0
[1] 1 1 2
COMM.RANK = 0
[1] 1 1 2
```

If you run the `allgather.r` test script successfully, then you should see the tail end of the `COMM.RANK` output as shown previously. The required command line options for running a `pbdMPI` test script is commented at the top of the given R script file; in this case, `-np 2` means to run with two MPI processes in the universe (this will launch two processes regardless of whether you only have a single-core machine).

The pbdMPI package on OS X Yosemite

It's possible that you may run into a specific compilation issue with `pbdMPI` on the Mac; I certainly did for OS X 10.10 Yosemite. The standard options for compiling the `pbdMPI` package may fail with an output similar to the following (note that the output is stripped for brevity):

```
mca: base: component_find: unable to open /usr/local/Cellar/open-mpi/1.10.0/lib/openmpi/mca_osc_sm: dlopen(/usr/local/Cellar/open-mpi/1.10.0/lib/openmpi/mca_osc_sm.so, 9): Symbol not found: _ompi_info_t_class
...
 in /usr/local/Cellar/open-mpi/1.10.0/lib/openmpi/mca_osc_sm.so (ignored)
...
No available pml components were found!
This is a fatal error; your MPI process is likely to abort.
...
```

A workaround for this is to make use of the OS X operating system's mechanism to inject dynamic libraries at runtime to ensure the core OpenMPI library is loaded to resolve the missing symbols. First, rebuild the `pbdMPI` package without the failing load test step, as follows:

```
mac:~ simon$ R CMD INSTALL pbdMPI --configure-args=''--with-mpi-type=OPENMPI'' --no-test-load
```

This should now build successfully and install the `pbdMPI` package into the standard R library location on your system. Now, whenever you run `mpiexec`, ensure that the dynamic loader shell environment variable `DYLD_INSERT_LIBRARIES` is set as follows (OpenMPI is installed to the standard `/usr/local` system directory on my system) via the following command:

```
mac:~ simon$ export DYLD_INSERT_LIBRARIES=/usr/local/lib/libmpi.dylib
```

You can also add this setting to your shell's start-up script in your home directory (`~/.bashrc`) so that it is automatically set up whenever you open a new terminal window.

The MPI API

We will divide our coverage of the MPI API into two: firstly, point-to-point communications followed by group-wise collective communications. Additional functionality beyond the core communication is described later in the advanced MPI API section.

First however, we need to explain some differences in the approaches to parallelism adopted by `Rmpi` and `pbdMPI`. We have already discussed that `Rmpi` can run within an interactive R session, whereas the `pbdMPI` R programs can only be run using `mpiexec` from a command shell (`Rmpi` programs can also be run with `mpiexec`).

`Rmpi` adopts the master/worker paradigm and dynamically launches worker processes internally using `MPI_Comm_spawn()`, where the launching R session is the master and the workers form the computational cluster. Code blocks that may include MPI communication are then issued by the master for remote execution by the worker cluster, which each execute an `Rmpi` daemon-style R script actively waiting for the next command to be broadcast to them with `MPI_Bcast()`. Upon completion, the results will be collectively returned back to the waiting master.

The `pbdMPI` package adopts the **Single Program Multiple Data (SPMD)** approach, whereby all parallel processes have equal billing and run the same code and MPI communications apply uniformly across all the processes in the MPI universe (unless explicitly programmed around). The `pbdMPI` R programs must be run via `mpiexec` to invoke the R runtime and for the MPI infrastructure to create the initial group of parallel processes.

Rmpi or pbdMPI – which is the best?

As ever with this type of question, the answer is: it depends.

`Rmpi` enables you to immediately spin up a cluster of master and workers on a single node from RStudio and run R functions effectively in parallel across split data on small clusters. Without some changes to the internals of `Rmpi`, which we will cover later, its default configuration makes it difficult to exploit communications between worker processes. `Rmpi` is compatible with R's core parallel package and can be used as the underlying framework for `makeCluster(""MPI"")`. Refer to the *Using parLapply()* section in *Chapter 1, Simple Parallelism with R*.

Programming with Big Data MPI (pbdMPI): R programs can only be launched through the external MPI runtime framework with the `mpiexec` command. It has greater flexibility in operating parallel processes, such as SPMD, and enabling larger-scale parallelism and does not impose restrictions on interprocess communication. The `pdbMPI` package is also part of a larger Big Data package that includes dense linear algebra libraries and distributed matrix classes.

The following sections include tables detailing the basic MPI functionality supported by `Rmpi` and `pbdMPI`, with reference to the corresponding MPI 3.0 standard's API call—the page reference in the PDF report is also given in case you want to look up the standard's definition for the C/Fortran language variant of the call (The MPI reference can be found at `http://www.mpi-forum.org/docs/mpi-3.0/mpi30-report.pdf`).

As you might expect, the naming conventions in the R packages are very similar. In essence, `pbdMPI` overloads a single API call name to work with multiple types of data, whereas `Rmpi` requires you to be more explicit and provides additional functions to support the different types of data. You'll also notice that `Rmpi` uses `"mpi."` as a standard function name prefix, whereas `pbdMPI` has no prefix. Unfortunately, this means that we cannot write a single program that is easily portable between these two package interfaces; we have to write separate code for each.

Point-to-point blocking communications

Let's jump straight in with a very simple test program that sends a message from the last ranked MPI process to its ranked predecessor. You'll need a machine with at least two cores for this example to work. When we start with `Rmpi`, a `pbdMPI` implementation also follows. Recall that `Rmpi` can be run in an interactive R session, as follows:

```
> library(Rmpi)
> mpi.spawn.Rslaves() # Spawn at least 2 workers
> rmpi_lastsend <- function() {
  myrank <- mpi.comm.rank(comm=1) # which MPI rank am I?
  sender <- mpi.comm.size(comm=1)-1 # msg is sent from last
  receiver <- mpi.comm.size(comm=1)-2 # to last''s predecessor
  buf <- ""long enough""
  if (myrank == sender) {
    msg <- paste(""Hi from:"",sender)
    mpi.send(msg,3,receiver,0,comm=1)
  } else if (myrank == receiver) {
    buf <- mpi.recv(buf,3,sender,mpi.any.tag(),comm=1)
  }
  return(buf)
}
> mpi.bcast.Rfun2slave(comm=1) # Master shares all its function
definitions with the Workers
```

```
> mpi.remote.exec(rmpi_lastsend()) # Workers (only) execute specific
function
$slave1
[1] ""long enough""
$slave2
[1] ""long enough""
$slave3
[1] ""Hi from: 4""
$slave4
[1] ""long enough""
```

You should see an output similar to the preceding. On my system, I have four cores, so `mpi.spawn.Rslaves()`, by default, creates a cluster of four workers. `Rmpi` creates the default communicator identified as `"1`," and this includes all the workers and the master—here, the master is at rank 0, and the last worker is at rank 4. As you can note from the previous code, we used `mpi.comm.rank()` to obtain the unique rank number of the calling process in the default communicator and `mpi.comm.size()` to determine how many processes there are in total in the default communicator, which in this case is the entire MPI universe. We also used the special `Rmpi` function, `mpi.bcast.Rfun2slave()`, to transmit our `lastsend()` function definition (and any other user-defined functions on the master) to all the workers so that they can subsequently execute it remotely. If at any time we change our function definition, we would need to retransmit it to the workers before we execute it again.

Let's focus on the `mpi.send` call, as follows:

```
mpi.send(msg, 3, receiver, 0, comm=1)
```

The `Rmpi` package's `mpi.send()` method has four mandatory arguments, which are:

- The R object you are sending, `msg`.
- A value that determines what (simple) type of data the R object is [`3`] (`Rmpi` defines 1=integer, 2=numeric, and 3=character string). Shortly, we will take a look at how to send and receive complex R objects.
- The rank of the MPI process you are sending to [`receiver`].
- The tag to label the send [`0`]. The receiver can choose to make its matching `mpi.recv()` selective on the value of tag. The tag is only typically used when different types of messages or a sequencing of messages received from a given sender is important to determine. It tends to be more applicable for the disambiguation of non-blocking communication, which we will come to later.

Optionally, you can define which communicator will be the scope for the send. In this case, we explicitly set it to the default "1" just for the purpose of clarity.

Now, let's examine the `mpi.recv` call:

```
buf <- mpi.recv(buf, 3, sender, mpi.any.tag(), comm=1)
```

The `Rmpi` package's `mpi.recv()` method also has four mandatory arguments:

- An R object of the same type as the one being sent and of sufficient size to accommodate the sent object [`buf`]. The next example will illustrate this aspect further.
- A value that determines what (simple) type of data the R object is [`3`], in which `3` indicates a character string.
- The rank of the MPI process you are receiving from [`sender`].
- The tag to match with the [`mpi.any.tag()`] send. We chose to use the special value defined by `mpi.any.tag()`, which means that this receive will match any tagged send from the specified sender.

Again, for this receive, we chose to explicitly set the communicator scope to its default value, "1".

To illustrate the `mpi.recv()` function's first "buffer" argument, it is instructed to modify the `lastsend()` function and then rerun it as follows:

```
> rmpi_lastsend <- function() {
  ...
  receiver <- mpi.comm.size(comm=1)-2 # to last''s predecessor
  buf <- ""too short""
  if (myrank == sender) {
  ...
  return(buf)
}
> mpi.bcast.Rfun2slave(comm=1) # Distribute updated function
> mpi.remote.exec(rmpi_lastsend()) # Workers execute function
$slave1
[1] ""too short""
$slave2
[1] ""too short""
```

```
$slave3
[1] ""Hi from: ""
$slave4
[1] ""too short""
```

As you can note, `Rmpi` reuses the object's memory supplied as the first argument to receive the value transmitted in the send, and in this case, it is one character too short. However, for this case, we do know how large we need to make the receiving buffer in order for us to get the complete message, so it is simple to fix. In the next chapter, when we review the more advanced MPI API, we will take a look at how to query the size of a message we are about to receive before we actually receive it using `MPI_Probe`.

For now, we can easily bypass this particular problem by choosing to use the `Rmpi` pair of `send`/`recv` functions that enable complex R objects to be communicated, namely `mpi.send.Robj()` and `mpi.recv.Robj()`, as follows:

```
rmpi_lastsend2 <- function() {
  myrank <- mpi.comm.rank(comm=1)
  sender <- mpi.comm.size(comm=1) - 1
  receiver <- mpi.comm.size(comm=1) - 2
  buf <- ""N/A""
  if (myrank == sender) {
    msg <- paste(""Hi from:"", sender)
    mpi.send.Robj(msg, receiver, 0, comm=1)
  } else if (myrank == receiver) {
    buf <- mpi.recv.Robj(sender, mpi.any.tag(), comm=1)
  }
  return(buf)
}
```

Note how with these functions, we do not need to specify the type of the R object we are sending/receiving and also how with `mpi.recv.Robj()`, we do not need to set a receive buffer object because the received object is created for us and returned from the function call directly. While `mpi.send.Robj()` and `mpi.recv.Robj()` are a little less performant for R data that is simply numeric or string, they are in general easier to use, and you are less likely to program it incorrectly.

As promised, here is the `pbdMPI` implementation of the "lastsend" example. Remember that `pbdMPI` must be run with `mpiexec` from a command shell—for example, from an OS X terminal, as follows:

```
# File: chapter2_pbdMPI.R
library(pbdMPI, quietly=TRUE)
init()
pbdmpi_lastsend <- function() {
  myrank <- comm.rank()
  sender <- comm.size() - 1
  receiver <- comm.size() - 2
  if (myrank == sender) {
    msg <- paste(""Hi from:"", sender)
    send(msg, rank.dest=receiver)
  } else if (myrank == receiver) {
    buf <- recv(rank.source=sender)
  }
  comm.print(buf, rank.print=receiver)
}
pbdmpi_lastsend() # This is SPMD so all processes execute the same
finalize()
```

The output from running this command will be displayed in the terminal window, as follows:

```
mac$ mpiexec -np 4 Rscript chapter2_pbdMPI.R
COMM.RANK = 2
[1] ""Hi from: 3""
```

Note how the last process is at rank `3`; there is no separate master process as we are running SPMD. Also, note that the `pbdMPI` package's `send()` and `recv()` functions have default argument settings for both the tag and communicator. Nor is any explicit typing required as `pbdMPI` checks the argument type of the sent data and internally switches to the most efficient MPI call to use. We also chose to not set the communicator explicitly, so the default `MPI_COMM_WORLD` communicator is used, which contains all of the MPI processes that started up and returned successfully from their `init()` calls.

pbdMPI `comm.print()`: In the preceding pbdMPI example, we used the `comm.print()` function to display the message string as received by the receiver only by setting the `rank.print` argument to the receiver's rank number. It is important to recognize that all MPI processes in the particular communicator must call `comm.print()` even if they are not going to print anything themselves; otherwise, a deadlock will result (internally, `comm.print()` would call `MPI_Barrier`. Refer to the *Collective Communications* section later in the chapter). It's quite easy to forget this, place `comm.print()` inside a conditional statement, and then wonder why your program hangs forever.

If you do want all the MPI processes in the same communicator to print something with `comm.print()`, simply call it with the argument setting `all.rank=TRUE`; this overrides `rank.print` if also set.

`MPI_Init` and `MPI_Finalize`: All MPI programs require an initialization and termination phase in order to set up and tear down the MPI communications subsystem. Unsurprisingly, `pbdMPI` calls `MPI_Init` within its `init()` function and `MPI_Finalize` within its `finalize()` function. However, as `Rmpi` is designed to work within the context of an interactive R session, it runs `MPI_Init` when the library is loaded and provides distinct MPI termination functions to handle three specific circumstances:

`Rmpi::mpi.finalize()`: This cleanly terminates the MPI. `Rmpi` remains available in the R session, so you can decide to launch more MPI workers and run in parallel again.

`Rmpi::mpi.exit()`: This executes `mpi.finalize()` but also detaches the `Rmpi` library, so you cannot use MPI again. R continues to run, and you could decide to reload the `Rmpi` library in the session and carry on.

`Rmpi::mpi.quit()`: This executes `mpi.exit()` but also terminates the R session entirely; it is final!

The MPI point-to-point send and receive routines that we used are known as *blocking*, which means that the send operation routine *may* not complete until the data being sent is transferred to the intended receiving process, implying that the process has executed a matching receive operation. From the sender's perspective, once the send function call returns, it is safe for the sender to modify the object that was just sent. If no matching receive operation for a given send occurs, then the sender may block and never return from the send function call. Consequently, the sending process will hang indefinitely. This is a situation known as *deadlock* and is discussed in more detail in *Chapter 6, The Art of Parallel Programming*. For now, it is enough for us to know that we must have a matching receive executed for each send from across all the MPI parallel processes in our program.

The point-to-point blocking communications are summarized in the following table:

BLOCKING COMMUNICATIONS		
MPI V3.0 API Call	**pbdMPI equivalent**	**Rmpi equivalent**

`MPI_Send` (*MPI Ref: p.24*
• `buf`: This is the address pointer to the first object in the buffer of contiguous memory, in the sending process
• `count`: This is the number of objects in the memory buffer to send
• `datatype`: This is the enum defining type of the object from which the size of object is inferred
• `dest`: This is the rank of destination processes in the communicator sending to
• `tag`: This is a non-negative integer that only means something to the caller
• `comm`: This is the communicator within which this message will be transferred)
	`send(`
	`Robject,`
	`rank.dest=1,`
	`tag=0,`
	`comm=0`
	`)`
	returns: NULL
	The default argument values for `pbdMPI::send` are defined in `$SPMD.CT` and can be changed there.
		`mpi.send(`
		`x, type, dest, tag,`
		`comm=1`
		`)`
		returns: NULL
		`mpi.send.Robj(`
		`Robject, dest, tag,`
		`comm=1`
		`)`
		returns: NULL
		The valid values for `type` are:
		• 1 = integer
		• 2 = numeric
		• 3 = character

`MPI_Send` is a blocking operation; there must be a matching `MPI_Recv` or `MPI_Irecv`; otherwise, the process executing `MPI_Send` will deadlock. Both `pdbMPI::send` and `Rmpi::mpi.send.Robj` are higher-level functions that internally compute the quantity of data that is to be transferred. `Rmpi::mpi.send` is used to send integer / int, numeric / double or character / char vectors only.		

<table>
<tr><th colspan="3">BLOCKING COMMUNICATIONS</th></tr>
<tr>
<td>MPI_Recv (MPI Ref: p.28
<ul>
<li>buf: This is an address pointer to the first object in the buffer of contiguous memory in the receiving process</li>
<li>count: This is the number of objects in the memory buffer to receive</li>
<li>datatype: This is the enum defining type of the object from which the size of the object is inferred</li>
<li>srce: This is the rank of source process in the communicator receiving from</li>
<li>tag: This is a non-negative integer that only has meaning for the caller</li>
<li>comm: This is the communicator within which this message will be transferred</li>
<li>status: This is an MPI_Status object that can be queried after the receive for details such as srce and tag)</li>
</ul>
</td>
<td>recv(
x.buffer=NULL,
rank.srce=0,
tag=0,
comm=0,
status=0
)
returns: Robject

The default argument values for pbdMPI::recv are defined in $SPMD.CT and can be changed there.</td>
<td>mpi.recv(
x, type, srce, tag,
comm=1,
status=0
)
returns: NULL

mpi.recv.Robj(
srce, tag,
comm=1,
status=0
)
returns: Robject

The valid values for type are:
<ul>
<li>1 = integer</li>
<li>2 = numeric</li>
<li>3 = character</li>
</ul>
</td>
</tr>
</table>

<table>
<tr><th colspan="3">BLOCKING COMMUNICATIONS</th></tr>
<tr><td colspan="3">

`MPI_Recv` is a blocking operation; there must be a matching `MPI_Send` or `MPI_Isend`, otherwise the process executing `MPI_Recv` will deadlock.

The `pbdMPI::recv` method can optionally be provided with an empty presized R object to receive the equivalent format of data from the sender. It always returns the received object.

`Rmpi::mpi.recv` requires you to provide it with a presized R vector of the correct type to match the one being sent. Once it is completed, the vector supplied to the call will be filled with the received data.

To make a wildcard receive that will capture an R object sent to the receiving process from any other in the same communicator with any `tag` value, use the following:

```
pbdMPI::recv(rank.srce=anysource(), anytag())
Rmpi::mpi.recv.Robj(mpi.any.source(), mpi.any.tag())
```

You can then query the `status` object used for the receive (default=`0`) to find out who the sender was and which `tag` was used:

```
st <- pbdMPI::get.sourcetag(status=0)
st <- Rmpi::mpi.get.sourcetag(status=0)
# st[1]=sender''s rank, st[2]=tag value sent
```

</td></tr>
<tr><td>

`MPI_Sendrecv` (*MPI Ref: p.79*
`sendbuf, sendcount, sendtype,`
`dest, sendtag,`
`recvbuf, recvcount, recvtype,`
`srce, recvtag,`
`comm, status`
)

`MPI_Sendrecv_replace(`
MPI Ref: p.80
`buf, count, datatype,`
`dest, sendtag,`
`srce, recvtag,`
`comm, status`
)

See `MPI_Send/MPI_Recv` previously in this table for explanation of the arguments used by these functions.

</td><td>

```
sendrecv(
Robject,
x.buffer=NULL,
rank.dest=see below,
send.tag=0,
rank.srce=see below,
recv.tag=0,
comm=0,
status=0
)
```

returns: `Robject`

```
sendrecv.replace(
Robject,
rank.dest=see below,
send.tag=0,
rank.srce=see below,
recv.tag=0,
comm=0,
status=0
)
```

returns: `Robject`

</td><td>

```
mpi.sendrecv(
senddata, sendtype,
dest, sendtag,
recvdata, recvtype,
srce, recvtag,
comm=1,
status=0
)
```

returns: `recvdata`

```
mpi.sendrecv.replace(
x, type, dest, sendtag,
srce, recvtag,
comm=1,
status=0
)
```

returns: `x`

</td></tr>
</table>

BLOCKING COMMUNICATIONS
Unsurprisingly, `MPI_Sendrecv` combines both a send and a receive by the calling process in a single call. Its equivalent to doing separate independent send and receive, such that each aspect can be with different processes and for different types of data, except that both the send and the receive must complete, before control is returned back to the program and the next R statement can be executed. `MPI_Sendrecv` is therefore a blocking operation; there must be matching `MPI_Sendrecv` or a set of `MPI_Send/MPI_Isend` and `MPI_Recv/MPI_Irecv` called by other processes. The `pdbMPI` library sets the defaults for `rank.dest` and `rank.srce` such that each process sends to its immediate ranked successor and receives from its immediate ranked predecessor, enabling a single-step-forward chain exchange among all the processes in the communicator to be trivially implemented. For a related code example using `MPI_Sendrecv`, refer to *Chapter 6, The Art of Parallel Programming*.

If you have loaded either the `Rmpi` library or the `pbdMPI` library into your R session (you can load `pbdMPI` but not actually run it this way), then typing `??sendrecv` (the standard R help syntax) will bring up the corresponding help page including a simple example; there are many more brief MPI examples you can access this way.

MPI intracommunicators

We have already touched on the concept of a matched send and receive. There are four key attributes of a communication on which we can be selective, namely:

- **Communicator**: This is the communicator that will be used to convey the message. If it helps, you can think analogously of the communicator being the equivalent of a radio channel. You have to be tuned into the correct channel if you want to hear a specific message broadcast to you (and as with most analogies, we can only take it so far...).
- **Source**: This is the rank of the process sending the message (that is, who is "transmitting").
- **Tag**: This is the tag label for the message, a program-defined interpretation of what is being sent.
- **Destination**: The sender also gets to choose the rank of the process that is the recipient for the message (that is, who is "listening").

The type of communicator we are using is an **intracommunicator**, meaning only processes that are members of this communicator—that is, have a rank within it—can communicate with one another. Within the context of a specific intracommunicator, all communication is private. The MPI standard provides a rich interface to support exotic process group hierarchies, enabling the overlapping, intersecting, and creating of combined process membership communicators and allowing processes in different groups to communicate via the construction of an **intercommunicator**. However, both `Rmpi` and `pbdMPI` are designed to serve more straightforward use cases, so both packages limit their exposure of this `MPI_Comm` family of API functions essentially to the duplication of an existing communicator with `MPI_Comm_dup`.

Duplicating an MPI communicator is a fundamental requirement enabling different parallelized functions to keep their own pattern of communications entirely separate from any other code (an analogy of this would be two different radio stations that are not permitted to broadcast on the same channel). Out of the box, `Rmpi` does not make it possible to create a workers-only communicator, and this can limit or at least complicate some of our programming options (refer to the following breakout box). However, it is instructive to show how we can make `Rmpi` a little more flexible in this regard, so this is what we will explore next.

The Rmpi workerdaemon.R script

We will implement an `Rmpi MPI_Comm_dup` fix by creating a new behind-the-scenes `Rmpi` worker daemon script. When `Rmpi` spawns a new set of worker processes, by default, it makes use of a special process launch script called `slavedaemon.R`. We will make a copy of this and edit it to introduce a duplicated communicator that spans just the set of worker processes and excludes the master. This will enable us to safely separate our own worker communications from what `Rmpi` does internally between the master and workers. It will also provide us with a communicator that we can use for the special *MPI Collective Communications* API calls just among the spawned workers.

First, identify the location of your `Rmpi` installation. From an R session, type the following:

```
> .libPaths()
[1] ""/Library/Frameworks/R.framework/Versions/3.2/Resources/library""
```

You should see an output similar to the previous one, particularly if you are running on a Mac device. Next, open a terminal window and type the following at the console prompt:

```
mac$ cd /Library/Frameworks/R.framework/Versions/3.2/Resources/library/
Rmpi
mac$ cp slavedaemon.R workerdaemon.R
```

Then, open a text editor on the new `workerdaemon.R` file and modify it to add in some additional lines as highlighted in the following code snippet. Your file may look a little different depending on the version of `Rmpi`:

```
#File: workerdaemon.R
# Copied from slavedaemon.R and modified to create workers'' Wcomm
communicator
if (!library(Rmpi,logical.return = TRUE)){
    warning(""Rmpi cannot be loaded"")
    q(save = ""no"")
}
options(error=quote(assign("".mpi.err"", TRUE, envir = .GlobalEnv)))
.comm <- 1
.intercomm <- 2
Wcomm <- 3 ### 1
invisible(mpi.comm.dup(0,Wcomm)) ### 2
invisible(mpi.comm.set.errhandler(Wcomm)) ### 3
print(paste(""Worker rank:"",mpi.comm.rank(comm=Wcomm),""of"",mpi.
comm.size(comm=Wcomm),""on Wcomm[=3]"")) ### 4
invisible(mpi.comm.get.parent(.intercomm))
invisible(mpi.intercomm.merge(.intercomm,1,.comm))
invisible(mpi.comm.set.errhandler(.comm))
mpi.hostinfo(.comm)
invisible(mpi.comm.disconnect(.intercomm))
.nonblock <- as.logical(mpi.bcast(integer(1),type=1,rank=0,comm=.
comm))
.sleep <- mpi.bcast(double(1),type=2,rank=0,comm=.comm)
repeat
    try(eval(mpi.bcast.cmd(rank=0,comm=.comm, nonblock=.nonblock,
sleep=.sleep),envir=.GlobalEnv),TRUE)
print(""Done"")
invisible(mpi.comm.disconnect(Wcomm)) ### 5
invisible(mpi.comm.disconnect(.comm))
invisible(mpi.comm.set.errhandler(0))
mpi.quit()
```

As you can note in the preceding script, at [### 2], all the workers (but not the master) duplicate the special communicator value 0. This is interpreted by Rmpi::mpi.comm.dup() as representing MPI_COMM_WORLD. When MPI processes are spawned by a parent process, MPI_COMM_WORLD references the group of child processes that have been spawned but excludes the parent. We created a duplicate communicator of MPI_COMM_WORLD, attached it to the internal Rmpi reference handle number 3, and recorded this handle index in the global Wcomm variable so that it can be clearly referenced in any Rmpi function we wish to call within the broadcast commands, which each worker receives from the master in their near-perpetual repeat loop. Note how we introduced code to set the error handler for this new worker communicator [### 3] and to generate some additional debugging output to the workers' log files [### 4]. Note also that to be tidy and release resources correctly, we explicitly disconnected from Wcomm prior to the worker process exiting [### 5]. The exit itself is triggered from the master when it calls mpi.close.Rslaves().

Having done all of the previous work, we can now go back to our R session and make a specific call to Rmpi::mpi.spawn.Rslaves() to use our modified launch script, as follows:

```
> mpi.spawn.Rslaves(Rscript=system.file(""workerdaemon.R"",
package=""Rmpi""))
    4 slaves are spawned successfully. 0 failed.
master (rank 0, comm 1) of size 5 is running on: Simons-Mac-mini
slave1 (rank 1, comm 1) of size 5 is running on: Simons-Mac-mini
slave2 (rank 2, comm 1) of size 5 is running on: Simons-Mac-mini
slave3 (rank 3, comm 1) of size 5 is running on: Simons-Mac-mini
slave4 (rank 4, comm 1) of size 5 is running on: Simons-Mac-mini
> tailslave.log(nlines=2)
==> Simons-Mac-mini.28857+1.32231.log <==
[1] ""Worker rank: 0 of 4 on Wcomm[=3]""
    Host: Simons-Mac-mini     Rank(ID): 1 of Size: 5 on comm 1
```

```
==> Simons-Mac-mini.28857+1.32232.log <==
[1] ""Worker rank: 1 of 4 on Wcomm[=3]""
    Host: Simons-Mac-mini      Rank(ID): 2 of Size: 5 on comm 1
==> Simons-Mac-mini.28857+1.32234.log <==
[1] ""Worker rank: 2 of 4 on Wcomm[=3]""
    Host: Simons-Mac-mini      Rank(ID): 3 of Size: 5 on comm 1
==> Simons-Mac-mini.28857+1.32237.log <==
[1] ""Worker rank: 3 of 4 on Wcomm[=3]""
    Host: Simons-Mac-mini      Rank(ID): 4 of Size: 5 on comm 1
```

Note that we can view the most recent entries made by workers in their respective log files using `Rmpi::tailslave.log()`. As a final step, to test, let's invoke a collective operation across just the workers as broadcast from the master and terminate the workers cleanly via the following code:

```
> mpi.remote.exec(mpi.barrier(comm=Wcomm))
  X1 X2 X3 X4
1  1  1  1  1
> mpi.close.Rslaves()
[1] 1
```

Voila! Here, we executed the simplest of all collective operations, `MPI_Barrier`, which causes all the processes in the `Wcomm` communicator—that is, all the workers—to effectively synchronize to the same point of program execution. Later in this chapter, we will explore the full set of MPI collective communications.

Rmpi: mpi.bcast.cmd() versus mpi.remote.exec()

As we discussed, `Rmpi` utilizes a master/worker cluster. It provides two alternate means of executing a specific function in parallel across the workers, as follows:

- `mpi.bcast.cmd(cmd=NULL, ..., rank=0, comm=1, nonblock=FALSE, sleep=0.1)`: This Rmpi call is typically only used when all the workers are quiescent and are (or will be) waiting for their next R function to execute (`cmd`), which is issued by the master. With the default setup for `Rmpi`, each worker calls this repeatedly with `nonblock=TRUE` and a short idle sleep of 0.1 seconds in order to reduce the CPU overhead. However, `mpi.bcast.cmd()` does not incorporate the return of results from the workers to the master; for this, you need `mpi.remote.exec()`.
- `mpi.remote.exec(cmd, ..., simplify=TRUE, comm=1, ret=TRUE)`: This `Rmpi` call will collect the computed function (`cmd`) results (if `ret=TRUE`) as its return value from all of the workers either as a list (`simplify=FALSE`) or, if possible, as an R dataframe (`simplify=TRUE`).

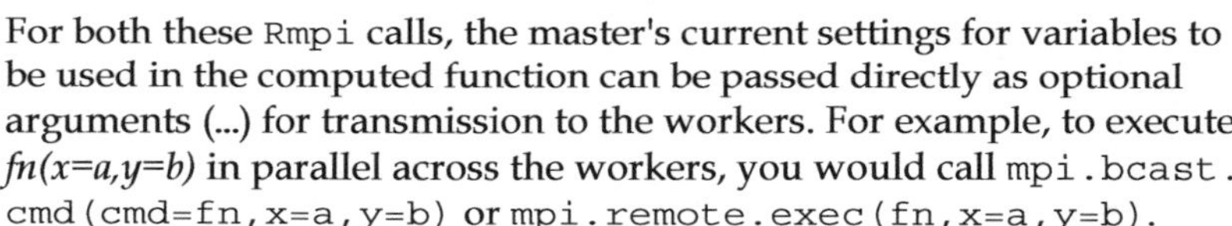

For both these `Rmpi` calls, the master's current settings for variables to be used in the computed function can be passed directly as optional arguments (...) for transmission to the workers. For example, to execute *fn(x=a,y=b)* in parallel across the workers, you would call `mpi.bcast.cmd(cmd=fn,x=a,y=b)` or `mpi.remote.exec(fn,x=a,y=b)`.

It should be noted, also, that in neither of these calls does the master execute the parallel function itself, and in fact, it could not do so with `mpi.remote.exec(cmd,ret=TRUE)` as it must wait until it has gathered all the results from each of the workers. If you do need to do this, then the usual pattern is for the master to execute the parallel function immediately after it calls `mpi.bcast.cmd()`. Be aware of this requirement in particular where the parallel function internally includes a call to an MPI collective communication across the default communicator as the master will have to participate in order to prevent a deadlock from occurring.

Point-to-point non-blocking communications

In the previous section, you learned about `MPI_Send` and `MPI_Recv`. These are blocking communications and present us with a couple of issues. Firstly, if we don't have a matching receive for a given send, then our program will hang; it will be in a state of deadlock (for a discussion of the issue of deadlock that can arise in the context of blocking communications, refer to *Chapter 6, The Art of Parallel Programming*). Secondly, the two processes involved in a data transfer have to wait for each other to be ready in order to make the transfer happen. This can be very inefficient if the processes are not closely synchronized—if, for example, they have imbalanced workloads or functionally perform different types of calculation. Thankfully, MPI's **non-blocking communications** can help alleviate some of these issues, and this is what we will explore next.

`MPI_Isend` and `MPI_Irecv` are the non-blocking send and receive variants. The "`I`" prefix stands for "*Immediate*", which means that the program flow of control is immediately returned to the calling process once the send or receive is initiated within the MPI communications subsystem. However, it is important to understand that even though `MPI_Isend` or `MPI_Irecv` is returned, this does not mean that the data is transferred; we need to make a separate MPI API call, `MPI_Wait` (or one of its variants), to determine when a specific non-blocking send or receive is completed. Until we determine that the non-blocking send is completed, we cannot change the state of the object we are sending; it is essentially off-limits. Likewise, until a non-blocking receive is completed, we cannot read the state of the object that we set aside to be modified by a matching send. Note that a non-blocking receive can be matched with a blocking send, and likewise, a blocking receive can be matched with a non-blocking send.

The following code snippets present the basic pattern for two processes engaging in non-blocking communications for both `Rmpi` (`rmpi_vectorSum`) and `pbdMPI` (`pdbmpi_vectorSum`). The example calculates a combined vector sum on the data held locally with the data received from the ranked predecessor MPI process. The key thing to note is that we will assign a unique request number to each non-blocking send and receive we launch so that we have a way of referring to it in order to be able check it later for completion:

```
# Run these code snippets with at least two MPI processes
# For Rmpi you must use the workers-only communicator: Wcomm
rmpi_vectorSum <- function(com) {
  np <- comm.size(comm=com)
  myrank <- comm.rank(com)
  succ <- (myrank+1) %% np
```

```
  pred <- (myrank-1) %% np
  dataOut <- as.integer(1:10 + (myrank * 10))
  dataIn <- vector(mode=""integer"", length=10)
  mpi.isend(dataOut, 1, succ, 0, comm=com, request=1)
  mpi.irecv(dataIn, 1, pred, 0, comm=com, request=2)
  mpi.wait(2, status=2) # wait on receive
  dataSum <- dataOut + dataIn
  mpi.wait(1, status=1) # wait on send
  return(dataSum)
}

pbdmpi_vectorSum <- function(com) {
  np <- comm.size(comm=com)
  myrank <- comm.rank(com)
  succ <- (myrank+1) %% np
  pred <- (myrank-1) %% np
  dataOut <- as.integer(1:10 + (myrank * 10))
  dataIn <- vector(mode=""integer"", length=10)
  isend(dataOut, rank.dest=succ, comm=com, request=1)
  irecv(x.buffer=dataIn, rank.source=pred ,comm=com, request=2)
  wait(2, status=2) # wait on receive
  dataSum <- dataOut + dataIn
  wait(1, status=1) # wait on send
  return(dataSum)
}
```

By now, you have all the knowledge to embed the preceding functions in the necessary code structure to make them run and display the output. The complete working code examples are available at the book's website.

In the following reference table, all of the non-blocking communications and additional `MPI_Wait` variants are described in detail:

<table>
<tr><th colspan="3">NON-BLOCKING COMMUNICATIONS</th></tr>
<tr><th>MPI API Call</th><th>pbdMPI equivalent</th><th>Rmpi equivalent</th></tr>
<tr>
<td><code>MPI_Isend</code>(MPI Ref: p.49
• <code>buf</code>: This is the address pointer to the first object in the buffer of contiguous memory local to sender
• <code>count</code>: This is the number of objects in the memory buffer to send
• <code>datatype</code>: This is the enum defining the type of object from which the size of the object is inferred
• <code>dest</code>: This is the rank of the destination process the in communicator that is being sent to
• <code>tag</code>: This is the a non-negative integer that only has meaning for the caller
• <code>comm</code>: This is the communicator within which this message will be transferred
• <code>request</code>: This is the handle for a communication request that will be associated with this immediate send)</td>
<td><code>isend(</code>
<code>Robject,</code>
<code>rank.dest=1,</code>
<code>tag=0,</code>
<code>comm=0,</code>
<code>request=0</code>
<code>)</code>
returns: NULL

The default argument values for <code>pbdMPI::isend</code> are defined in <code>$SPMD.CT</code> and can be changed there.</td>
<td><code>mpi.isend(</code>
<code>x, type, dest,</code>
<code>tag,</code>
<code>comm=1,</code>
<code>request=0</code>
<code>)</code>
returns: NULL

<code>mpi.isend.Robj(</code>
<code>Robject, dest,</code>
<code>tag,</code>
<code>comm=1,</code>
<code>request=0</code>
<code>)</code>
returns: NULL

The valid values for <code>type</code> are:
• 1 = integer
• 2 = numeric
• 3 = character</td>
</tr>
<tr><td colspan="3"><code>MPI_Isend</code> is a non-blocking send operation that returns to the caller immediately. It requires either a matching blocking <code>MPI_Recv</code> or non-blocking <code>MPI_Irecv</code> operation. The completion of an <code>MPI_Isend</code> operation is determined by calling <code>MPI_Wait</code> or <code>MPI_Test</code> on the request handle that was associated with the send. It is only safe to change the state of the object being transmitted once the non-blocking send is known to be completed.

Refer to <code>MPI_Send</code> described in the previous table. For <code>pbdMPI</code> and <code>Rmpi</code>, their <code>Isend</code> functions are equivalent to their blocking variants with the addition of the integer request handle that is uniquely associated with the non-blocking communication.</td></tr>
</table>

<table>
<tr><th colspan="3">NON-BLOCKING COMMUNICATIONS</th></tr>
<tr>
<td>MPI_Irecv(MPI Ref: p.51
<ul>
<li>buf: This is the address pointer to the first object in the buffer of contiguous memory local to receiver</li>
<li>count: This is the number of objects in the memory buffer to receive</li>
<li>datatype: This is the enum defining the datatype of the object from which the size of the object is inferred</li>
<li>srce: This is the rank of source process in the communicator that it is receiving from</li>
<li>tag: This is the a non-negative integer that only has meaning to the caller</li>
<li>comm: This is the communicator within which this message will be transferred</li>
<li>request: This is the handle for a communication request that will be associated with this immediate receive)</li>
</ul>
</td>
<td>irecv(
x.buffer=NULL,
rank.srce=0,
tag=0,
comm=0,
request=0
)
returns: Robject

The default argument values for pbdMPI::recv are defined in $SPMD.CT and can be changed there.</td>
<td>mpi.irecv(
x, type, srce,
tag,
comm=1,
request=0
)
returns: NULL</td>
</tr>
<tr><td colspan="3">MPI_Irecv is a non-blocking receive operation that returns to the caller immediately. It requires either a matching blocking MPI_Send or non-blocking MPI_Isend operation. The completion of an MPI_Irecv operation is determined by calling MPI_Wait or MPI_Test on the request handle that was associated with the send. It is only safe to read the state of the object being received once the non-blocking receive is known to be completed.

Refer to MPI_Recv described in the previous table. For pbdMPI and Rmpi, their Irecv functions are equivalent to their blocking variants with the addition of the integer request handle that will be uniquely associated with the non-blocking communication. Note that Rmpi does not implement an mpi.isend.Robj() method equivalent for mpi.irecv.Robj ().</td></tr>
</table>

NON-BLOCKING COMMUNICATIONS		

`MPI_Wait` (*MPI Ref: p.53*
• `request`: This is the handle for the `Isend`/ `IRecv` communication to wait for completion
• `status`: This is the information about the completed communication)
	`wait(`
	`request=0,`
	`status=0`
	`)`
	returns: NULL
		`mpi.wait(`
		`request=0,`
		`status=0`
		`)`
		returns: NULL

`MPI_Waitall` (*MPI Ref: p.59* `count`: This is the number of requests to wait on `requests`: This is the array of handles for the `Isend`/ `IRecv` communications to wait on completing `statuses`: This is the information about each of the corresponding requests' completion)	`waitall(count)` returns: NULL	`mpi.waitall(count)` returns: NULL

`MPI_Waitany` (*MPI Ref: p.57*
• `count`: This is the number of requests to wait on
• `requests`: This is the array of handles for the `Isend`/ `IRecv` communications to wait on completing the count
• `index`: This is the an array index of a request in requests that is completed
• `status` - information about the completed communication)
	`waitany(`
	`count,`
	`status=0`
	`)`
	returns: NULL
		`mpi.waitany(`
		`count,`
		`status=0`
		`)`
		returns: NULL

`MPI_Waitsome` (*MPI Ref: p.60* • `count`: This is the number of requests to wait on • `requests` This is the array of handles for the `Isend`/ `IRecv` communications to wait on completing the count • `countComplete` This is the number of requests completed • `requestsComplete`: This is the array of completed request handles • `statuses`: This is the information about each of the corresponding requests' completion)	`waitsome(count)` returns: list(countComplete, indices[count Complete]) The default argument values are defined in `$SPMD.CT` and can be changed there.	`mpi.waitsome(count)` returns: list(countComplete, indices[countComplete])

NON-BLOCKING COMMUNICATIONS

`MPI_Wait` comes in several flavors. The basic `mpi.wait()` function enables you to wait for a single specific non-blocking communication request and optionally set the supplied status handle with information about the completed communication (`source` and `tag`), which you can subsequently access with `MPI_Probe`.

You are free to create as many outstanding non-blocking communications as you want (within resource limits, of course), so your code can choose to wait for any single or subset of the outstanding communications to complete.

`Rmpi` and `pbdMPI` simplify the use of `wait` by maintaining their own per MPI process internal arrays of the `MPI_Request` and `MPI_Status` objects, which (at the time of writing) are the compile time limits for `Rmpi` of 2,000 each, and for `pbdMPI`, it is 10,000 and 5,000, respectively. Be aware that when using the bulk `wait` functions, the `count` parameter effectively determines the range of request handles that will be scanned from 0 up to `count` -1. With this in mind and assuming you assign the request handle numbers incrementally in your own R code, the collective `wait` functions will operate as follows:

The `mpi.waitany()` function will wait for the first of the supplied `count` parameter of the currently outstanding non-blocking sends/recvs to be completed and set the supplied `status` parameter to enable you to inspect the information about the communication that is completed (with `MPI_Probe`).

The `mpi.waitsome()` function will wait on the supplied `count` parameter of the outstanding communications and return a list of the number of requests and a vector of the request handles for those that are completed.

The `mpi.waitall()` function simply waits for all of the supplied `count` parameter of the outstanding communications to be completed.

Collective communications

We already encountered the simplest of the MPI collective communication calls, namely `MPI_Barrier`. The remaining MPI collective communications are explained visually in the following figure illustrating a communicator with three processes—that is, which rank(s) send which data and which rank(s) receive which data. In the following figure, rank zero is colored red, rank one is colored blue, and rank two is green:

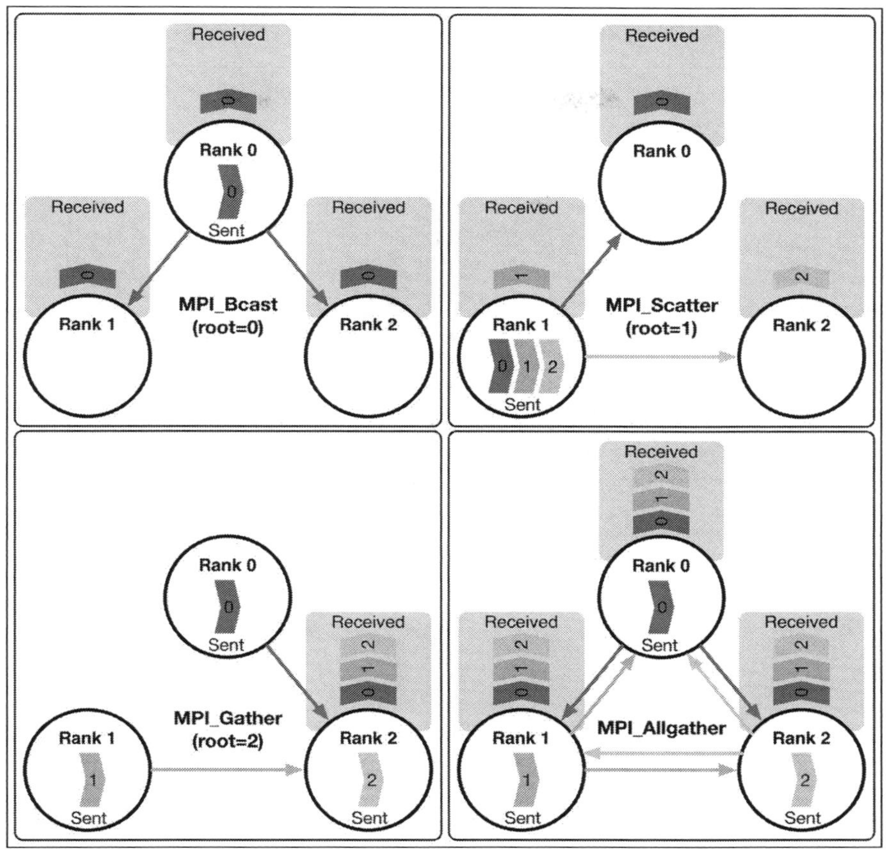

Figure 2: A diagram depicting the MPI collective operations Bcast, Scatter, Gather, and Allgather for a communicator with three processes. Using these operations, data can be distributed and combined in a number of different patterns to support a wide variety of algorithms.

In many of the collective communications, one of the participating processes is designated as the *root* and will have a special role within the operation as the overall message source or destination, distributing and combining data according to a specific pattern.

The set of MPI collective communications exposed by `pbdMPI` and `Rmpi` are detailed in the following table:

GROUP-WISE COMMUNICATIONS (refer to the preceding figure)		
MPI API Call	**pbdMPI equivalent**	**Rmpi equivalent**
`MPI_Barrier` (*MPI Ref: p.147* `comm`: This is the communicator across which the barrier will be executed.)	`barrier (comm= 0)` returns: NULL The default argument values are defined in `$SPMD.CT` and can be changed there.	`mpi.barrier(comm =1)` returns: NULL
`MPI_Barrier` is the simplest of the collective communication calls. It blocks all the processes in the given communicator from proceeding until all processes call `MPI_Barrier`. It is used to create a shared code execution synchronization point among all the processes. If any one of the processes in the communicator fails to call `MPI_Barrier`, then all processes that called `MPI_Barrier` will be blocked indefinitely.		

GROUP-WISE COMMUNICATIONS (refer to the preceding figure)		

`MPI_Bcast`(*MPI Ref: p.148*
• `buf`: This is the base address of the first object in the contiguous memory local to caller
• `count`: This is the number of objects in the memory buffer to send or receive
• `datatype`: This is the enum defining the type of the object from which the size of the object is inferred
• `root`: This is the rank of the source process transmitting its data to all the others in the communicator
• `comm`: This is the communicator within which this message will be broadcast
)
	`bcast(`
	`Robject,`
	`rank.`
	`source=0,`
	`comm=0`
	`)`
	returns: `Robject`
		`mpi.bcast(x, type, rank=0, comm=1, buffunit=100)`
		returns: NULL on root and x vector on other processes
		`mpi.bcast.Robj(Robject, rank=0, comm=1)`
		returns: NULL on root and Robject on other processes
		
		`mpi.bcast.Rfun2slave(comm=1)`
		`mpi.bcast.Robj2slave(Robject=null, comm=1, all=FALSE)`
		`mpi.bcast.data2slave(R matrix or vector of type double, comm=1, buffunit=100)`
		
		The valid values for `type` are:
		• 1 = integer
		• 2 = numeric
		• 3 = character

GROUP-WISE COMMUNICATIONS (refer to the preceding figure)
All the processes must call `MPI_Bcast` with the same value for root and communicator; otherwise, a deadlock may occur. The root process transmits its data to each of the other processes, each of which must have sufficient memory buffer space to receive the data being sent. In `pbdMPI`, `rank.source` is the root. In `Rmpi`, `rank` is the root, and `buffunit` is the number of `type` data items in the vector to be broadcast. The `Rmpi.bcast` call is used to transfer simple vector data of the integer, numeric, or character type. The `Rmpi Robj2slave` (which transfers all the master objects to the slave if `all=TRUE`), `Rfun2slave` (which transmits all of the master's R function definitions to the slaves), and `Rdata2slave` (which transmits a double-type array held on the master fast) convenience functions are part of the built-in `Rmpi` cluster framework and always transmit data from the master to the workers. As we discussed earlier in this chapter, the workers, when not processing a task, always wait for the next broadcast message from the master.

<table>
<tr><th colspan="3">GROUP-WISE COMMUNICATIONS (refer to the preceding figure)</th></tr>
<tr>
<td>

<code>MPI_Scatter</code> (MPI Ref: p.159
<ul>
<li><code>Sendbuf</code>: This is the base address of objects in the contiguous memory local to caller</li>
<li><code>sendcount</code>: This is the number of objects to send</li>
<li><code>sendtype</code>: This is the datatype of the objects being sent</li>
<li><code>recvbuf</code>: This is the address pointer for the buffer to receive data into</li>
<li><code>recvcount</code>: This is the number of objects that can be received into the buffer</li>
<li><code>recvtype</code>: This is the datatype of the objects being received</li>
<li><code>root</code>: This is the rank of source process transmitting data</li>
<li><code>comm</code>: This is the communicator for this scatter operation</li>
</ul>
)
Similarly, take a look at the following:
<code>MPI_Scatterv</code> (MPI Ref: p.161
<code>sendbuf,</code>
<code>sendcounts[comm.size]</code>: This is the array of counts of data to send to the associated ranked process
<code>displs[comm.size]</code>: This is the displacement offsets applied to <code>sendbuf</code> from which to send ith data to ith ranked process
<code>sendtype, recvbuf, recvcount, recvtype, root, comm</code>
)
</td>
<td>
<code>scatter(x,
x.buffer=NULL,
x.count=NULL,
displs=NULL,
rank.source=0,
comm=0)</code>
</td>
<td>
<code>mpi.scatter(x,
type, rdata,
root=0, comm=1)</code>

<code>mpi.scatterv(x,
scounts, type,
rdata, root=0,
comm=1)</code>

The valid values for <code>type</code> are:
<ul>
<li>1 = integer</li>
<li>2 = numeric</li>
<li>3 = character</li>
</ul>
</td>
</tr>
<tr><td colspan="3">

<code>MPI_Scatter</code> is essentially a more complex form of <code>MPI_Bcast</code>, in which each receiving process is sent its own separate subset of the broadcast data. Essentially, where there are N processes in the MPI communicator, the root's data is segmented sequentially into i=1..N equal-sized parts (the size of each part is defined by <code>sendcount</code> and <code>type</code>), and the ith part is sent to the matching ith ranked process.

<code>MPI_Scatterv</code> extends the basic scatter operation to enable the root to send differently sized segments of data to each of the other processes. The <code>displs</code> displacement offsets array also enables noncontiguous segments of data to be distributed from the send buffer.

In R, the scatter operations are normally used with numeric vectors and matrices.
</td></tr>
</table>

GROUP-WISE COMMUNICATIONS (refer to the preceding figure)		

`MPI_Gather(`
• `sendbuf`: This is the base address of objects in the contiguous memory local to caller
• `sendcount`: This is the number of objects to send
• `sendtype`: This is the datatype of the objects being sent
• `recvbuf`: This is the base address of the buffer to receive data into
• `recvcount`: This is the number of objects that can be received into the buffer
• `recvtype`: This is the datatype of the objects being received
• `root`: This is the rank of the destination process receiving the data
• `comm`: This is the communicator for this gather operation
`)`
Similarly, take a look at the following:
`MPI_Allgather(`
`sendbuf, sendcount, sendtype, recvbuf, recvcount, recvtype, comm`
`)`
`MPI_Gatherv(`
`sendbuf, sendcount, sendtype, recvbuf,`
`recvcounts[comm.size]`: This is the array of counts of the data to receive from to the associated ranked process
`displs[comm.size]`: This is the displacement offsets applied to `recvbuf` from which to receive the ith data from the ith ranked process
`recvtype, root, comm`
`)`
Similarly, take a look at the following:
`MPI_Allgatherv(`
`sendbuf, sendcount, sendtype, recvcounts, displs, recvtype, comm`
`)`
	`gather(x , x.buffer =NULL, x.count= NULL, displs=NULL, rank.dest=0, comm=1, unlist=FALSE)`
	returns: NULL
	
	`allgather(x, x.buffer =NULL, x.count =NULL, displs =NULL, comm=1, unlist =FALSE)`
	returns: NULL
		`mpi.gather(x, type, rdata, root=0, comm=1)`
		`mpi.gatherv(x, type, rdata, rcounts, root=0, comm=1)`
		
		`mpi.allgather(x, type, rdata, comm=1)`
		
		`mpi.allgatherv(x , type, rdata, rcounts, comm=1)`
		The valid values for type are:
		• 1 = integer
		• 2 = numeric
		• 3 = character

<table>
<tr><th colspan="3">GROUP-WISE COMMUNICATIONS (refer to the preceding figure)</th></tr>
<tr><td colspan="3">MPI_Gather is the inverse of MPI_Scatter, and likewise, MPI_Gatherv is the inverse of MPI_Scatterv. MPI_Gather collects an identical quantity of data from all the processes in the communicator to the designated root process. MPI_Gatherv extends this to enable different amounts of data to be collected from each process and for the data to be placed at noncontiguous offsets within the aggregate receive buffer.
In R, gather operations are normally used with numeric vectors and matrices.</td></tr>
<tr><td>MPI_Reduce (MPI ref p.174
• sendbuf: This is the data elements being sent
• recvbuf: This is the buffer into which the aggregated reduced data will be placed
• count: This is the total number of data elements
• datatype: This is the type of data element
• op: This is the reduction operation to apply to the data
• root: This is the rank of the process receiving the reduced data
• comm: This is the communicator for this reduction
)
Similarly, take a look at the following:
MPI_Allreduce (MPI ref p.187
sendbuf, recvbuf, count, datatype, op, comm)</td><td>reduce(x,
x.buffer
=NULL,
op=""sum"",
rank.dest=0,
comm=1)

allreduce(
x, x.buffer
=NULL,
op=""sum"",
comm=1
)</td><td>mpi.reduce(x,
type=2, op,
dest=0, comm=1)

mpi.allreduce(
x, type=2, op,
comm=1
)
The valid values for type are:
• 1 = integer
• 2 = numeric</td></tr>
<tr><td colspan="3">MPI_Reduce may be considered an extension of MPI_Gather. It additionally performs a reduction on the data sent by all the processes to the root according to one of the following mathematical operations: sum, prod, max, min, maxloc, and minloc. In R, the reduce operations are intended for use with numerical data. The summation, product, maximum, and minimum operations should be self-explanatory. The maxloc operation returns a sequence of pairs in the reduced vector with the maximum value and the rank of the process that hold the maximum value. Similarly, minloc returns the minimum value and rank of the process that holds the value.
MPI_Allreduce extends the behavior such that all the processes in the communicator receive the final result rather than just a single process.</td></tr>
</table>

PBD: This is a higher-level abstraction for Programming with Big Data in R. For even more information about message passing with R, refer to the excellent pbdR book *Speaking Serial R with a Parallel Accent*. This gives a very thorough exposition of the additional useful higher-level Programming Big Data packages that are designed specifically to work with `pbdMPI`. It's available online for free from this CRAN link:

`https://cran.r-project.org/web/packages/pbdDEMO/vignettes/pbdDEMO-guide.pdf.`

Summary

Right, it's time to take a wee breather. In this chapter, we covered the basic concepts and the API for MPI. You learned how to utilize both the `Rmpi` and `pbdMPI` packages in conjunction with OpenMPI. We explored a number of simple examples of both blocking and non-blocking communications in R and also introduced the collective communications operations in MPI. We looked into the low-level implementation of `Rmpi` package's own master/worker scheme to manage the execution of R code in parallel. You now have sufficient grounding to write a wide variety of highly scalable MPI programs in R.

In the next chapter, we will complete our discussion on MPI, work through a particular MPI example that introduces spatial grid-style parallelism, and cover the remaining slightly more esoteric MPI API functions available to us in R.

3 Advanced Message Passing

We continue our tour of MPI in this chapter by focusing on the more advanced aspects of message passing. In particular, we explore a specific structured approach to distributed computing for efficiently processing spatially organized data, known as *Grid Parallelism*. We will work through a detailed example of image processing that will illustrate the use of non-blocking communications, including localized patterns of inter-process message exchange, based on appropriately configuring an `Rmpi` master/worker cluster.

In this chapter, we will cover additional MPI API calls, including `MPI_Cart_create()`, `MPI_Cart_rank()`, `MPI_Probe`, and `MPI_Test`, and briefly revisit `parLapply()` which we first encountered in *Chapter 1, Simple Parallelism with R* (and even snow gets a mention).

So, without further ado, let's discover how to perform spatially oriented parallel processing using MPI in R.

Grid parallelism

Grid parallelism is naturally aligned to image processing, where operations can be cast in a form that acts on a specific localized region for each and every individual cell value of data. Commonly, the cell value is referred to as a pixel in the case of 2D image data, and voxel in the case of 3D image data. Grids can, of course, be N-dimensional matrix structures, but as human beings, it's somewhat difficult for us to wrap our heads around more than 4D.

The key to efficient grid parallelism is the distribution mapping of data across the set of parallel processes, and the interactions between each process, as they may exchange data with one another to accommodate iterative operations that require access to more of the data than each process holds locally. Consider a simple but very large square 2D image, and that we have a cluster of nine independent computational cores available. To illustrate the point, we will add the constraint that each of the computational nodes only has sufficient data memory to hold a little more than one-ninth of the total image. There are now two obvious ways in which we can decompose the image amongst the nine MPI processes in the cluster. Either we can distribute the data as nine equal-sized tiled squares where the cluster acts as a 3x3 grid, or as nine equal-sized abutting stripes (effectively, a 1x9 grid). These two options are depicted in the following diagrams:

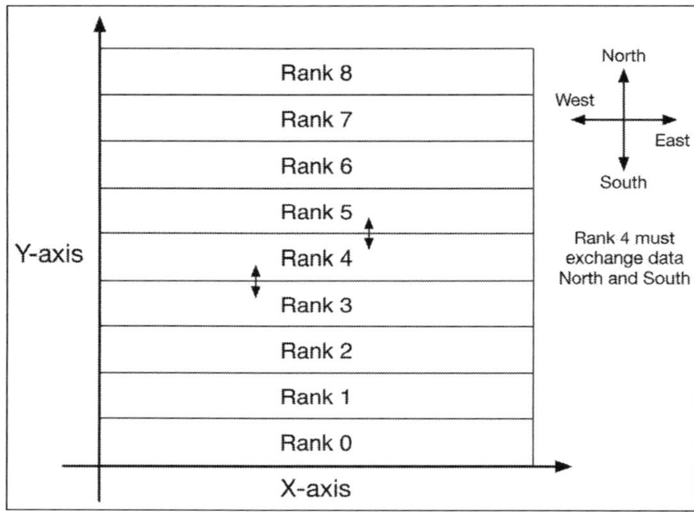

Figure 1: Image split into 9 equal stripes.

As can be seen, the striped option implies fewer communication exchanges between processes at the stripe boundaries as compared to the tiled approach. In the former case, rank 4 must exchange with its two neighbors (3 and 5), and in the latter case, rank 4 may need to exchange with all of the other eight processes, assuming that exchange is required on the diagonal, and not just with the cardinal neighbors:

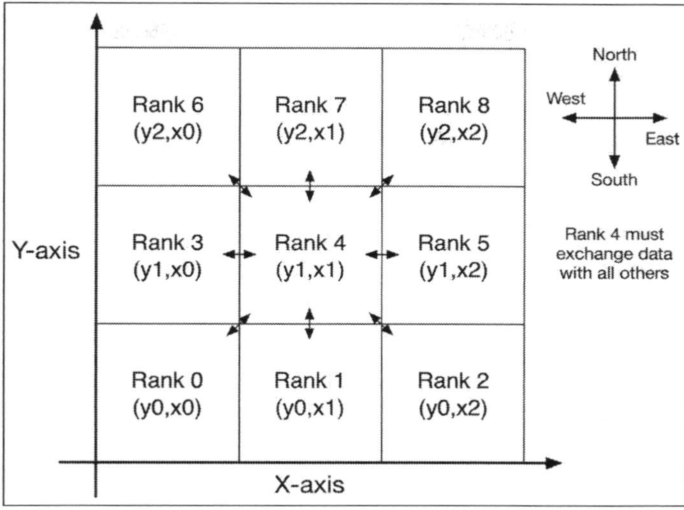

Figure 2: Image split into nine equal square tiles. The co-ordinate order is *(y, x)* to reflect R code.

We should also recognize that there is an imbalance in the amount of communication required between processes in these two different approaches. In the striped case, only rank 0 and rank 8 have one exchange to perform, the rest all have two exchanges. In the tiled case, ranks 0, 2, 6, and 8 (the corners) have three exchanges; ranks 1, 3, 5, and 7 (the cardinals) have five exchanges, and rank 4 alone has eight exchanges. This implies that in the tiled case, the overall efficiency of the processing is dictated by rank 4, which has twice as many exchanges to perform compared to the average, and therefore, the other processes will inevitably end up waiting on it to exchange their data.

This is indeed likely to be the case at this scale. However, one should also note that the amount of data being exchanged is less between neighbors in the tiled case as compared to the striped case. The differential in volume of data exchanged between neighbors also favors the tiled case, since as we increase the number of processes in the grid, the average number of exchanges increases (there are more inner tiles). Additionally, the volume of data exchanged decreases in the tiled case (tile size reduces and edge perimeter decreases), whereas in the striped case, the length of the stripe edge remains constant. Also, if the type of data processing requires data exchange to wrap around at the boundaries of the grid, then all the processes in the grid will need to engage in the same number of exchanges with its neighbors. This example highlights why it is important to consider how data is distributed and mapped for a given scale of parallelism, and how this may affect the efficiency of communication, and therefore, impact the overall runtime.

Now that you have a pretty good idea about grid parallelism, let's get some code running.

Creating the grid cluster

Usually, MPI includes a variety of utility functions to help configure the MPI universe as a grid. Essentially, what this boils down to is mapping a linear set of MPI process ranks to a multidimensional coordinate system.

The following `Rmpi`-based code sets up a square grid of the given dimension. It also associates a specific new `comm` handle with this grid in order to isolate the grid communications from other comms, in particular to isolate those comms from the `Rmpi` master which have no role to play in the grid computation itself:

```
Worker_makeSquareGrid <- function(comm,dim) {
  grid <- 1000 + dim     # assign comm handle for this size grid
  dims <- c(dim,dim)     # dimensions are 2D, size: dim X dim
  periods <- c(FALSE,FALSE)  # no wraparound at outermost edges
  if (mpi.cart.create(commold=comm,dims,periods,commcart=grid))
  {
    return(grid)
  }
  return(-1) # An MPI error occurred
}
```

You'll note the use of `mpi.cart.create()` that constructs a Cartesian rank/grid mapping from a group of existing MPI processes, and associates a new specific communicator handle with the grid. Recall that `Rmpi` maintains its own internal arrays of MPI handle references, and the handle reference we are using for the communicator association must be a currently unused index within this array (hence, the 1000 offset). Though this is not ideal coding on our part, it is pragmatic given the nature of the interface exposed by `Rmpi`.

Now that we have a grid association set up through `Rmpi`, we can use its `mpi.cart.coords()` and `mpi.cart.rank()` functions on each process to figure out which cell of the grid it is, and the ranks of its neighbors. Without this information, we could not determine with which other ranked processes we should be exchanging image boundary information. It is not a given that a specific rank will be automatically assigned a specific coordinate in the grid, so instead, we need to explicitly query what association has been created.

```
worker_initSpatialGrid <- function(dim,comm=Wcomm)
{
  Gcomm <- worker_makeSquareGrid(dim,comm)
  myRank <- mpi.comm.rank(Gcomm)
  myUniverseRank <- mpi.comm.rank(1) # Lookup rank in cluster
  myCoords <- mpi.cart.coords(Gcomm,myRank,2)
```

```
    myY <- myCoords[1]; myX <- myCoords[2]; # (y^,x>)
    coords <- vector(mode="list", length=8)
    neighbors <- rep(-1,8)
    if (myY+1 < dim) {
      neighbors[N] <- mpi.cart.rank(Gcomm,c(myY+1,myX))
    }
    if (myX+1 < dim && myY+1 < dim) {
      neighbors[NE] <- mpi.cart.rank(Gcomm,c(myY+1,myX+1))
    }
    if (myX+1 < dim) {
      neighbors[E] <- mpi.cart.rank(Gcomm,c(myY,myX+1))
    }
    if (myX+1 < dim && myY-1 >= 0) {
      neighbors[SE] <- mpi.cart.rank(Gcomm,c(myY-1,myX+1))
    }
    if (myY-1 >= 0) {
      neighbors[S] <- mpi.cart.rank(Gcomm,c(myY-1,myX))
    }
    if (myX-1 >= 0 && myY-1 >= 0) {
      neighbors[SW] <- mpi.cart.rank(Gcomm,c(myY-1,myX-1))
    }
    if (myX-1 >= 0) {
      neighbors[W] <- mpi.cart.rank(Gcomm,c(myY,myX-1))
    }
    if (myX-1 >= 0 && myY+1 < dim) {
      neighbors[NW] <- mpi.cart.rank(Gcomm,c(myY+1,myX-1))
    }
    # Store reference for neighbor comms
    assign("Neighbors", neighbors, envir=.GlobalEnv)
    # Store reference for grid communicator
    assign("Gcomm", Gcomm, envir=.GlobalEnv)
    return(list(myY,myX,myUniverseRank))
  }
```

The preceding `initSpatialGrid()` function determines the calling MPI process, its rank, grid coordinates, and the ranks of each of its eight neighbors. Where it does not have a neighbor, its neighbor's rank will be set to `-1`, because the calling MPI process is located at the edge of the grid. We return the coordinate to rank mapping in the MPI universe back to the master so that it can determine which image tile is to be sent to which ranked worker. We also store the neighbor and grid communicator as globals for ease of reference in the worker's separate processing loop when that is subsequently invoked by the master.

Boundary data exchange

The pattern of data exchange is depicted in the following Figure 3. Each individual process has its own section of image to operate over with an additional external one pixel boundary that is populated with the inner one pixel boundary of its neighboring process's section of the image. The coloration in Figure 3 is designed to show how each process contributes data to the overlap with each of its neighbors. The processes which own a region of the image that is at the real edge of the complete image—in this case, all processes except rank 4—have an artificial overlap boundary at this edge (colored gray) that is populated with values that are out of range of the normal pixel image values (in our grayscale image, the normal valid range of pixel value is 0 to 255). This simplifies the coding of the median filter function without interfering with the filter results generated:

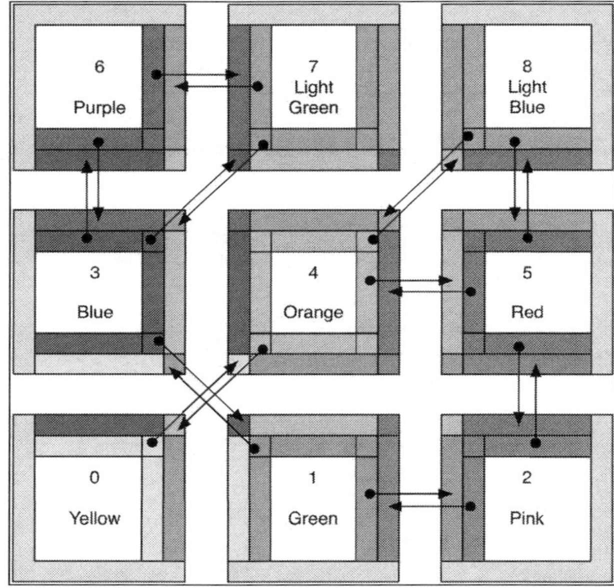

Figure 3: Pattern of boundary data exchange between processes, with some of the exchanges highlighted with arrows for clarity.

The median filter is a 3x3 window operator. If we used a larger window operator, then we would have to enlarge our overlap boundaries by the requisite number of pixels.

As can be seen in the preceding image, there is a little bit of complexity in setting up the pattern of data access to enable the set of exchanges.

The following is an implementation that executes the boundary exchange based on a local square image array (`img`) that directly includes the single pixel overlap. Here we present the series of non-blocking sends:

```
% local image tile has one pixel shared border
edge <- ncol(img)-1 # image is square: ncol=nrow
sbuf <- vector(mode="list", length=8) # 8 send buffers
req <- 0
# non-block send my tile data boundaries to my neighbors
if (neighbors[N]>=0) { # north
  sbuf[[N]] <- img[2,2:edge]
  mpi.isend(sbuf[[N]],1,neighbors[N],N,comm=comm,request=req)
  req <- req + 1
}
if (neighbors[NE]>=0) { # ne
  sbuf[NE] <- img[2,edge] # top-right inner cell
  mpi.isend(sbuf[[NE]],1,neighbors[NE],NE,
            comm=comm,request=req)
  req <- req + 1
}
... # Sends to East, South-East and South not shown
if (neighbors[SW]>=0) { # sw
  sbuf[[SW]] <- img[edge,2] # bottom-left inner cell
  mpi.isend(sbuf[[SW]],1,neighbors[SW],SW,
comm=comm,request=req)
  req <- req + 1
}
if (neighbors[W]>=0) { # west
  sbuf[[W]] <- img[2:edge,2] # leftmost inner col
  mpi.isend(sbuf[[W]],1,neighbors[W],W,comm=comm,request=req)
  req <- req + 1
}
if (neighbors[NW]>=0) { # nw
  sbuf[[NW]] <- img[2,2] # top-left inner cell
  mpi.isend(sbuf[[NW]],1,neighbors[NW],NW,
comm=comm,request=req)
  req <- req + 1
}
```

Each non-blocking send is associated with a separate request handle from 0 to 7, numbered similarly as 1 to 8 from north, clockwise round to northwest. We also set the tag associated with the sends to 1 to 8 as an explicit direction marker.

Next we present the non-blocking receives, although note that the data we receive from our neighbor in the north, for example, is its innermost sent south data. We need to ensure that we match up these opposite placements correctly for each direction pairing, but since we only have a single message coming in from each compass cardinal and inter-cardinal neighbor, then it is not necessary to set the `tag` on the receive, that is, we can just use `mpi.any.tag()`:

```
# Set-up non-blocking receives for incoming boundary data
# Local image tile has one pixel shared border
len <- ncol(img)-2
rbuf <- vector(mode="list", length=8) # 8 receive buffers
for (i in 1:8) {
  if (neighbors[i]>=0) {
    rbuf[[i]] <- integer(length=len)
    tag <- mpi.any.tag()
    mpi.irecv(rbuf[[i]],1,neighbors[i],tag,
  comm=comm,request=req)
    req <- req + 1
  }
}
```

Receive buffer sizes

Note that we have simplified the code by not bothering to size each receive buffer precisely, but making each of them as large as the maximum amount of data we'll receive from any sender.

The next step in an image processing iteration is to complete the boundary exchange. This requires us to simply wait on all of the outstanding communication requests we have created and have effectively kept count of with the value of the `req` variable:

```
mpi.waitall(req)
```

Nice and simple—we just have to wait on the total number of outstanding requests (both sends and receives), which we assigned to the request handle range 0 to 15, to complete.

All we are left with to do now is to remap the data received into the various buffers back into our image array, ready for the next processing iteration:

```
# Unpack received boundary data into my image tile
n <- ncol(img)
if (neighbors[N]>=0) { # north
  img[1,2:edge] <- rbuf[[N]] # top row
}
if (neighbors[NE]>=0) { # ne
  img[1,n] <- rbuf[[NE]][1] # top-right cell
}
if (neighbors[E]>=0) { # east
  img[2:edge,n] <- rbuf[[E]] # rightmost column
}
if (neighbors[SE]>=0) { # se
  img[n,n] <- rbuf[[SE]][1] # bottom-right cell
}
if (neighbors[S]>=0) { # south
  img[n,2:edge] <- rbuf[[S]] # bottom row
}
if (neighbors[SW]>=0) { # sw
  img[n,1] <- rbuf[[SW]][1] # bottom-left cell
}
if (neighbors[W]>=0) { # west
  img[2:edge,1] <- rbuf[[W]] # leftmost column
}
if (neighbors[NW]>=0) { # nw
  img[1,1] <- rbuf[[NW]][1] # top-left cell
}
```

To put all of this together, we now need to implement the operator to be applied to the section of the image held on each process. In our example, we are going to use a median filter, so let us explore what that is next.

The median filter

There are a large number of localized, neighborhood-oriented processing operators used in image processing. For our example, we will use a median filter: a smoothing operator that is classically used to remove noise in images. It's a relatively straightforward operation to implement, and can be applied in multiple passes over an image, so it is ideal for our pedagogical purposes. As you may well be able to intuit, the operation sets the target pixel value in the output to the middle value of the ordered ranking of the pixel and its surrounding pixel values in the input (see: `https://en.wikipedia.org/wiki/Median_filter`). The Following Figure 4 depicts the operation in terms of a 3x3 neighborhood window, centered on the target pixel:

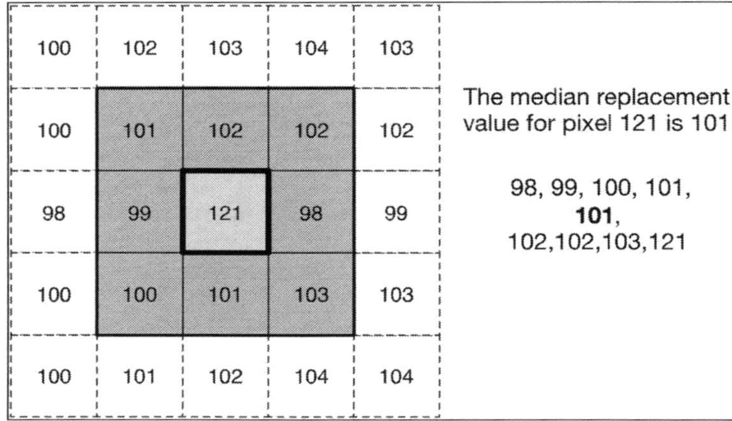

Figure 4: The median filter with a 3x3 pixel window applied to a single pixel in a larger grayscale image

Our simple implementation of the median filter is given as follows:

```
medianFilterPixel3 <- function(y,x,img) {
  v <- vector("integer",9) # bottom-left to top-right
  v[1]<-img[y-1,x-1]; v[2]<-img[y-1,x]; v[3]<-img[y-1,x+1];
  v[4]<-img[y,  x-1]; v[5]<-img[y,  x]; v[6]<-img[y,  x+1];
  v[7]<-img[y+1,x-1]; v[8]<-img[y+1,x]; v[9]<-img[y+1,x+1];
  s <- sort(v); # sort by pixel value (default ascending)
  return (s[5]) # return the middle value of the nine
}
```

This should be easy to understand: the nine pixel values for the window are placed in a vector, which is then sorted, and the value positioned in the middle is selected.

Distributing the image as tiles

The final part of the picture, excuse the pun, is the image itself. For testing purposes, we create a large example square grayscale image, and then apply some random noise for the median filter to smooth. This large image is then distributed in *P* equal-sized tiles from the master, across the `Rmpi` grid of *P* worker processes, to form local tile arrays. The picture boundary data is then initialized with out-of-range data values in preparation for processing on the worker. The following is the code executed by the master:

```
# We create large B/W image array with values in range 101-111
height <- Height; width <- Width;
image1 <- matrix(sample(101:111,height*width,replace=TRUE),
                 height,width)
# We add a bit of white saturation noise (pixel value=255)
image1[height/6,width/6] <- 255
...
image1[height/1.5,width/1.5] <- 255

# Tell the workers to process the image (3 pass MedianFilter)
# The Workers first wait to receive their local tile from the
# Master,then do their multi-pass image processing, then finally #
send their processed tiles back to the Master.
mpi.bcast.cmd(worker_gridApplyMedianFilter(3))
Start <- proc.time()

# We split the image into non-overlapping square grid tiles
# and distribute one per Worker
twidth <- width/dim # tile width
theight <- height/dim # tile height
for (ty in 0:(dim-1)) { # bottom-left to top-right
  sy <- (ty * theight) +1
  for (tx in 0:(dim-1)) {
    sx <- (tx * twidth) +1
    tile <- image1[sy:(sy+theight-1),sx:(sx+twidth-1)]
    # Send tile to the appropriate Worker
    worker <- workerRanks[ty+1,tx+1]
    mpi.send.Robj(tile,worker,1,comm=1)
  }
}
```

The master then simply waits to receive the processed tiles back from the grid workers, and places them to reform the image:

```
# Master receives output tiles in sequence and unpacks
# each into its correct place to form the output image
for (ty in 0:(dim-1)) { # bottom-left to top-right
  sy <- (ty * theight) +1
  for (tx in 0:(dim-1)) {
    sx <- (tx * twidth) +1
    # Receive tile from the appropriate Worker
    worker <- workerRanks[ty+1,tx+1]
    tile <- mpi.recv.Robj(worker,2,comm=1)
    image2[sy:(sy+theight-1),sx:(sx+twidth-1)] <- tile
  }
}
```

Processing the image tiles

The following is the code executed by the grid workers—in the complete code, this is wrapped in a function that the master executes across the worker grid with `mpi.bcast.cmd()`:

```
# Worker Grid Function: worker_gridApplyMedianFilter()
# Receive tile from Master on Rmpi default comm
tile <- mpi.recv.Robj(0,1,comm=1,status=1)

# Create local image with extra pixel boundary
theight <- nrow(tile); iheight <- theight+2;
twidth <- ncol(tile); iwidth <- twidth+2;
img <- matrix(0L,nrow=iheight,ncol=iwidth)

# Initialize borders with out-of-bound pixel values
# These values will be sorted to the ends of the set of 9
# and so will not interfere with the real image values
img[1,1:iwidth] <- rep(c(-1,256),times=iwidth/2)
img[1:iheight,1] <- rep(c(-1,256),times=iheight/2)
img[iheight,1:iwidth] <- rep(c(256,-1),times=iwidth/2)
img[1:iheight,iwidth] <- rep(c(256,-1),times=iheight/2)

# Set internal bounded area to the received tile
img[2:(theight+1),2:(twidth+1)] <- tile
...
```

Once the image has been constructed, each worker enters its processing sequence, using the code snippets described previously. The processing sequence is as follows:

1. Each worker exchanges boundary data, consisting of the set of non-blocking sends and non-blocking receives, with its neighbors:
2. It then applies the Median filter operator to all pixels within the inner tile square.
3. Steps 1 and 2 are repeated for some chosen number of iterations.
4. The resultant filtered tile data is then back to the master.

The full commented code for the entire grid-based median filter processing program is provided in the following section.

Median filter grid program

The code listing in the next few pages describes the entire program for implementing the grid-based Median filter with `Rmpi`, and is broken into sections reflecting the various steps through which we developed the code previously in this chapter:

```
##
## Copyright 2016 Simon Chapple
##
## Packt: "Mastering Parallelism with R"
## Chapter 3 - Advanced MPI Grid Parallelism Median Filter
##
library(Rmpi)

# Useful constants
Height<-200; Width<-200; # Size of image
Dim<-2; # Square size of grid
N<-1; NE<-2; E<-3; SE<-4; # Neighbor compass directions
S<-5; SW<-6; W<-7; NW<-8;
```

Creating the grid cluster:

```
worker_makeSquareGrid <- function(dim,comm)
{
  print(paste0("Base grid comm=",comm," dim=",dim))
  grid <- 1000 + dim    # assign comm handle for this size grid
  dims <- c(dim,dim)    # dimensions are 2D, size: dim X dim
  periods <- c(FALSE,FALSE)  # no wraparound at outermost edges
```

```
  if (mpi.cart.create(commold=comm,dims,periods,commcart=grid))
  {
    return(grid)
  }
  return(-1) # An MPI error occurred
}

worker_initSpatialGrid <- function(dim,comm=Wcomm)
{
  Gcomm <- worker_makeSquareGrid(dim,comm)
  myRank <- mpi.comm.rank(Gcomm)
  myUniverseRank <- mpi.comm.rank(1) # Lookup rank in cluster
  print(paste("myRank:",myRank))
  myCoords <- mpi.cart.coords(Gcomm,myRank,2)
  print(paste("myCoords:",myCoords))
  # (y^,x>) co-ordinate system
  myY <- myCoords[1]; myX <- myCoords[2];
  coords <- vector(mode="list", length=8)
  neighbors <- rep(-1,8)
  if (myY+1 < dim) {
    neighbors[N] <- mpi.cart.rank(Gcomm,c(myY+1,myX))
  }
  if (myX+1 < dim && myY+1 < dim) {
    neighbors[NE] <- mpi.cart.rank(Gcomm,c(myY+1,myX+1))
  }
  if (myX+1 < dim) {
    neighbors[E] <- mpi.cart.rank(Gcomm,c(myY,myX+1))
  }
  if (myX+1 < dim && myY-1 >= 0) {
    neighbors[SE] <- mpi.cart.rank(Gcomm,c(myY-1,myX+1))
  }
  if (myY-1 >= 0) {
    neighbors[S] <- mpi.cart.rank(Gcomm,c(myY-1,myX))
  }
  if (myX-1 >= 0 && myY-1 >= 0) {
    neighbors[SW] <- mpi.cart.rank(Gcomm,c(myY-1,myX-1))
  }
  if (myX-1 >= 0) {
    neighbors[W] <- mpi.cart.rank(Gcomm,c(myY,myX-1))
  }
  if (myX-1 >= 0 && myY+1 < dim) {
    neighbors[NW] <- mpi.cart.rank(Gcomm,c(myY+1,myX-1))
  }
```

```
    # Store reference for neighbor comms
    assign("Neighbors", neighbors, envir=.GlobalEnv)
    # Store reference for grid communicator
    assign("Gcomm", Gcomm, envir=.GlobalEnv)
    return(list(myY,myX,myUniverseRank))
  }
```

Boundary data exchange:

```
  worker_boundaryExchange <- function(img,neighbors,comm)
  {
    # More efficient to set-up non-blocking receives then sends
    neighbors <- Neighbors; comm <- Gcomm;

    # Set-up non-blocking receives for incoming boundary data
    # Local image tile has one pixel shared border
    len <- ncol(img)-2
    rbuf <- vector(mode="list", length=8) # 8 receive buffers
    req <- 0
    for (i in 1:8) {
      if (neighbors[i]>=0) {
        rbuf[[i]] <- integer(length=len)
        tag <- mpi.any.tag()
      mpi.irecv(rbuf[[i]],1,neighbors[i],tag,
      comm=comm,request=req)
        req <- req + 1
      }
    }

    edge <- ncol(img)-1 # image is square: ncol=nrow
    sbuf <- vector(mode="list", length=8) # 8 send buffers
    # non-block send my tile data boundaries to my neighbours
    if (neighbors[N]>=0) { # north
      sbuf[[N]] <- img[2,2:edge]
      mpi.isend(sbuf[[N]],1,neighbors[N],N,comm=comm,request=req)
      req <- req + 1
    }
    if (neighbors[NE]>=0) { # ne
      sbuf[NE] <- img[2,edge] # top-right inner cell
      mpi.isend(sbuf[[NE]],1,neighbors[NE],NE,
    comm=comm,request=req)
      req <- req + 1
    }
```

```
if (neighbors[E]>=0) { # east
  sbuf[[E]] <- img[2:edge,edge] # rightmost inner col
  mpi.isend(sbuf[[E]],1,neighbors[E],E,comm=comm,request=req)
  req <- req + 1
}
if (neighbors[SE]>=0) { # se
  sbuf[[SE]] <- img[edge,edge] # bottom-right inner cell
  mpi.isend(sbuf[[SE]],1,neighbors[SE],SE,
comm=comm,request=req)
  req <- req + 1
}
if (neighbors[S]>=0) { # south
  sbuf[[S]] <- img[edge,2:edge] # bottom inner row
  mpi.isend(sbuf[[S]],1,neighbors[S],S,comm=comm,request=req)
  req <- req + 1
}
if (neighbors[SW]>=0) { # sw
  sbuf[[SW]] <- img[edge,2] # bottom-left inner cell
  mpi.isend(sbuf[[SW]],1,neighbors[SW],SW,
comm=comm,request=req)
  req <- req + 1
}
if (neighbors[W]>=0) { # west
  sbuf[[W]] <- img[2:edge,2] # leftmost inner col
  mpi.isend(sbuf[[W]],1,neighbors[W],W,comm=comm,request=req)
  req <- req + 1
}
if (neighbors[NW]>=0) { # nw
  sbuf[[NW]] <- img[2,2] # top-left inner cell
  mpi.isend(sbuf[[NW]],1,neighbors[NW],NW,
comm=comm,request=req)
  req <- req + 1
}

mpi.waitall(req) # Wait for all boundary comms to complete

# Unpack received boundary data into my image tile
n <- ncol(img)
if (neighbors[N]>=0) { # north
  img[1,2:edge] <- rbuf[[N]] # top row
}
if (neighbors[NE]>=0) { # ne
  img[1,n] <- rbuf[[NE]][1] # top-right cell
```

```
    }
    if (neighbors[E]>=0) { # east
      img[2:edge,n] <- rbuf[[E]] # rightmost column
    }
    if (neighbors[SE]>=0) { # se
      img[n,n] <- rbuf[[SE]][1] # bottom-right cell
    }
    if (neighbors[S]>=0) { # south
      img[n,2:edge] <- rbuf[[S]] # bottom row
    }
    if (neighbors[SW]>=0) { # sw
      img[n,1] <- rbuf[[SW]][1] # bottom-left cell
    }
    if (neighbors[W]>=0) { # west
      img[2:edge,1] <- rbuf[[W]] # leftmost column
    }
    if (neighbors[NW]>=0) { # nw
      img[1,1] <- rbuf[[NW]][1] # top-left cell
    }
    return(img)
  }
```

The median filter:

```
medianFilterPixel3 <- function(y,x,img) {
  v <- vector("integer",9) # bottom-left to top-right
  v[1]<-img[y-1,x-1]; v[2]<-img[y-1,x]; v[3]<-img[y-1,x+1];
  v[4]<-img[y,  x-1]; v[5]<-img[y,  x]; v[6]<-img[y,  x+1];
  v[7]<-img[y+1,x-1]; v[8]<-img[y+1,x]; v[9]<-img[y+1,x+1];
  s <- sort(v); # sort by pixel value (default ascending)
  return (s[5]) # return the middle value of the nine
}
```

Processing the image tiles:

```
worker_gridApplyMedianFilter <- function(niters)
{
  # Receive tile from Master on Rmpi default comm
  tile <- mpi.recv.Robj(0,1,comm=1,status=1)

  # Create local image with extra pixel boundary
  theight <- nrow(tile); iheight <- theight+2;
  twidth <- ncol(tile); iwidth <- twidth+2;
  print(paste("Received tile:",theight,twidth))
```

```
  img <- matrix(0L,nrow=iheight,ncol=iwidth)

  # Initialize borders with out-of-bound pixel values
  # These values will be sorted to the ends of the set of 9
  # and so will not interfere with the real image values
  img[1,1:iwidth] <- rep(c(-1,256),times=iwidth/2)
  img[1:iheight,1] <- rep(c(-1,256),times=iheight/2)
  img[iheight,1:iwidth] <- rep(c(256,-1),times=iwidth/2)
  img[1:iheight,iwidth] <- rep(c(256,-1),times=iheight/2)

  # Set internal bounded area to the received tile
  img[2:(theight+1),2:(twidth+1)] <- tile

  # Apply multi-pass image operation
  for (i in 1:niters) {
    print(paste("Iteration",i))
    img <- worker_boundaryExchange(img)
    for (y in 2:theight+1) {
      for (x in 2:twidth+1) {
        img[y,x] <- medianFilterPixel3(y,x,img)
      }
    }
  }

  # Send processed tile to Master on default comm
  tile <- img[2:(theight+1),2:(twidth+1)]
  mpi.send.Robj(tile,0,2,comm=1)
}


##############################################################
# Master co-ordinates creation and operation of the grid,
# but does not itself participate in any tile computation.

# Launch the Rmpi based grid with (dimXdim) worker processes
dim <- Dim;
np <- dim * dim # number of MPI processes in grid
mpi.spawn.Rslaves(
  Rscript=system.file("workerdaemon.R", package="Rmpi"),
  nslaves=np)

# Send all Master defined globals/functions to Workers
```

```
mpi.bcast.Robj2slave(all=TRUE)

# Map grid co-ords to cluster rank assignment of the Workers
map <- mpi.remote.exec(worker_initSpatialGrid(),dim,
                       simplify=FALSE,comm=1)
workerRanks <- matrix(-1,nrow=dim,ncol=dim)
for (p in 1:length(map)) {
  y <- map[[p]][[1]]
  x <- map[[p]][[2]]
  rank <- map[[p]][[3]]
  print(paste0("Map ",p,": (",y,",",x,") => ",rank))
  workerRanks[y+1,x+1] <- rank
}

# We create large B/W image array with values in range 101-111
height <- Height; width <- Width;
image1 <- matrix(sample(101:111,height*width,replace=TRUE),
                 height,width)
# We add a bit of white saturation noise (pixel value=255)
image1[height/6,width/6] <- 255
image1[height/5,width/5] <- 255
image1[height/4,width/4] <- 255
image1[height/3,width/3] <- 255
image1[height/2.1,width/2.1] <- 255
image1[height/1.1,width/1.1] <- 255
image1[height/1.2,width/1.2] <- 255
image1[height/1.3,width/1.3] <- 255
image1[height/1.4,width/1.4] <- 255
image1[height/1.5,width/1.5] <- 255

# Tell the workers to process the image (3 pass MedianFilter)
# The Workers first wait to receive their local tile from the
# Master,then do their multi-pass image processing, then finally #
send their processed tiles back to the Master.
mpi.bcast.cmd(worker_gridApplyMedianFilter(3))
Start <- proc.time()
```

Distributing the image as tiles:

```
# We split the image into non-overlapping square grid tiles
# and distribute one per Worker
twidth <- width/dim # tile width
theight <- height/dim # tile height
```

```
for (ty in 0:(dim-1)) { # bottom-left to top-right
  sy <- (ty * theight) +1
  for (tx in 0:(dim-1)) {
    sx <- (tx * twidth) +1
    tile <- image1[sy:(sy+theight-1),sx:(sx+twidth-1)]
    # Send tile to the appropriate Worker
    worker <- workerRanks[ty+1,tx+1]
    mpi.send.Robj(tile,worker,1,comm=1)
    print(paste0("Sent tile to ", worker,
          " y=",sy,"-",sy+theight-1," x=",sx,"-",sx+twidth-1))
  }
}

# Create processed output image, initially blank
image2 <- matrix(0L,nrow=height,ncol=width)

# Master receives output tiles in sequence and unpacks
# each into its correct place to form the output image
for (ty in 0:(dim-1)) { # bottom-left to top-right
  sy <- (ty * theight) +1
  for (tx in 0:(dim-1)) {
    sx <- (tx * twidth) +1
    # Receive tile from the appropriate Worker
    worker <- workerRanks[ty+1,tx+1]
    tile <- mpi.recv.Robj(worker,2,comm=1)
    print(paste0("Received tile from ", worker,
          " y=",sy,"-",sy+theight-1," x=",sx,"-",sx+twidth-1))
    image2[sy:(sy+theight-1),sx:(sx+twidth-1)] <- tile
  }
}

# Ta da!
Finish <- proc.time()
print(paste("Image size:",Height,"x",Width," processed
with",np,"Workers in",Finish[3]-Start[3],"elapsed seconds"))
# Saturated image=255
print(paste("Noisy image max pixel value",max(image1)))
# MedianFiltered image=111
print(paste("Clean image max pixel value",max(image2)))
mpi.close.Rslaves()
```

Performance

The following is some sample output running this program on my four-core MacBook laptop, with `Dim` set to `1`, that is, on a grid with a single MPI process (plus master), effectively running in serial versus `Dim` set to `2`, that is, on a grid with four MPI processes (plus master):

```
[1] "Map 1: (0,0) => 1"
[1] "Sent tile to 1 y=1-200 x=1-200"
[1] "Received tile from 1 y=1-200 x=1-200"
[1] "Image size: 200 x 200  processed with 1 Workers in 29.485 elapsed
seconds"
[1] "Noisy image max pixel value 255"
[1] "Clean image max pixel value 111"

[1] "Map 1: (0,0) => 1"
[1] "Map 2: (0,1) => 2"
[1] "Map 3: (1,0) => 3"
[1] "Map 4: (1,1) => 4"
[1] "Sent tile to 1 y=1-100 x=1-100"
[1] "Sent tile to 2 y=1-100 x=101-200"
[1] "Sent tile to 3 y=101-200 x=1-100"
[1] "Sent tile to 4 y=101-200 x=101-200"
[1] "Received tile from 1 y=1-100 x=1-100"
[1] "Received tile from 2 y=1-100 x=101-200"
[1] "Received tile from 3 y=101-200 x=1-100"
[1] "Received tile from 4 y=101-200 x=101-200"
[1] "Image size: 200 x 200  processed with 4 Workers in 4.786 elapsed
seconds"
[1] "Noisy image max pixel value 255"
[1] "Clean image max pixel value 111"
```

We always need to run tests multiple times to ensure that we recognize any other system resource effects influencing the timing figures. However, comparing the given elapsed times clearly demonstrates how effective grid-based computation can be for spatial/localized image/matrix operations.

Inspecting and managing communications

For most types of parallel algorithms implemented in R, where the focus is mainly on statistical numerical programming as opposed to more symbol-based processing or implementing exotic system architectures with more unpredictable communication patterns, the following "advanced" API calls are not often used. Nevertheless, they enable the MPI processes to deal with out-of-bound communication, and to avoid waiting unnecessarily for a communication to complete when other processing may usefully be performed; so if your context permits, then it can certainly be more efficient to make use of them. You may, for example, be able to interleave the communication between successive iterations in a long-running computation.

The following table covers `MPI_Probe` for retrieving information about a completed communication, `MPI_Test` to check for completion of a communication, and `MPI_Cancel` for enabling you to rescind an uncompleted communication:

INSPECTING / MANAGING COMMUNICATIONS - MPI_Probe		
MPI API Call	**pbdMPI equivalent**	**Rmpi equivalent**

`MPI_Probe` (*MPI Ref: p.64* `source`, `tag`, `comm`, `flag`, `status`)
Similarly:
`MPI_Iprobe` (*MPI Ref: p.65* `source`, `tag`, `comm`, `flag`, `status`)
	`probe(rank.srce, tag, comm=1, status=0)`
	
	`iprobe(rank.srce, tag, comm=1, status=0)`
	
	Wildcard values:
	`anysource()`
	`anytag()`
		`mpi.probe(source, tag, comm=1, status = 0)`
		
		`mpi.iprobe(source, tag, comm=1, status = 0)`
		
		Wildcard values:
		`mpi.any.source()`
		`mpi.any.tag()`

INSPECTING / MANAGING COMMUNICATIONS - MPI_Probe

`MPI_Probe` enables you to check for the presence of an incoming communication from a specific sender, marked with a specific tag. Wildcards can also be used to match on any sender and tag. This enables you to check for an incoming communication, work out its details, and then make a specific `MPI_Recv` to complete the communication. In this mode of behavior, your program can dynamically respond to incoming messages rather then being hard-coded with an explicit pattern of communication.

However, `MPI_Probe` is a blocking operation, and therefore, will not return until a matching communication has actually occurred—a qualifying message must have been sent.

`MPI_Iprobe`, on the other hand, is non-blocking, and therefore, will not wait to find a matching communication, but can be used to determine if a matching communication is pending, that is, waiting to be delivered to the caller as receiver at the specific moment in time.

Examples:

The following `pbdMPI` example illustrates a wildcard wait on the receiver until there is an incoming message from any rank with any tag on the default communicator, the details of which are returned in the default status handle:

```
# Wait for any incoming message
probe(anysource(),anytag())
# Retrieve vector with sender and tag of incoming message
st <- get.sourcetag(0)
# Selectively complete the pending communication
obj <- recv(rank.srce=st[1],st[2])
```

The following `Rmpi` example demonstrates the use of `MPI_Iprobe` to periodically test for any incoming communication (assumed here to be integer vectors) between iterations of background work:

```
# Computation is in the form of a series of subtasks
for (iter in 1:N) {
  # Check if a message is pending delivery to this process
  if (mpi.iprobe(mpi.anysource(),mpi.anytag())) {
     st <- mpi.get.sourcetag(0) # Default status: Who from?
     count <- mpi.get.count(0) # How many integers?
       dataIn <- vector(mode="integer",length=count)
       # receive the pending message with correct size buffer
       mpi.recv(dataIn,1,st[1],st[2])
       # process the message
       ...
  }
  # Continue to do background computational tasks
  doIteration(iter)
}
```

In reality, you would want to handle out-of-bounds communication in a more structured and engineered fashion than this—the preceding example is intended to explain how to use `MPI_Iprobe` in conjunction with other API calls.

INSPECTING / MANAGING COMMUNICATIONS - MPI_Status		
MPI API Call	**pbdMPI equivalent**	**Rmpi equivalent**

`MPI_Status` - *MPI Ref: p.30*
`MPI_SOURCE`
`MPI_TAG`
 	
`MPI_Get_Count(`
`status, type, count)`
	`get.sourcetag(`
	`status`
	`)`
		`mpi.get.sourcetag(`
		`status)`
		
		`mpi.get.count(`
		`status`
		`)`

The `MPI_Status` object provides information about a completed communication. In R, the message sender and message tag can be retrieved from a specific `status` handle with `[mpi.]get.sourcetag(status)`. The `Rmpi` package also provides `mpi.get.count(status)` to determine the number of elements in a pending message, where the message relates to a vector/array of typed data, and this enables you to size the receive buffer appropriately when completing the communication. Refer to the section on `MPI_Probe` given earlier for examples.		

INSPECTING / MANAGING COMMUNICATIONS - MPI_Test		
MPI API Call	**pbdMPI equivalent**	**Rmpi equivalent**
`MPI_Test` (*MPI Ref: p.54* `request, flag, status)`	Not implemented	`mpi.test(request, status=0)` **returns:** `flag` (`TRUE`/`FALSE`)
`MPI_Testall` (*MPI Ref: p.60* `flag, count, requests, statuses)`		`mpi.testall(count)` **returns:** `flag` (`TRUE`/`FALSE`)
`MPI_Testany` (*MPI Ref: p.58* `flag, count, requests, index, status)`		`mpi.testany(count, wstatus=0)` **returns:** `list` (`index, flag`)
`MPI_Testsome(` *MPI Ref: p.61* `count, requests, count, indices, statuses)`		`mpi.testsome(count)` **returns:** `list(count, indices[])`

INSPECTING / MANAGING COMMUNICATIONS - MPI_Test
Notably, only `Rmpi` exposes this aspect of the MPI API. `MPI_Test` is essentially a non-blocking variant of `MPI_Wait` (see *Chapter 2, Introduction to Message Passing*), and the entire family of `MPI_Test` is otherwise similar in behavior to their `MPI_Wait` namesakes. So, with this in mind, let's understand the following functions: `mpi.test()`: This selectively tests for completion of a previously launched non-blocking send or receive with reference to its specific request handle. When `mpi.test()` returns `TRUE`, then the referenced `status` handle will provide the details on the completed communication. `mpi.testall()`: This tests *all* the outstanding, currently incomplete communications to determine if they have all completed. Note that here, `all` refers to the internally held array of `Rmpi` request handles, up to the maximum number referred to by the supplied `count` parameter. Recall that `Rmpi` request handles are indexes into this internal array, and are numbered sequentially from 0. If any of the communications within the count range have not completed, then this function will return `FALSE`. `mpi.testany()`: This function checks by scanning for (but does not wait for) the first of the supplied `count` of the currently outstanding non-blocking `sends/recvs` to have completed, and sets the supplied `status` handle to enable you to inspect the information about this communication (with `MPI_Probe`). `mpi.testsome()`: It checks on the supplied `count` of outstanding communications, and returns a list of the number of requests and a vector of the request handles for those that have completed.

INSPECTING / MANAGING COMMUNICATIONS - MPI_Cancel		
MPI API Call	**pbdMPI equivalent**	**Rmpi equivalent**
`MPI_Cancel` (*MPI Ref: p.72* `request`)	Not implemented	`mpi.cancel(request)`
As its name suggests, `MPI_Cancel` can be used to cancel a current non-blocking send or receive operation that has not yet completed. In essence, you cannot know whether or not the operation has been cancelled successfully: in terms of the limited API exposed by `Rmpi`, and because the cancellation itself operates only within the confines of the calling process. In any case, you must subsequently call `MPI_Wait` (or `MPI_Test` repeatedly until it succeeds) on the request handle that you have cancelled in order that the internal resources within the underlying MPI subsystem are released correctly. The program logic associated with the use of `MPI_Cancel` can be difficult to implement correctly. `MPI_Cancel` has limited use in typical R programs.		

Variants on lapply()

And finally, to end our tour of MPI, we come almost full circle in a sense. Just as in *Chapter 1, Simple Parallelism with R*, where R's core `parallel` package provides specific versions of `lapply()` that make it very simple to run a function in parallel, `Rmpi` and `pbdMPI` also provide their own `lapply()` variants.

parLapply() with Rmpi

Here we revisit the basic operation of `parLapply()` (*Chapter 1, Simple Parallelism with R*) in conjunction with MPI. We hinted back then that an MPI cluster can be used with `parLapply()`, and this indeed can be done by introducing an additional package called `snow`, an abbreviation that stands for **Simple Network Of Workstations (SNOW)**. All that we need to do is to install the `snow` package from CRAN, load the libraries in the correct order, and create the cluster using `Rmpi` thus (note that `pbdMPI` is not compatible with `parLapply()`):

```
> library("snow")
> library("Rmpi")
> library("parallel")
Attaching package: 'parallel'
The following objects are masked from 'package:snow':
    clusterApply, clusterApplyLB, clusterCall, clusterEvalQ,
    ...
> cl <- makeCluster(detectCores(), type="MPI")
> parLapply(...) # apply parallelized function
> stopCluster(cl)
> mpi.exit()
```

Of course, the fact that you are using `Rmpi` to provide the underlying cluster means you can run parallelized functions that themselves contain `Rmpi` calls, such as the collective communications operations.

As its name suggests, SNOW can also be used to leverage a disparate set of networked computers that could all be very different machines, for example, a mix of networked laptops, desktop computers, and servers, sited in multiple offices (see the breakout box for more information on this aspect).

Let it SNOW!

There's nothing to stop you from using SNOW by itself. The `parallel` package effectively wraps the SNOW functionality, and this includes SNOW's ability to run across a potentially heterogeneous network of machines running various operating systems. For this, SNOW requires the use of sockets, which are built-in and selected with the cluster `type="SOCK"`. Alternatively, you can use the `nws` package that operates NetWorkSpaces and can be downloaded from CRAN:

For the R `nws` package, go to the following link:

`https://cran.r-project.org/web/packages/nws.`

The various systems in the network must be set up appropriately for both SOCK and NWS. While SOCK does not require additional software, NWS in its simplest form requires the lead computer running the R script that calls `parApply()`, a running NetWorkSpace server (written in Python), and R installed with the `nws` package in all other computers in the network.

The following link can be used to download the NetWorkSpace server:

`http://nws-r.sourceforge.net/.`

For ease of use, all other aspects of configuration, such as directory paths, version of R, and so on, should be common across all the computers, irrespective of which operating systems they run on, although it will be simpler if all computers are running some variant of UNIX. It is then necessary to supply a list of network hosts, which can be IP addresses if the local DNS host names are not resolvable, for the set of computers to be included in the call to `makeCluster()`. For example, for a three-host cluster, the following list can be provided:

```
> hosts <- c(list(host="charlie"),
     list(host="192.168.9.4"), list(host="fred"))
> cl <- makeCluster(hosts, type="SOCK") # or type="NWS"
```

Since all the parallel processes run on completely separate computers, it is important that `stopCluster()` is called at program termination. Otherwise, stray processes will be left dangling, and manual clean-up would have to be performed by logging into each separate machine.

Please refer to the `snow` package manual at the following link for more information:

`https://cran.r-project.org/web/packages/snow/snow.pdf.`

Summary

In this chapter, we explored several more advanced aspects of message passing through its application to grid-based parallelism, including data segmentation and distribution for spatial operations, use of non-blocking communications, localized communication patterns between MPI processes, and how to map an SPMD style grid on to a standard `Rmpi` master/worker cluster. Whilst the illustrative example in image processing may not seem the most natural home for R programming, the knowledge gained through this example will be applicable to a wide range of large matrix-iterative algorithms.

We also covered MPI in detail by explaining the additional API routines geared to inspecting and managing outstanding communications, including `MPI_Probe` and `MPI_Test`.

We finished the chapter by reviewing how `Rmpi` can be used in conjunction with `parLapply()`, and touched on how you can run an MPI cluster across a simple network of workstations.

The grid-based processing framework that we have constructed in this chapter is applicable to a wide range of image processing operators, particularly if we were to generalize the code to cope with larger-sized local pixel windows. The code is highly amenable for this further development, and for extension to deal with arbitrary-sized and non-square images. All of this I will leave as an exercise for you, dear reader.

In this chapter, our focus was on using `Rmpi` to implement grid-based image/matrix parallel processing. In the next chapter, our focus switches to `pbdMPI` applied to genome analysis on supercomputers for ultimate scalability, so buckle your seatbelts for maximum acceleration in parallel processing!

4
Developing SPRINT, an MPI-Based R Package for Supercomputers

In this chapter, we will learn how to use a form of parallelism called *message passing*, written in the widely adopted **Message Passing Interface (MPI)** standard, and how to utilize MPI-based parallel routines written in other programming languages directly from an R script.

We will start with a simple "Hello World" MPI program, and transform it into an R library package. This will demonstrate how you can take an existing MPI code written in C and make it directly callable from R.

We will then delve into the architecture of an MPI-based R package, commonly known as **Simple Parallel R Interface** (**SPRINT**). SPRINT provides a suite of MPI-parallel routines of particular use to bio-informaticians and life scientists for genomic analysis. We will show how you can further extend its utility by adding your own parallel functionality to the package.

Finally, we will explore the performance characteristics of a SPRINT-based genomics analysis program running on a massive scale on ARCHER, the UK's largest academic supercomputer.

Software versions

In this chapter, the MPI examples were run on an Apple Mac Book Pro, with a 2.4 GHz Intel Core i5 processor, 8 GB memory, running OS X 10.9.5, MPI mpich-3.1.2, C clang-600.0.57, and R version 3.1.1. For the genomics analysis case study, the examples were run on ARCHER. At the time of writing (March 2015), the ARCHER compute nodes contain two 2.7 GHz, 12-core E5-2697 v2 Ivy Bridge series processors. Each of the cores in these processors can support two hardware threads, also known as Hyper-threads. Within the node, the two processors are connected by two QuickPath Interconnect links. Each node has a total of 64 GB of memory. ARCHER has 4,920 compute nodes. The software versions used on ARCHER were: MPI cray-mpich version 7.1.1, C gcc version 4.9.2, and R version 3.1.0.

About ARCHER

ARCHER has more than 100,000 cores (`http://www.archer.ac.uk/about-archer/`). The following Figure 1 shows some of the physical cabinets that comprise the ARCHER supercomputer, occupying an entire dedicated room in a purpose-built facility.

Figure 1: The ARCHER supercomputer at Edinburgh Parallel Computing Centre.

Figure 2 illustrates how these thousands of cores are organized across the individual cabinets. Notice how each of the individual Intel-based compute node processors has *2x12* cores and 64 Gb of memory.

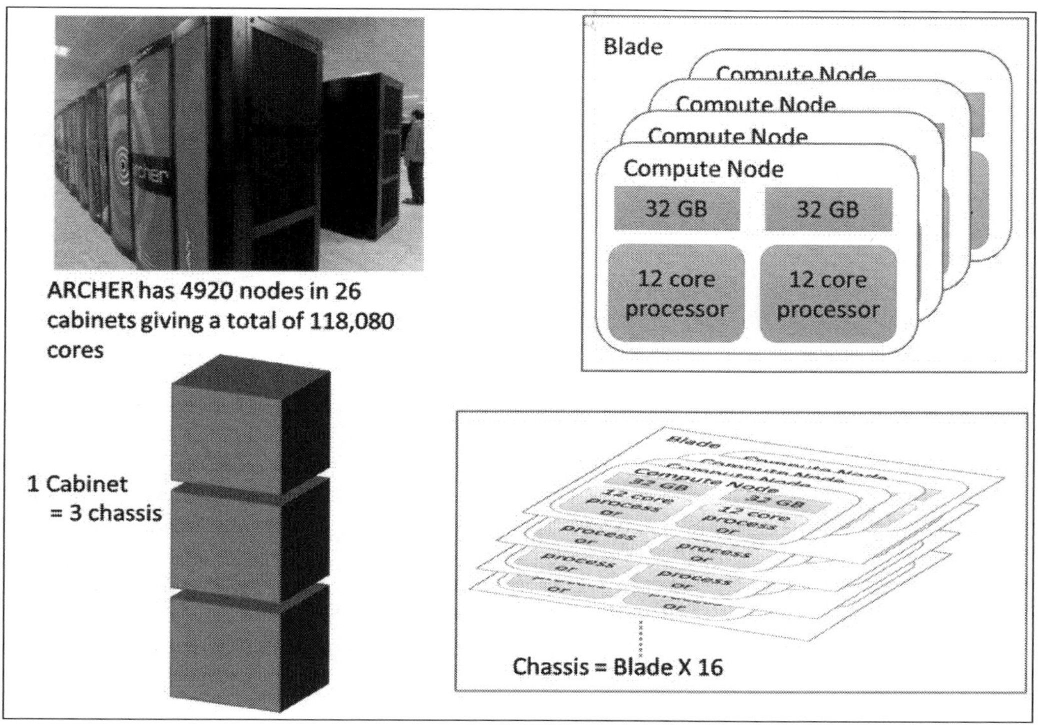

Figure 2: The composition of an ARCHER cabinet.

Calling MPI code from R

Let's look at how to call the existing MPI C code from R. What follows is an example that will help when you already have some C or C++ MPI code that you want to call from R. We will look at one simple way of doing this, but please note there are a number of ways this can be done. The definitive guide to calling code in C or other languages from R is the *Writing R Extensions* manual available from CRAN at `http://cran.r-project.org/doc/manuals/r-release/R-exts.html`.

If you are writing the MPI C code that you want to call from R from scratch, then you should consider using the `Rcpp` R package (see `http://cran.r-project.org/web/packages/Rcpp/index.html`). This package provides C++ wrappers for R data types, thus allowing easy data transfer between C++ and R. It also manages memory for you, and provides other helper methods.

MPI Hello World

Let's start with a simple "Hello World" MPI C program, where each separate process prints `hello` and its MPI rank number.

```
#include <stdio.h>
#include <mpi.h>

int hello(void);

int main(void)
{
   return hello();
}

int hello(void)
{
    int rank, size;

    // Standard MPI initialisation
    MPI_Init(NULL, NULL);

    MPI_Comm_size(MPI_COMM_WORLD, &size);
    MPI_Comm_rank(MPI_COMM_WORLD, &rank);

    // Prints out hello from each process
    printf("Hello from rank %d out of %d\n", rank, size);

    MPI_Finalize();
    return 0;
}
```

The preceding code contains a function `hello()` that:

- Initializes MPI
- Obtains the size (that is, the number of processes) in the default `MPI_COMM_WORLD` communicator that has been initialized by calling `MPI_Comm_size()`
- Gets the rank of the calling process in this `MPI_COMM_WORLD` communicator by calling `MPI_Comm_rank()`
- Prints out hello and the rank number of the calling process
- And finally, calls `MPI_Finalize()` to terminate the process

Assuming you have previously installed the mpich-3.1.2 version of MPI, you can save this program in a file called `mpihello.c`, then compile and run it (using four MPI processes) from the OS command line as follows:

```
$ mpicc -o mpihello.o mpihello.c
$ mpiexec -n 4 ./mpihello.o
```

You will see the following output (not necessarily in this order):

```
Hello from rank 0 out of 4
Hello from rank 1 out of 4
Hello from rank 2 out of 4
Hello from rank 3 out of 4
```

Calling C from R

To call a C program from R, you must first build a shared object that contains the compiled C code that you want to call. This shared object must be loaded into your R session using the R `dyn.load` function. You can then use the R function, `.Call`, to call the compiled C code from an R script. To illustrate how to do this, let's build a shared object for our MPI Hello World program, and then call it from within R.

Modifying C code to make it callable from R

First, let's make the necessary changes to the C code itself in order to make it callable from R. These changes are highlighted in the code that follows:

```
#include <mpi.h>
#include <R.h>
#include <Rinternals.h>
#include <Rdefines.h>

SEXP hello(void);

SEXP hello(void)
{

  int rank, size;

  MPI_Init(NULL, NULL);
  MPI_Comm_size(MPI_COMM_WORLD, &size);
  MPI_Comm_rank(MPI_COMM_WORLD, &rank);

  Rprintf("Hello from rank %d out of %d\n", rank, size);
```

```
    MPI_Finalize();

    // Create an R integer data type with value zero
    SEXP result = PROTECT(result = NEW_INTEGER(1));
    INTEGER(result)[0] = 0;
    UNPROTECT(1);
    return result;
}
```

As you can see in the preceding code, the necessary R header files have to be included, and the `main` routine has been removed. The various header files and their purpose are explained in detail in the *Writing R Extensions* manual, but for your convenience, here's a brief description. The `R.h` file is a header file that includes many other necessary files, `Rinternals.h` contains the definitions for using R's internal structures, and finally, `Rdefines.h` contains various useful macros.

The `hello()` function now returns an `SEXP` instead of `int`. As stated in the *Writing R Extensions* manual, an `SEXP` is a pointer to a structure that can handle all the usual types of R objects, that is, functions, vectors of various modes, environments, language objects, and so on.

Our `hello()` function must return an `SEXP` when it is called from the R `.Call()` function for two reasons. The first is that R requires that any C code called in this way must return a value. This means that even this simple example must return something to R. The second reason is that R is implemented in C, and all R data types are represented internally as `SEXP` data types in C. Therefore, when editing code to make it callable from R, you need to convert the input and output data between R and C.

Within the `hello()` function, the MPI calls are unchanged and `printf()` has been replaced by `Rprintf()`. As explained in the *Writing R Extensions* manual, `Rprintf()` is guaranteed to write to R's output whether that be a GUI console, a file, or a re-direction. It can be used in the same way as `printf()`. More importantly, using `Rprintf()` ensures that the output is redirected appropriately when using parallel computations.

After `MPI_Finalize()`, we create the value for `hello()` to return to R. This is an `SEXP` pointer—`result`—that we make point to an R integer data type. The R objects that you create in C are at a risk of being garbage-collected automatically by R. So, we protect the object pointed to by `result` by calling the `PROTECT()` macro. We can now set `result` to the value we wish the `hello()` function to return to R, in this case, `0`. Before returning this, we must use the `UNPROTECT()` macro to clear the stack of variables that we have previously protected from garbage collection by R; we can then return `result`. The `PROTECT()/UNPROTECT()` calls are not strictly necessary here, as no R code or macros (which could trigger garbage collection) run in between the calls. The `PROTECT/UNPROTECT()` calls are included here as an example.

Let's save our modified code into a file called `mpihello_fromR.c`.

Compiling MPI code into an R shared object

Now that we have modified our C code to make it callable from R, the next step is to compile it into an R shared object library that can be loaded into R. For this, we will use the standard R command `R CMD SHLIB` at the OS command line. This code should work with either the openMPI or the mpich implementations of MPI, but if you have any problems with openMPI, then you should try mpich instead.

Remember that the modified code for our MPI Hello World example is saved in a file called `mpihello_fromR.c`. Let's compile this, and make it into an R shared object library by executing the following at the OS command line:

```
$ MAKEFLAGS="CC=mpicc" R CMD SHLIB -o mpihello_fromR.so
mpihello_fromR.c --preclean
```

Since our code contains calls to MPI, we need to execute `R CMD SHLIB` with the compiler set to `mpicc` rather than `cc` using the argument `MAKEFLAGS="CC=mpicc"` in the preceding code. Executing the preceding code at the OS command line will produce a file called `mpihello_fromR.so`. Note that in Microsoft Windows, a dynamic link library needs to be produced, and so, the extension `.dll` must be used in place of `.so`.

Calling the MPI Hello World example from R

This is the final step. To call our modified MPI Hello World code from R, we must now load our shared object library `mpihello_fromR.so` that contains it, into R. We can then use `.Call` to call the `hello()` function contained in this shared object. The following is the R code to load the shared object into R and then call our modified `hello()` function:

```
dyn.load("mpihello_fromR.so")
.Call("hello")
```

Let's save these two lines of R code into a file called `mpihello.R`, and run it from the OS command line as follows:

```
$ mpiexec -n 4 R -f mpihello.R
```

In the preceding line, the `mpiexec -n 4` part specifies that four MPI processes are to be instantiated. `R -f mpihello.R` specifies that the R file `mpihello.R` is to be executed on each of these processes. The following is some of the output from executing this line at the OS command line. There will also be some output from R.

```
Hello from rank 0 out of 4
Hello from rank 1 out of 4
Hello from rank 2 out of 4
Hello from rank 3 out of 4
```

So you have now executed MPI C code from R, and you have learned how to write, compile, and then call the MPI code (written in C) from R.

Building an MPI R package – SPRINT

Now that we have built an R shared object library that contains MPI code which is callable from R, let's investigate how to create an R package that contains a number of MPI-enabled functions, each callable from R.

Building a package for this can be useful for various reasons, including the following:

- **Maintainability**: If each function has its own MPI setup and teardown, then you could end up with a lot of duplicate code to maintain.
- **Flexibility**: From one invocation of MPI in your R script, you can easily call multiple, different MPI-enabled functions according to your needs.
- **Efficiency**: If each function has its own separate shared object library, then each will go through their own `MPI_Init`/`MPI_Finalize` stages when called, thus adding to the runtime.

The SPRINT package provides an R user with just such a suite of parallelized functions callable from R that exploit MPI. In the following sections, we will show you how to add your own function to the SPRINT package, but first let's look at the premise behind SPRINT and how it works.

The Simple Parallel R Interface (SPRINT) package

Many existing R packages allow developers or interested parties with sufficient expertise and resources to make use of code parallelization in order to solve their computational problems. The R SPRINT package is based on a different philosophy. The SPRINT package is designed for big data processing, seamlessly exploiting both multi-node and multi-core computing architectures, and efficiently utilizing disk space as additional out-of-core memory. It has been developed specifically by expert parallel programmers to provide prebuilt parallelized solutions to common analysis problems for R users. SPRINT particularly focuses on solving problems that are difficult for non-experts to parallelize. SPRINT is fully open source, and experienced users can make use of SPRINT to develop their own parallelized functionality. The SPRINT team welcomes contributions from the wider community back into the project.

At the time of writing, the latest version of SPRINT, v1.0.7, is available from CRAN at `http:// cran.r-project.org/web/packages/sprint/index.html`. It is also available directly from the SPRINT team's website at `http://www.r-sprint.org/`.

Using a prebuilt SPRINT routine in an R script

SPRINT contains a function called `ptest()` that is equivalent to our previous MPI Hello World example. It checks if the SPRINT package has been installed correctly by simply printing a message identifying each parallel process that has been instantiated.

Assuming the SPRINT package has previously been installed on your local R installation, the following sample R script can be used to call `ptest()`.

```
library("sprint") # load the sprint package


ptest()


pterminate() # terminate the parallel processes


quit()
```

The `pterminate()` function in this script is a SPRINT function that terminates all the parallel processes. This internally calls `MPI_Finalize` to shut down the instantiated parallel processes. All SPRINT-enabled scripts require that `pterminate()` is called before the final `quit()` command.

If this sample R script is stored in a file called `sprint_test.R`, then it can be run from the OS command line as follows:

```
$ mpiexec -n 5 R -f sprint_test.R
```

This will result in the following output (Note: the exact order may be different):

```
[1] "HELLO, FROM PROCESSOR: 0"
[2] "HELLO, FROM PROCESSOR: 2"
[3] "HELLO, FROM PROCESSOR: 1"
[4] "HELLO, FROM PROCESSOR: 3"
[5] "HELLO, FROM PROCESSOR: 4"
```

The architecture of the SPRINT package

The core of SPRINT is an MPI harness that manages a number of processes in the Master/Worker paradigm, which can either be assigned different tasks to execute or can be put to sleep while the sequential part of an R script runs, instead. It is relatively straightforward to add your own parallel MPI function to SPRINT. SPRINT is implemented in R and C. Figure 3 illustrates how SPRINT uses the Master/Worker paradigm at runtime. Let's explain how this works using our previous example execution of an R script containing the SPRINT `ptest()` function.

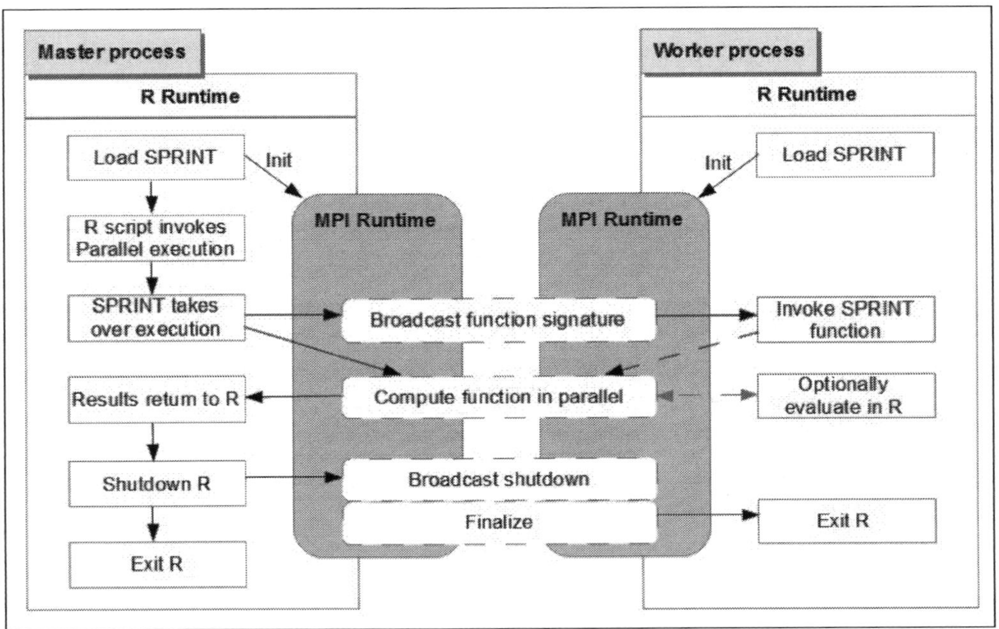

Figure 3: The flow of execution between Master and Worker processes when an R script uses SPRINT.

When the following command is executed at the OS command line, this results in all the instantiated processes initializing the R Runtime environment, as shown in Figure 3:

```
$ mpiexec -n 5 R -f sprint_test.R
```

Each of these processes then start executing the `sprint_test.R` script, the first line of which is `library("sprint")`. This line loads the SPRINT package on each of these processes, and more importantly, also initializes the MPI environment on each. At this point, SPRINT uses the MPI rank of each process to determine if a process is to be the Master process, or if it is to be one of the Worker processes. If a process is designated as a Worker, then it effectively sits in a wait state until a command code is sent from the Master process. Meanwhile, the Master process executes the remainder of the `sprint_test.R` script.

When the Master process executes the SPRINT `ptest()` function, this results in a command code representing the `ptest()` function (that is, the function signature) being broadcast from the Master to all the Worker processes. All the processes can then participate in the parallel execution of the function, and can interact with each other via MPI.

The fact that MPI is initialized in the R memory space (that is, via the `library("sprint")` line in the R script) means that the R runtime environment can be accessed on all the processes. This allows the handling of native R objects in C, and most importantly, it means that R expressions can be evaluated from C. This feature provides flexibility when adding new functions to SPRINT—this means that parallel SPRINT-enabled functions can either consist of a complete parallel re-implementation of the function, or utilize the existing serial R implementation of a function within a parallel harness.

After all the computation is completed on the Worker processes, results are sent back to the Master process, which returns these to the R environment running on it. The Worker processes return to their waiting state, and the Master process continues execution of the remainder of our `sprint_test.R` script.

The next line in this is `pterminate()`. This shuts down the MPI environment by broadcasting the appropriate command code to all the Worker processes, whereupon each process calls `MPI_Finalize` and terminates. Within `pterminate()`, the Master process also calls `MPI_Finalize`, and then continues executing the remainder of the R script.

Adding a new function to the SPRINT package

Let's now add our own function to the SPRINT package. This new function will be called `phello()`. We will use our earlier MPI Hello World example as the basis for this. This will involve the following tasks:

- Downloading the SPRINT source code.
- Creating the R stub file: This enables the desired functionality to be callable from R on the Master process. It calls the interface function for this functionality.
- Adding the interface function: The interface function is the C equivalent of the R stub. It is also executed on the Master process. It is responsible for broadcasting the command code for the implementation function that the Worker processes are to execute.
- Adding the implementation function: Each command code has a corresponding implementation function. On receipt of the command code, this function is executed on the Worker processes. Additionally, it is also executed on the Master process.
- Connecting the stub and functions: Update the relevant SPRINT header and configuration files to enable the stub, interface, and implementation functions to interact properly.

Downloading the SPRINT source code

First of all we have to download the SPRINT source code. You can download the latest version of the SPRINT source code from the CRAN website at `http://cran.r-project.org/web/packages/sprint/index.html`. It is also available directly from the SPRINT team at `http://www.r-sprint.org/`.

Use the following OS commands to download and unpack this source code:

```
$ Wget http://cran.r-project.org/src/contrib/sprint_1.0.7.tar.gz
$ tar -xvf sprint_1.0.7.tar.gz
```

The unpacked SPRINT source code has the following directory structure:

```
/sprint dir         Contains configure scripts, etc
    |
    |- inst         Documentation and tests
    |
    |- man             R documentation
```

```
    |
    |- R           Contains the R stubs
    |
    |- src           Functions header files, Makefile and sprint
itself.
        |
        |- algorithms
        |
            |- common    Functions used by all of the sprint
functions
            |
            |- papply
                |- implementation
                |- interface
            |- pboot
                |- implementation
                |- interface
            |- ...     All of the sprint functions have their own
folder
                         with implementation and interface sub-
folders.
    |
    |- tools
```

Creating a stub in R – phello.R

This stub contains the actual R wrapper function called by a user in their R script. This is executed on the SPRINT Master process, and this, in turn, uses the R `.Call()` function to call the MPI C code on this Master process. This function can be used to perform sanity checking on parameters and other programming housekeeping before activating the MPI C code.

To create this stub, let's navigate to the R directory in the SPRINT source code directory.

```
cd sprint/R
```

Now create a file called `phello.R`. The use of `p` in the filename is purely a SPRINT convention to help distinguish this implementation from any other existing R implementation of the function.

The following are the contents for `phello.R`:

```
phello <- function()
{
  return_val <- .Call("phello")
  return(return_val)
}
```

In the preceding code, the R function `phello()` is defined. This function contains the `.Call("phello")` that will call our C MPI code.

Notice how `phello.R` differs from our earlier `mpihello.R` file for the MPI Hello World shared object library example. This had the following contents:

```
dyn.load("mpihello_fromR.so")
.Call("hello")
```

With SPRINT, the `dyn.load()` call to load the shared object is not necessary, because as we will see later, the C code will be compiled as part of the SPRINT package, and loaded into the user's R script with the `library("sprint")` command.

Adding the interface function – phello.c

In SPRINT, an interface function is the C function called by an R stub. It is executed only by the SPRINT Master process. The purpose of the interface function is to broadcast the command code for the parallel function that is to be executed to all the SPRINT Worker processes. After broadcasting the command code, the interface function then starts executing on the Master process itself, the parallel function associated with the command code. Like the R stub that it mirrors, an interface function can perform argument checking and general housekeeping.

Let's create the interface function corresponding to our `phello.R` stub. As per the instructions given next, first we navigate to the `sprint/src/algorithms` directory, where we create a `phello` directory. In this `phello` directory, we create two further directories: the `implementation` directory and the `interface` directory.

```
$ cd sprint/src/algorithms
$ mkdir phello
$ mkdir phello/implementation
$ mkdir phello/interface
```

In the `interface` directory, let's create the file `phello.c` to hold our interface function. In SPRINT, the interface functions are all quite similar. Let's add the following contents to `phello.c`:

```
#include <Rdefines.h>
#include "../../../sprint.h"
#include "../../../functions.h"
extern int hello(int n, ...);
```

```
/* ****************************************************************
 *  The stub for the R side of a very simple hello world command
 *  Simply issues the command and returns 0 for successful      *
 *  completion of command or -1 for failure.
 * ***************************************************************/

// Note that all data from R is of type SEXP.
SEXP phello()
{
    SEXP result;
    int response, intCode;
    enum commandCodes commandCode;

    // Check MPI initialisation
    MPI_Initialized(&response);
    if (response) {
        DEBUG("MPI is init'ed in phello\n");
    } else {
        DEBUG("MPI is NOT init'ed in phello\n");

        // return -1 if MPI is not initialised.
        PROTECT(result = NEW_INTEGER(1));
        INTEGER(result)[0] = -1;
        UNPROTECT(1);
        return result;
    }

    // broadcast command to other processes
    commandCode = PHELLO;
    intCode = (int)commandCode;
    DEBUG("commandCode in phello is %d \n", intCode);
    MPI_Bcast(&intCode, 1, MPI_INT, 0, MPI_COMM_WORLD);

     // Call the command on this process too.
    response = hello(0); // We are passing no arguments.
    // If we wanted to pass 2 arguments, we'd write
    // response = hello(2, arg1, arg2);

     // Convert result into an R datatype (SEXP)
    result = PROTECT(result = NEW_INTEGER(1));
    INTEGER(result)[0] = response;
    UNPROTECT(1);
    return result;
}
```

Let's look at the preceding code in a little more detail.

At the top of the file, a number of header files are included, and the `hello()` function is declared as an extern, that is, it will be resolved at the final step of compilation during the linking phase.

```
#include <Rdefines.h>
#include "../../../sprint.h"
#include "../../../functions.h"
extern int hello(int n, ...);
```

As mentioned previously, `Rdefines.h` contains various macros. The next two header files, `sprint.h` and `functions.h`, are SPRINT header files that include header files and macros, respectively. These header files are required by SPRINT and the command codes for the various functions available in the SPRINT package.

Following this is the code for the `phello()` function itself. This starts by sanity checking that MPI is already initialized. Remember, in our SPRINT `ptest()` example given earlier, MPI is initialized in the calling R script by `library("sprint")`. This means that each call to a SPRINT function can use MPI without having to initialize it each time.

After this sanity checking, the `PHELLO` command code is broadcast via MPI, with `MPI_Bcast()`, to all the SPRINT Worker processes. The Master can now itself execute the parallel function associated with the broadcast command code. In this specific case, it is the `hello()` function. Finally, its output is converted into a `SEXP` pointer to an R integer data type so that it can be returned to the R stub `phello.R`, and the various macros dealing with garbage collection are also called.

Adding the implementation function – hello.c

In SPRINT, the implementation function is the function called by the interface function on the Master process after it has broadcast the command code to the Worker processes. It is also the function called by the Worker processes on receiving the command code for that function. So, for our `phello` example, this C code is placed in a file in the `sprint/src/algorithms/phello/implementation` directory that we have created.

Let's create a file called `hello.c` in this directory that will contain the implementation of the actual parallel algorithm we want to perform. This will use MPI for communication. As mentioned earlier, we are using our MPI C Hello World example as the basis for this. The following code is to be added to `hello.c`:

```
#include <mpi.h>
#include <R.h>
```

```
#include <Rinternals.h>
#include <Rdefines.h>
#include "../../../sprint.h"

int hello(int n, ...)
{
// ignore input args.We don't need them in this example.
  int rank, size, result;

  MPI_Comm_size(MPI_COMM_WORLD, &size);
  MPI_Comm_rank(MPI_COMM_WORLD, &rank);

  DEBUG("MPI is initiated in phello rank %d \n", rank);
  Rprintf("Hello from rank %d out of %d\n", rank, size);

  MPI_Barrier(MPI_COMM_WORLD);
  result = 0; // successful execution

  return result;
}
```

The code is almost exactly the same as in our `mpihello.c` example, but without `MPI_Init()` and `MPI_Finalize()`. As mentioned previously, SPRINT now handles the MPI initialization and termination. Note also the addition of an `MPI_Barrier()` function to ensure that the Master and all the Worker processes are synchronized to the same point in execution before the result is returned.

Connecting the stub, interface, and implementation

Now we get to the final steps to including our function in SPRINT. These involve updating the various configurations and header files.

The files to be updated are as follows:

- `functions.h`
- `functions.c`
- `NAMESPACE`
- `Makefile`
- The man page, `pHello.Rd`, for our new function.

Let's deal with each in turn.

functions.h

Let's navigate to `sprint/src`, where you will find this file. This is one of the files included in the interface function (see the `phello.c` description given earlier). It contains the command codes for the functions available in the SPRINT package. These are the command codes sent by the SPRINT Master process to the Worker processes to instruct them on which function to execute.

Let's add a command code for `phello()` to the command code list by adding `PHELLO` to the enumerated list `commandCodes` in `functions.h` as follows:

```
enum commandCodes {TERMINATE = 0, PCOR, PMAXT, PPAM, PAPPLY,
PRANDOMFOREST, PBOOT, PSTRINGDIST, PTEST, INIT_RNG, RESET_RNG,
PBOOTRP, PBOOTRPMULTI, PHELLO, LAST};
```

Note that any new code must be added immediately prior to `LAST`. Internally, SPRINT uses `LAST` as a marker to indicate the range of implemented command codes for error checking.

functions.c

This file contains the declarations for the implementation functions corresponding to the command codes in `functions.h`. It also contains the pointers for these functions. These functions are declared as `extern`, and with a variable number of arguments.

Let's navigate to `sprint/algorithms/common` and edit `functions.c`. Firstly, let's add the declaration of the `hello()` function highlighted as follows:

```
/*
 * Declare the various command functions as external
 */

extern int test(int n,...);
//extern int svm_call(int n,...);
extern int correlation(int n,...);
extern int permutation(int n,...);
extern int pamedoids(int n,...);
extern int apply(int n,...);
extern int random_forest_driver(int,...);
extern int boot(int,...);
extern int stringDist(int,...);
extern int init_rng_worker(int n, ...);
extern int reset_rng_worker(int n, ...);
extern int boot_rank_product(int n, ...);
extern int boot_rank_product_multi(int n, ...);
extern int hello(int n, ...);
```

Next, let's add the function pointer for `hello` to `functions.c`. This function pointer is of type `commandFunction`. The `typedef` for this is located in `sprint/src/functions.h`.

Please note that this function pointer must be added to the array of function pointers in the position corresponding to its command code within the enumerated list `commandCodes` in `sprint/src/functions.h`.

Let's add the function pointer for `hello` to `functions.c`, as highlighted next. Notice how the function pointers are in the *same order* as the enumeration in `functions.h`.

```
/**
 * This array of function pointers ties up with the commandCode
   enumeration found in src/functions.h
 **/

commandFunction commandLUT[] = {voidCommand,
//                               svm_call,
                                 correlation,
                                 permutation,
                                 pamedoids,
                                 apply,
                                 random_forest_driver,
                                 boot,
                                 stringDist,
                                 test,
                                 init_rng_worker,
                                 reset_rng_worker,
                                 boot_rank_product,
                                 boot_rank_product_multi,
                                 hello,
                                 voidCommand};
```

Namespace

As explained in the *Writing R Extensions* manual, R has a namespace management system for code in packages. This allows the package writer to specify which variables in the package are to be exported, and hence, made available to package users. It also specifies the variables to be imported from other packages.

For all R packages, a namespace is specified by the `NAMESPACE` file located in the top-level directory for a package. For SPRINT, this is the `sprint` directory in our downloaded and unpacked source code.

Let's now add `phello()` to this `NAMESPACE` file so that after loading SPRINT, an R user can call `phello()` in order to execute the R code located in our `phello.R` file, and hence, the corresponding interface and implementation function.

Highlighted in the following code snippet is the line to be added to the SPRINT `NAMESPACE` for this:

```
# Namespace file for sprint

useDynLib(sprint)

export(phello)
export(ptest)
export(pcor)
```

Makefile

This file is used to compile and link the SPRINT package. We need to update this for our `phello()` function.

Let's navigate to the `sprint/src` directory, and add the text highlighted in the following code to `Makefile`, in the positions indicated:

```
SHLIB_OBJS = sprint.o

ALGORITHM_DIRS = algorithms/phello algorithms/common …

INTERFACE_OBJS = algorithms/phello/interface/phello.o algorithms/
papply/interface/papply.o …

IMPLEMENTATION_OBJS = algorithms/phello/implementation/hello.o
algorithms/papply/implementation/apply.o…

phello.Rd
```

The source code for an R package has a subdirectory, `man`, which contains the documentation files for the user-level object contents of that package. Let's add the `man` page for our new function. Navigate to `sprint/man/`, and create the file `phello.Rd` in this directory. Now let's add the following contents to this file:

```
\name{phello}
\alias{phello}
\title{SPRINT Hello World}
\description{
Simple example function demonstrating adding a method to the SPRINT
library.
Prints a 'hello from processor n' message.
}
\usage{
phello()
}
\arguments{
None
}
\seealso{
\code{\link{SPRINT}}
}
\author{
University of Edinburgh SPRINT Team
    \email{sprint@ed.ac.uk}
    \url{www.r-sprint.org}
    }
\keyword{utilities}
\keyword{interface}
```

This file is written in the R documentation format. More information about this format and how to write R documentation files can be found in the *Writing R Extensions* manual.

Compiling and running the SPRINT code

Now that all the required files have been updated to include our new function, we need to compile and install the SPRINT package so we can execute it.

The SPRINT library can be compiled and installed in R as follows:

```
$ cd sprint/src/
$ make clean
$ cd ../../
$ R CMD INSTALL sprint
```

Let's now run our new function. The R code for running `phello()` from SPRINT is very simple. The `sprint` library is loaded, `phello()` is called, and the SPRINT worker processes are closed down with a call to `pterminate()`. Here's the R code to do all this.

```
library(sprint)
phello()
pterminate()
```

Save this R code in file called `testHello.R` and execute it as follows:

```
mpiexec -n 4 R -f testHello.R
```

You will see the following output.

```
Welcome to SPRINT
 Please help us fund SPRINT by filling in
 the form at http://www.r-sprint.org/
 or emailing us at sprint@ed.ac.uk and letting
 us know whether you use SPRINT for commercial
 or academic use.
> phello()
Hello from rank 0 out of 4
Hello from rank 1 out of 4
Hello from rank 2 out of 4
Hello from rank 3 out of 4
[1] 0
> pterminate()
```

The following Figure 4 shows the flow of execution through the various files for this on the SPRINT Master process in more detail. Notice how the Master initiates commands, broadcasts them to the workers, and then waits for each of their results.

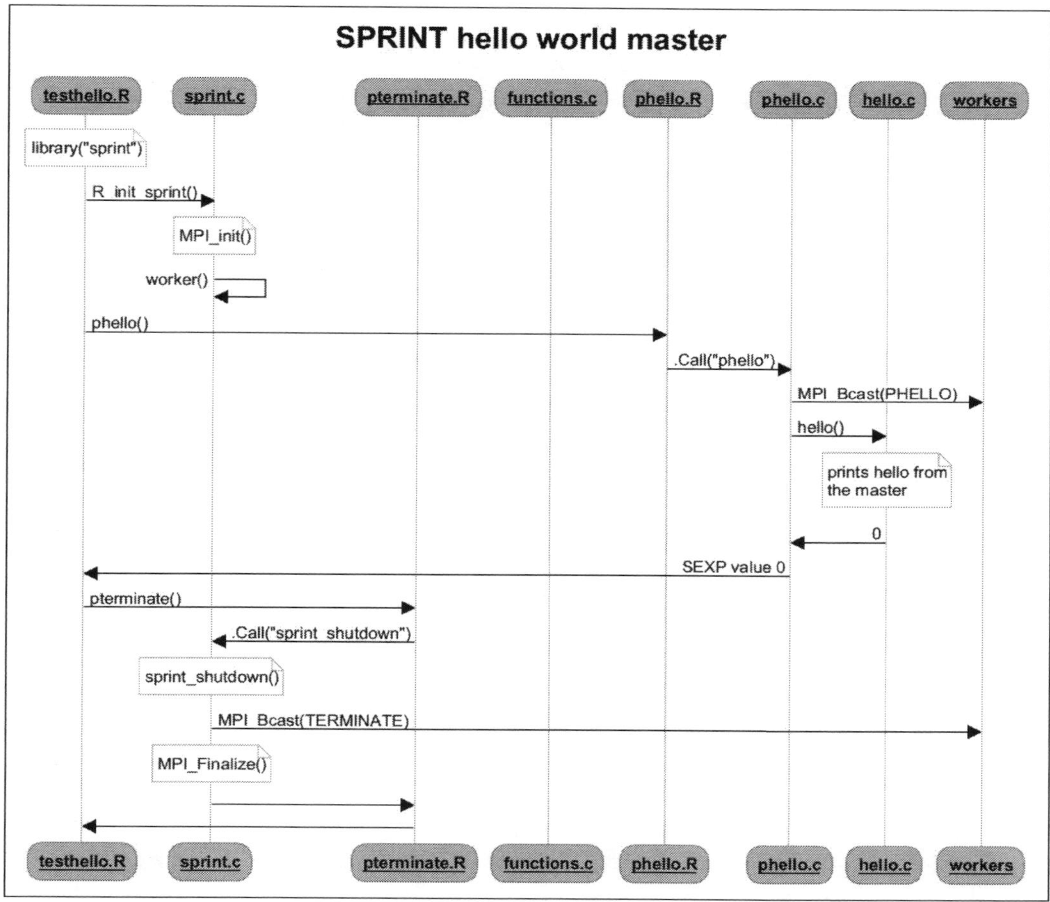

Figure 4: A sequence diagram showing the execution flow for `pHello()` on the Master process.

The next figure, similarly shows the execution flow on a SPRINT Worker process. Notice how the worker cycles through a loop, waiting for the next command from the Master to execute and return a result, until it receives the explicit TERMINATE command, at which point it exits.

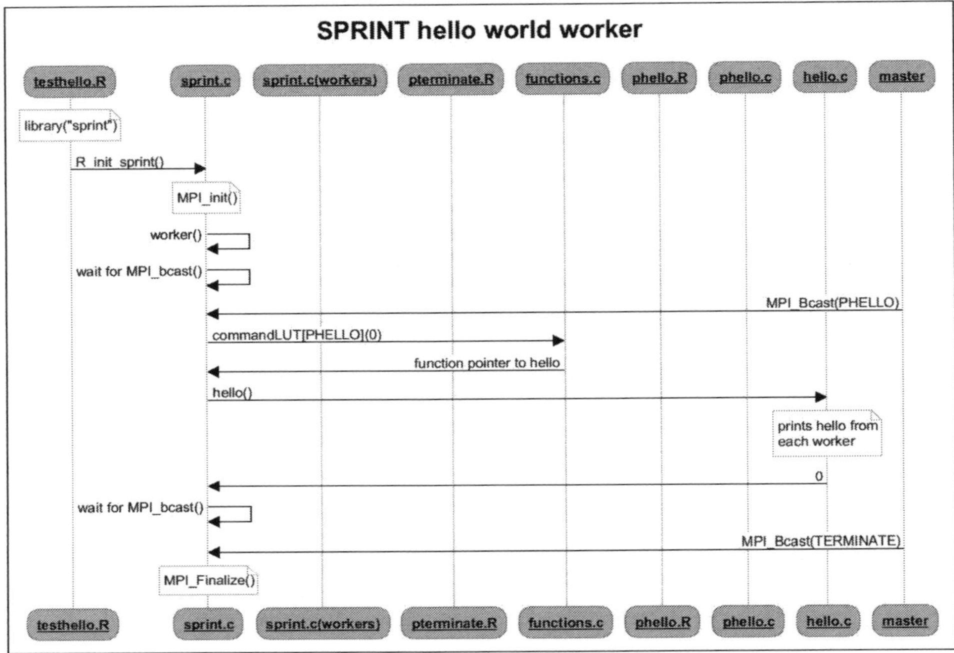

Figure 5: A sequence diagram showing the execution flow for phello() on a Worker process.

Genomics analysis case study

So far in this chapter, you have learned how to write MPI parallel routines, access these directly from your R scripts, and turn these routines into reusable R packages. In the remainder of this chapter, we will show you how this capability has been used to exploit supercomputers in the quest to identify signs of bacterial infection and sepsis in blood samples of newborn babies.

Genomics helps us find those genes in a baby that have increased or decreased levels of activity in response to a bacterial infection. By knowing which genes are involved in the immune system's response to bacterial infection (or indeed, how the immune system is subverted by bacteria), we can (a) look at how the activity of these genes differ from baby to baby, and (b) use them to diagnose a bacterial infection from the gene expression measurements in a blood sample.

The remainder of this chapter, therefore, comprises a brief introduction to Genomics followed by a description of how an MPI-based R package such as SPRINT, discussed earlier in this chapter, allows R to exploit a supercomputer, and so assist researchers in the fight against bacterial infection in newborn babies.

Genomics

Genomics is the collective term for the study of the structure and functions of the genome. The **genome** is the totality of deoxyribonucleic acid, that is, DNA, in each cell of most organisms. In humans, this DNA consists of a string of around 3.2 billion organic molecules that are called nucleotides.

A **nucleotide** consists of a molecule of sugar, a molecule of phosphoric acid, and a chemical called a **base**. In DNA, there are four bases: **Adenine** (**A**), **Guanine** (**G**), **Thymine** (**T**), and **Cytosine** (**C**). A DNA string is therefore represented by a sequence of these abbreviations.

Any stretch of DNA that is known to contain biological instructions for making a particular protein is called a gene. The remaining stretches of the genome are referred to as non-coding sequences, although many of these sequences do actually have another biological function. In humans, the total number of genes in the genome is currently thought to be around 19,000.

Genomics allows the monitoring of the activity, and in some cases the structure, of all or a large number of these genes, or indeed any nucleotide sequences, for a given biological tissue or cell. As a field and technology within the life sciences, genomics has reached the stage whereby relatively large datasets, some potentially terabytes in size, are routinely generated or obtained by non-specialists. This has resulted in an explosion in both the size and volume of data to analyze.

As an example of this, the **Gene Expression Omnibus** (**GEO**) currently hosts a repository of around 55,900 studies with a total of 1.36 million biological samples. With file size for an individual sample ranging from approximately 20 Mb to 60 Mb or higher, the size of the study data sets range from as little as 200 Mb to more than 100 GB.

Genomics is often called **post-genomics**, in the sense that we work in an era where full genomes are already sequenced, and we now simply measure under what circumstances a particular sequence (that is, a gene) is used to carry out a biological function.

A genome is said to be **sequenced** when the sequence of nucleotides from the start to the end of the DNA is known.

Measuring the genome is important, because this gives a detailed view of how an organism responds to a given circumstance like infection, injury, or treatments. As part of this response, the biological instructions contained in a gene are read by other components (ribosomes) in a biological cell. This process is referred to as transcription, and is an intermediary step in the conversion of these instructions into actions carried out by proteins, for example, chemical reactions, binding and recognizing bacteria, building cell structures, or transporting molecules. The presence of proteins could also be measured directly, but there are far more possible proteins than genes in an organism, and the three dimensional structure of a protein also plays a role in determining its function. Using the proteome to understand biological processes is, therefore, far more complex compared to measuring the genome.

In the same way that the totality of all the genes in a cell of an organism is referred to as the genome, the totality of all the proteins in the cell of an organism is referred to as **proteome**.

Take a look at the following figure. It illustrates how the DNA of an organism is used to produce proteins.

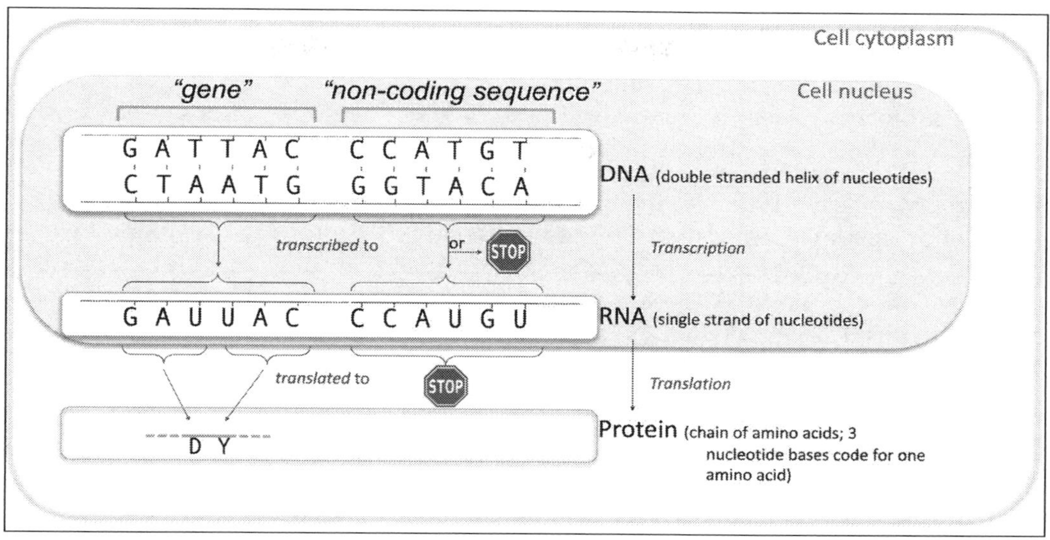

Figure 6: To produce a protein, a gene in the DNA of an organism first undergoes transcription into RNA and then translation.

As you can see in the preceding diagram, a set of instructions is first transcribed from a gene in the DNA to RNA, that is, a ribonucleic acid. DNA is a double-stranded helix of nucleotides, whereas RNA is a single-sequence strand of nucleotides. This single RNA strand, as opposed to DNA, can leave the cell nucleus. This means the instructions contained in the gene on how to put together a protein, can be transported to where they are needed.

In the second step in Figure 6, these instructions (comprising three RNA nucleotide bases at a time) are used to string together the correct amino acids to make up a protein. For example, the three bases (also called a 'codon') G-A-U are the instruction to make amino acid 'D' in Figure 6. This step of stringing together the correct amino acids is known as translation.

Genomic data

Currently, the genome is most frequently measured with two types of genomic laboratory technology: **Microarrays** and **Next-Generation Sequencing (NGS)**.

Microarrays measure the expression level of each gene in a given biological sample. The expression level refers to the number of RNA strings present for a given gene. For each biological sample, they can return the expression level of each of approximately 19,000 or more genes, plus several hundreds or thousands of non-coding sequences.

NGS allows the counting of millions to billions of short nucleotide sequences that are present in a given biological sample, that is, not just genes. These so-called "short reads" can, in turn, provide data on other aspects of a biological sample, such as the expression level of genes, alternative versions of genes, the interactions of DNA with proteins, and the composition of previously unknown genomes.

With either type of technology, the dataset size obtained is the number of entities (genes, short reads) measured, multiplied by the number of biological samples in the study or experiment. Sample numbers usually range from a handful to several hundred. For example, 19,000 genes measured by microarray on 100 biological samples results in 1,900,000 data points. A large NGS study with many hundreds or thousands of samples may produce terabytes of data.

Although this is not yet comparable to physics or imaging problems, the size and volume of genomic data sets is sufficient to present analysts with many CPU speed and memory allocation problems. This is particularly so because one of the driving forces in genomic data analysis is the identification of potential relationships between genes or between biological samples. This involves investigating all possible pairs of individual observations (genes or samples), meaning that the number of required computations and space is the square of the original data dimension. For example, measuring the similarity between the 19,000 genes in the previous microarray example, results in $19{,}000^2$, that is, 361 million computations of a correlation or other similarity metric. A further complication is that such investigations do not easily lend themselves to simple "task farming" parallelization solutions.

As these laboratory technologies develop further, not only will the dataset size increase due to the number of sequences that can be measured, but so too will the sheer volume of results produced as more research groups become adept at using these increasingly inexpensive technologies. Next-generation sequencing, in particular, will likely be responsible for much of these increases, and provide interesting computational software parallelization problems for the foreseeable future.

Genomics with a supercomputer

Now that you have some knowledge about Genomics, let's look at how a supercomputer can help an R user investigating bacterial infection in newborn babies.

The goal

It is possible to use genomic data (like microarray gene expression data) to identify sets of genes that, taken together, can predict if a new biological sample belongs to a particular class sample (that is, a healthy sample or a diseased sample). In the case study presented here, we will look at the research by the Division of Infection and Pathway Medicine at The University of Edinburgh into diagnosing bacterial infection in young infants by measuring gene expression in blood samples. We want to look at how effectively a supercomputer can be used by R to process the large gene expression datasets involved.

The ARCHER supercomputer

The supercomputer used is Cray XC30 MPP. This forms part of ARCHER, the UK's academic national supercomputing service. At the time of writing, (March 2015), this service consists of the Cray XC30 MPP supercomputer, external login nodes, post-processing nodes, and associated file systems.

The supercomputer itself comprises 4,920 compute nodes, which each contain two 12-core Intel Ivy Bridge series processors, giving a total of 118,080 processing cores. 4,544 of these compute nodes each have a total of 64 GB of memory, with the remaining 376 compute nodes having 128 GB of memory.

Running a program or script on a supercomputer is different from running it on a laptop or personal computer. In the case of ARCHER, a user logs in to one of the external login nodes, and creates a submission script that contains the instructions for executing the desired program or application. The user then submits this script for execution as a job on one or more of ARCHER's compute nodes using the PBS batch job scheduling system. Few jobs, if any, make use of all of ARCHER's thousands of compute nodes and tens of thousands cores. Instead, through PBS, ARCHER is organized into queues consisting of various numbers of nodes. In this way, multiple jobs can be executed simultaneously on ARCHER, with each of these jobs having exclusive access to the subset of compute nodes associated with the queue it has been submitted to.

> In order to make best use of their computational capacity, supercomputers such as ARCHER often have access to their compute nodes organized into a series of **queues**. Each queue will have different constraints, for example, a queue might be restricted to jobs that have an elapsed time of 10 minutes or less and have requested 2 nodes or less. Another queue might be restricted to jobs that have a minimum elapsed time of 6 hours and require up to 150 nodes. Often, the queue configuration changes over 24 hours to reflect the different usage profiles for the supercomputer. For example, only those queues that utilize large numbers of nodes are active overnight.
>
> In the case of ARCHER, the smallest queue consists of one node. This means that even if a job uses only one core on that node, the whole node is reserved for the user, and so no other job will run on that node at the same time.

Let's submit the `sprint_test.R` script to ARCHER's compute nodes for executing the SPRINT `ptest()` function. This script and the `ptest()` function were both described earlier in this chapter.

```
library("sprint") # load the sprint package

ptest()

pterminate() # terminate the parallel processes

quit()
```

Here's the submission script for this. This contains a mixture of comments, directives for PBS and shell script.

```
#!/bin/bash -login
# ! Edit the job name to identify separate job
#PBS -N ptest
# ! Edit number of nodes to fit your job
#PBS -l select=2
# ! Edit time to fit your job
#PBS -l walltime=00:09:00
# Replace with your own budget
#PBS -A a01

# Load R & SPRINT library
module swap PrgEnv-cray PrgEnv-gnu
module load R

# Change to the directory that the job was submitted from
```

```
cd $PBS_O_WORKDIR

# Replace $TMP with your own temporary directory.
export TMP=~/work/tmp

# Launch the job
aprun -n 48 R -f sprint_test.R
```

The first line of this script, `#!/bin/bash -login`, indicates the flavor of the Linux shell to be used to execute the instructions in the submission script. In this case, it is bash. Those lines beginning with `#PBS` are directives to PBS. All other lines beginning with `#` are comments.

Line 3 of the submission script contains `#PBS -N ptest`. This is a directive that instructs PBS to run the contents of this script as a batch job called `ptest`. The directive in line 5, `#PBS -l select=2`, instructs PBS that the job wants to use two of ARCHER's compute nodes. On ARCHER, this will mean that the job has exclusive access to these nodes; no other job will run concurrently on those nodes. The line 7 directive, `#PBS -l walltime=00:09:00`, requests that the job have these nodes exclusively for nine minutes of elapsed time, with the line 9 directive, `#PBS -A a01`, indicating the cost of running this job on these nodes is to be charged to a budget with the code `a01`. On ARCHER, like many supercomputers, a user has to pay for executing their program or application. In ARCHER's case, this is managed by means of budgets, whereby a user can be granted a certain amount of compute time. For a successful submission, the budget code must be valid, and the budget must contain sufficient time to fulfil the elapsed time requested in line 7. Look at lines 12 and 13:

```
module swap PrgEnv-cray PrgEnv-gnu
module load R
```

These contain shell commands to load the appropriate application development environments to be used on the compute nodes. On ARCHER, these environments are controlled by means of modules, which allow the loading and switching of compilers, libraries, and software. In the case of our R script that uses the SPRINT package, this means swapping from the Cray to the GNU programming environment and loading the module for the R installation on ARCHER. Lines 15 and 18 respectively change the working directory to the one where the submission script is submitted from, and set the temporary directory to be used during execution. Finally, take a look at the last line of the file:

```
aprun -n 48 R -f sprint_test.R
```

It contains the ARCHER instruction equivalent to the following OS command line instruction that we described earlier in this chapter when executing `sprint_test.R`:

```
$ mpiexec -n 5 R -f sprint_test.R
```

On ARCHER, the submission script uses a call to `aprun` rather than `mpiexec` to instantiate the MPI processes. Here the `aprun` call instantiates 48 processes, one for each core on the two nodes that have been requested. There are 24 cores on each ARCHER compute node.

If this submission script is saved in a file called `ptest.pbs`, typing the following at the OS command line on an ARCHER login node instructs PBS to use the file to create a job for execution on two ARCHER compute nodes. This job is placed by PBS in a queue while it awaits execution.

```
$ qsub test.pbs
```

On the ARCHER, the PBS `qstat` command can be used to monitor the status of a job in queue. The following is the output from running this for our submission. The argument `-u $USER` instructs PBS to return a list of only those jobs for the current user.

```
$ qstat -u $USER


sdb:


Req'd     Req'd     Elap
Job ID              Username  Queue      Jobname  SessID NDS TSK Memory
Time   S Time
---------------      --------         --------         ----------
------      ---      ---   ------        -----     -   -----
2761436.sdb   user A       S2755804  ptest          --          2
48      --            00:09  Q   —
```

Under `Job ID`, the output shows the identifier PBS has given the job to, in this case it is `2761436.sdb`. Under `Username` is the name of the user, `user A`, who submitted the job. The queue the job is waiting in is listed under `Queue (S2755804)`. Under `Jobname` is the name given to the job in the submission script, that is, `ptest`. Under `SessID` is the identifier of the session if the job is running. In our preceding example, the job is not yet running, so it contains `--`. Under `NDS` is number of compute nodes requested, that is, `2`.

Under `TSK` is listed the number of tasks or cores requested—`48`. The memory requested and the elapsed time requested are listed under `Req'd Memory` and `Req'd Time`; these are given as `"--"` to indicate that no specific amount of memory was requested, and `00:09` to indicate that up to 9 minutes of elapsed time was requested, respectively. The job's current state is listed under `S`, and here it contains `Q` indicating that the job is queued. Finally, `Elap Time` indicates the elapsed time used thus far. Since the job is in the queued state, waiting to be executed, this contains "–", which means that no elapsed time has been spent thus far.

After the job actually gets executed, its output and any errors encountered are listed in two files in the directory from which the submission script was submitted. The output is found in the file called `ptest.o2761436`, and the file containing any errors encountered during execution is called `ptest.e2761436`. As you can see, the names of these are derived from the job name specified in the line `#PBS -N ptest` in the submission script and the Job Identifier, as shown in the `qstat` output.

Opening the `ptest.o2761436` reveals 48 R startup and library load messages as well as the 48 `ptest()` output messages. The following is an extract from that file:

```
[1] "HELLO, FROM PROCESSOR: 0"  "HELLO, FROM PROCESSOR: 22"
[3] "HELLO, FROM PROCESSOR: 17" "HELLO, FROM PROCESSOR: 24"…
```

Random Forests

There are several algorithms that can be used to classify blood samples as infected or healthy. Random Forests is one such classification algorithm. Based on a set of known sample classes, Random Forests will predict the class membership of a new sample. With large data sets, Random Forests are not usually used as an applied diagnostic test. Instead, it is used to identify those genes that best predict the class of an unknown sample. These genes are of interest to biologists studying the immune reaction to infection, and are also prime candidates for creating a diagnostic test.

The Random Forests algorithm is an ensemble tree classifier that constructs a forest of classification trees from bootstrap resamples of a dataset. More information on Random Forests can be found in Breiman's paper of the same title in Volume 5, Issue 1 of the journal, *Machine Learning*.

In Random Forests, a **classification tree** consists of nodes, each of which splits the dataset based on the value of some variable (selected at random). Once the tree is constructed, we can classify an observation case by sending it down the tree from the root node. At each branching of the tree, the decision is made by comparing the value of the variable with the rule on that node of the tree. For example, at one node all of the observations where variable A had a value greater than 1.4 would be sent down the right-hand branch, and the other observations would be sent down the left-hand branch. The predicted class of the observation is the leaf node it ends up in. The Random Forests algorithm randomly selects many observations from the original dataset to create a forest of classification trees that can then classify the data. These also provide useful information on which variables are most significant in correctly classifying the data. Observations are classified by sending them down each of these trees in the forest. If 1000 trees vote that observation *X* is of class AB, whereas 200 trees vote that it is of class CD, then observation *X* is classified as class AB. There is some debate about the minimum number of trees to generate for a particular size of dataset, but the general view is that subject to computational constraints, the more trees generated, the greater the confidence in the classifications produced.

A *bootstrap* resample of a dataset is created by randomly selecting observations from the dataset until the bootstrap dataset has the same number of observations as the original dataset. Resampling with replacement is where an observation can be selected more than once for inclusion in the same bootstrap resample. That is, the observation remains in the pool of possible observations that can be selected from the original dataset for that bootstrap resample.

Mitchell's paper (see `http://onlinelibrary.wiley.com/doi/10.1002/cpe.2928/full`), describes the two options for parallelizing Random Forest. You can either parallelize the bootstrap phase or the generation of a single tree.

This latter option of parallelizing single tree growth is the more complicated of the two. Even so, a number of existing algorithms for growing decision trees in parallel do exist. All these approaches are, however, designed for the data encountered in the social sciences where there are typically very many samples (hundreds of thousands or millions) but only a small number of variables (tens or hundreds) describing each sample. These algorithms exploit the parallelism available in the samples, dividing them between parallel processes. Unfortunately, these algorithms do not map well onto microarray or NGS data where the number of samples is low (typically tens or hundreds) while the number of variables is large (typically thousands or millions). Furthermore, since each split in a tree only considers a subset of all the variables, if we were to parallelize across variables (rather than cases), the load balance would be poor.

Given the SPRINT R package's origins as a collaboration between life scientists from the Division of Infection and Pathway Medicine and HPC experts from the Edinburgh Parallel Computing Centre at the University of Edinburgh, its implementation of Random Forest uses a task parallel approach. In this task parallel approach, the bootstrap samples are distributed amongst the parallel processes, and the results combined. This approach is, however, constrained in that the original microarray or NGS data must fit in the memory of a single R process.

This task parallel nature of the SPRINT implementation of Random Forest means it can reuse the existing R code for serial Random Forest generation. That is, it uses Breiman and Cutler's `randomForest` R package available from CRAN (see `http://cran.r-project.org/web/packages/randomForest/randomForest.pdf`). This allows the user interface of the SPRINT implementation to exactly mimic the calling conventions of the serial code. However, due to the nature of the random bootstrapping, whilst the results in parallel may not be numerically identical to the results from serial execution, they are within statistical norms.

Data for the genomics analysis case study

In this chapter, we will use the SPRINT parallel implementation of Random Forests executing on the ARCHER supercomputer to test the hypothesis that bacterial infection in newborn babies can be identified via gene transcription profiling.

Following image processing and initial data processing, an example of small analysis-ready gene expression dataset may consist of a data matrix of size 25,000 genes by 20 samples. A large genotyping data set may consist of 2 million **Single Nucleotide Polymorphism (SNP)** probes by 2,000 samples. Dimensionality is of concern to most analysis approaches, with the number of variables (that is, the numbers of genes, SNPs, or sequences) vastly outweighing the number of samples. This differs from the sort of dataset that would be produced in social science, where a typical dataset would be made up of a small number of variables with a large number of samples. As mentioned previously, the SPRINT implementation of Random Forests is designed to handle a biological dataset with a very large number of variables.

To study bacterial infection, Division of Infection and Pathway Medicine collected blood samples from 62 infants—27 of these have a confirmed bacteriological infection, and 35 are non-infected controls. The overall goal is to determine sets of genes that can reliably identify an unknown blood sample as infected or not infected.

The blood samples were processed to RNA level, and each sample hybridized to an Illumina human gene expression microarray. Each array contains 23,292 probe sequences that measure the expression of all known genes in the human genome.

Random Forests performance on ARCHER

Using a single core of the ARCHER supercomputer on a 64 GB memory node, the serial Random Forests implementation took approximately 168 seconds of elapsed time to generate a forest of 8,192 trees (64 * 128) on the data derived from the collected blood samples.

Figure 7 shows the elapsed time for running the serial implementation on 1 core, and the SPRINT implementation of Random Forests on 2, 4, 8, 16, 32, 64, 128, 256, 512, and 912 cores on the ARCHER 64 GB compute nodes on the same data.

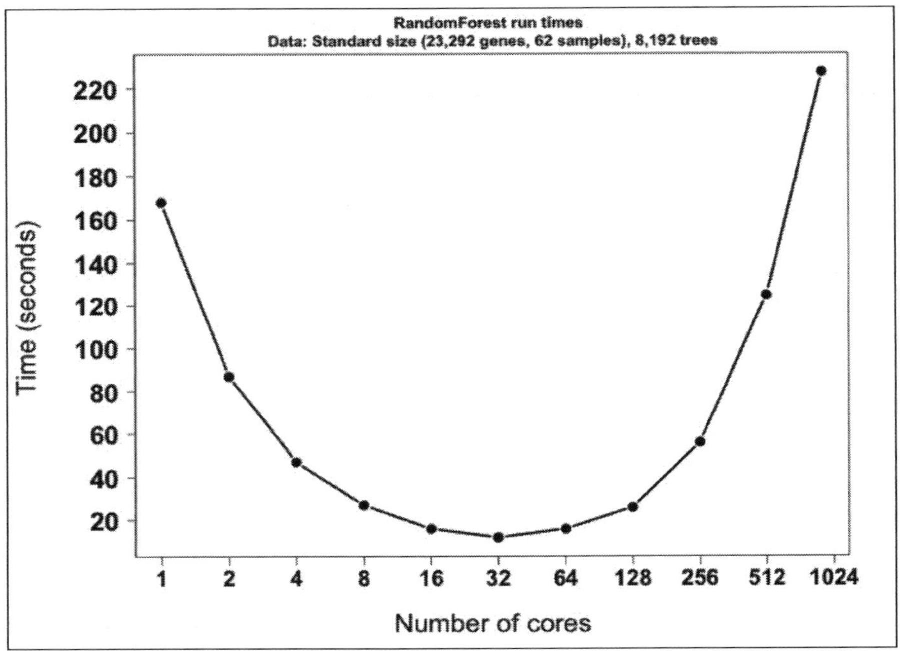

Figure 7: Elapsed (run) time of Random Forests generating 8,192 trees from data consisting of on 23,292 genes and 62 samples. The *x*-axis is log-scaled to show the full sequence of cores used in each execution.

The next graph shows the speed-up of the SPRINT implementation relative to the serial execution (Speed-Up and Amdahl's Law are explained in *Chapter 6, The Art of Parallel Programming*.)

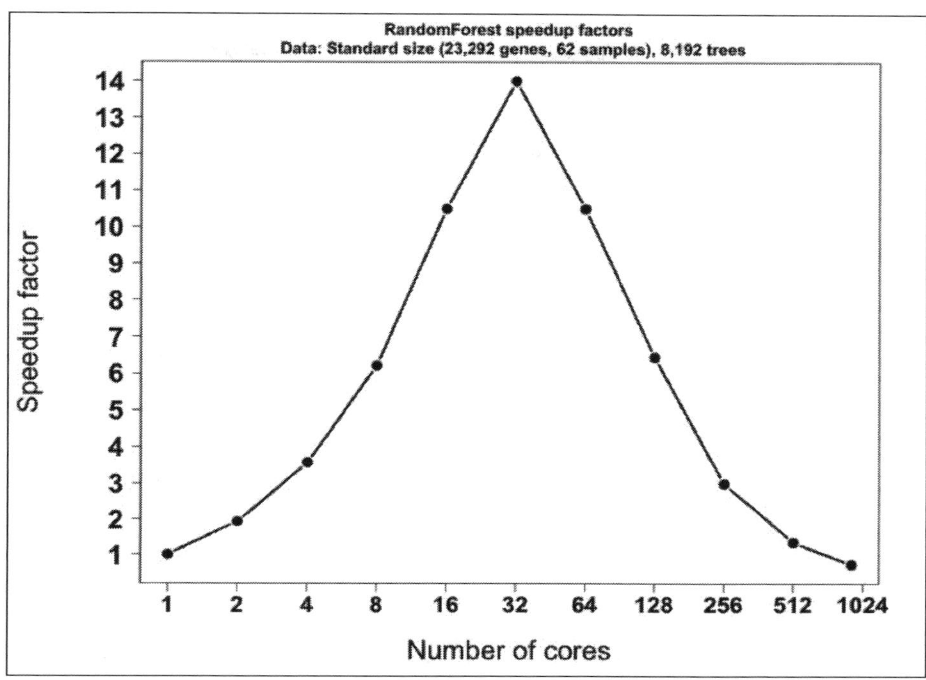

Figure 8: Speed-up of SPRINT implementation of Random Forests relative to the serial code. The *x*-axis is log-scaled to show the full sequence of cores used in each execution.

As can be seen in Figure 8, the speed-up is quite modest, reaching a peak of 14 at 32 cores and a fastest elapsed time of 12 seconds. Beyond 32 cores, for this size of data set, the overhead of communicating partial results and recombining them outweighs the gains from generating the trees in parallel. This effect is further illustrated in Figure 9.

The SPRINT Random Forest implementation uses a task parallel approach, whereby each core is tasked with executing random forest on a subset of the total bootstrap samples (that is, trees) following which, these results are combined. Figure 9 shows the elapsed time for executing SPRINT Random Forest on the same data, but this time, varying the number of bootstrap samples (that is, trees) according to the number of cores being used. When there is 1 core, only 128 trees are used, for 2 cores it is 256 trees, and so on up to 512 cores, where 65,536 trees are used. That is, each core used is always generating 128 trees. The figure shows the total elapsed time divided by the number of cores for each run, that is, the time for calculating 128 trees per core in each execution.

This, therefore, helps show the impact of communicating the partial results and recombining them. Above 32 cores, the overhead of communication and recombination far outweighs the overall performance benefit on this size of dataset.

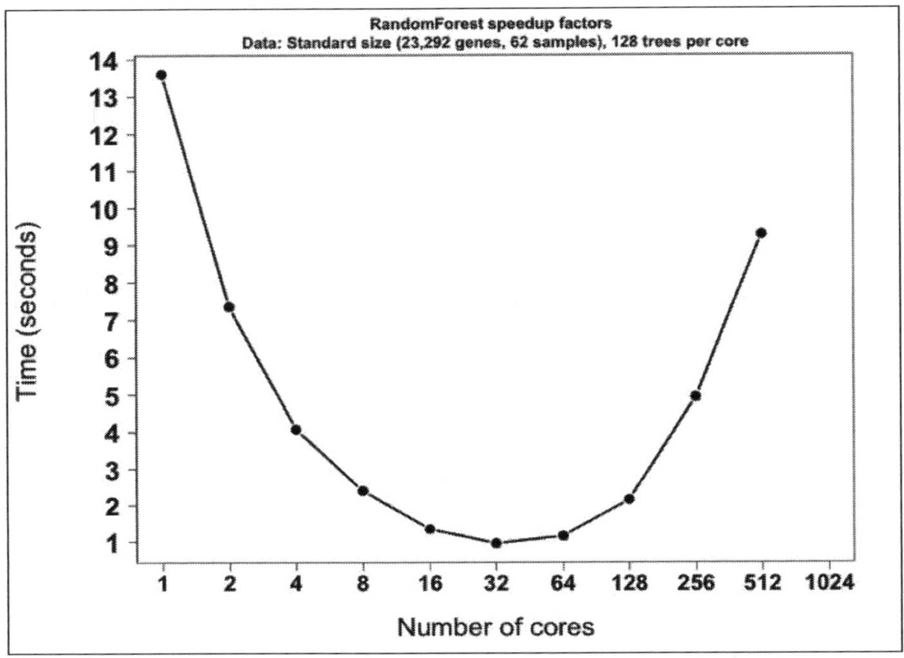

Figure 9: Executing SPRINT Random Forest with 128 trees per core (and a fixed dataset size of 23,292 genes and 62 samples). The *x*-axis is log-scaled to show the full sequence of cores used in each execution.

As mentioned earlier in this chapter, NGS datasets are significantly bigger, so let's use the data from the study on bacterial infection in newborn babies to generate a dataset of a size comparable to an NGS dataset. Figure 10 shows the elapsed times for a dataset comprising 512,000 variables (when actually generated through NGS technology, such a number could include non-coding sequences, single nucleotide polymorphisms, gene splice variants, and so on) derived from our original 23,292 genes. Again 8,192 trees have been generated.

Here, the serial elapsed time is over 100 minutes, but on running this with the SPRINT parallel implementation on 128 cores, the elapsed time reduces to just over a minute and a half. Again, these were executed on ARCHER's 64 GB memory compute nodes.

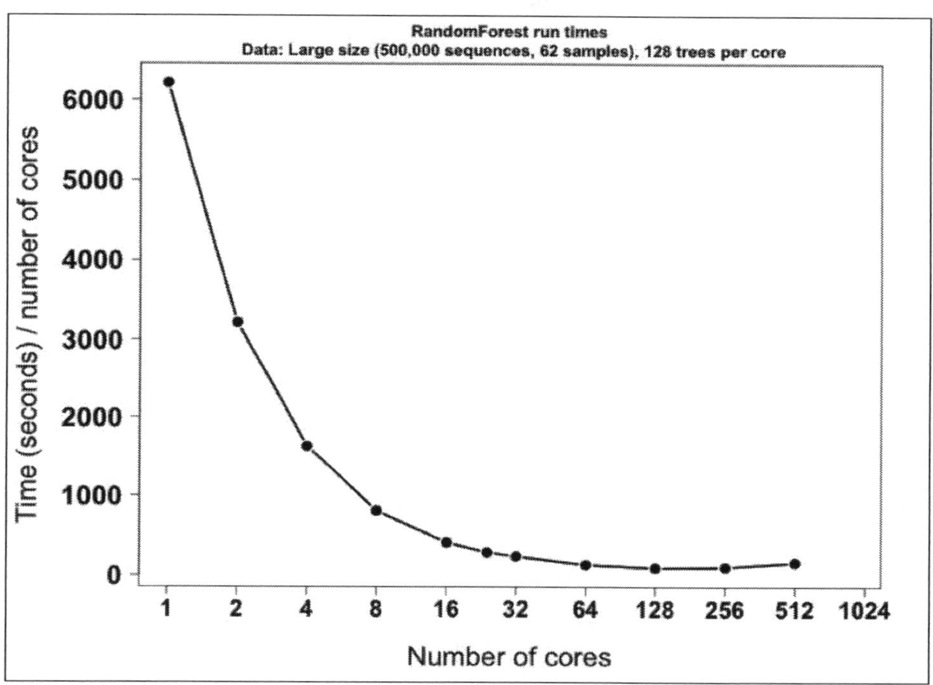

Figure 10: Parallel Random Forest elapsed (run) times to generate 8,192 trees from a dataset of 512,000 variables and 62 samples. The *y*-axis shows the elapsed time in seconds for each execution, while the *x*-axis is log-scaled to show the full sequence of cores used in each execution.

In Figure 11 the speed-up relative to the serial implementation is shown. At 128 cores a speed-up of at least 64 is achieved. Beyond that number of cores, as with the smaller dataset, the overhead of communicating partial results and recombining them outweighs the gains from generating the trees in parallel.

The smaller dataset achieved the maximum speed using 32 cores; the larger dataset achieves the maximum speed using 128 cores. The ideal number of cores to use will depend on your dataset.

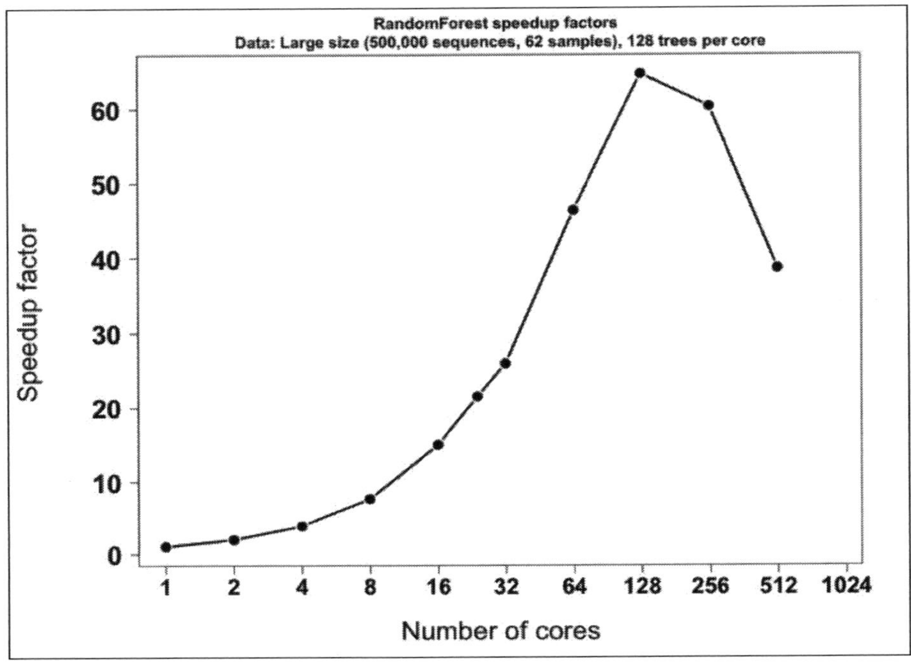

Figure 11: Speedup relative to the serial implementation for parallel random forest generating 8,192 trees from a dataset of 512,000 variables and 62 samples. The *x*-axis is log-scaled to show the full sequence of cores used in each execution.

The jobs run to produce Figure 12 are similar to those in Figure 9, that is 128 trees per core, but this time with a larger dataset, containing 500,000 sequences. This confirms how with this larger dataset, it is a higher number of cores at which the overhead of communication and recombination of trees outweighs the benefits of parallelization.

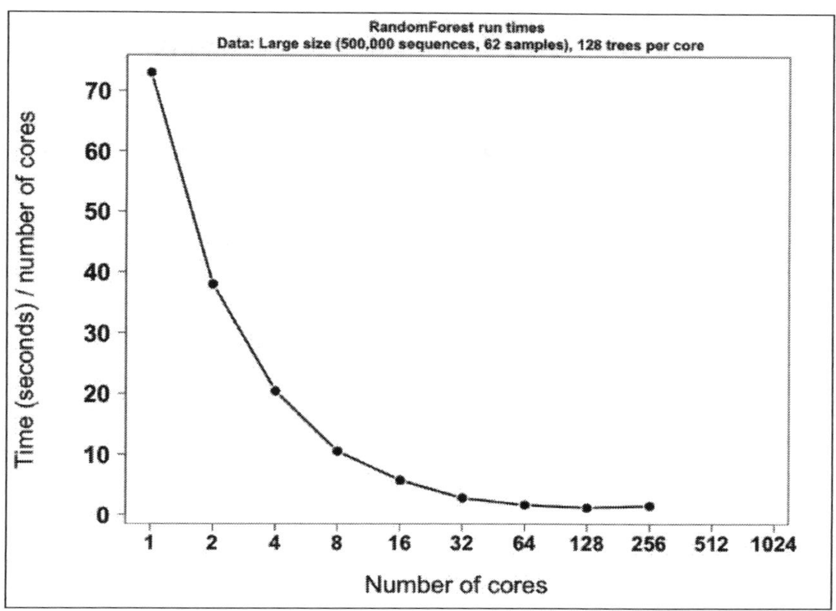

Figure 12: Executing SPRINT Random Forest with 128 trees per core on a larger dataset of 500,000 sequences and 62 samples. The *x*-axis is log-scaled to show the full sequence of cores used in each execution.

Rank product

Gene expression data is often used to simply identify which individual genes show statistically significant changes of expression between groups, for example, between healthy and diseased samples. Although in standard scenarios, the frequently used `limma` package with its empirical Bayes moderated *t* test is sufficient for most analyses, for some scenarios (non-parametric data assumptions, meta-analyses) the rank product test is an alternative example of a statistically robust test with focus on fold changes in gene expression (in essence, measuring the stability of fold changes directly rather than a group-specific gene expression mean and associated gene variability).

Rank product is therefore considered to be a feature selection method capable of identifying important genes. (For more information on the details of rank product, see Breitling et al's 2004 paper titled, "*Rank products: a simple, yet powerful, new method to detect differentially regulated genes in replicated microarray experiments.*" This is freely available at `http://www.ncbi.nlm.nih.gov/pubmed/15327980`.)

As explained by Mitchell et al refer to the URL mentioned in the *Random Forests* section of this chapter, rank product is applicable to experiments comparing two different experimental conditions, for example, class A and class B, and in effect, comprises three steps:

1. For each gene, a rank product is calculated by:
    - Ranking the fold-change value of that gene in all pairwise comparisons of class A against class B
    - Taking the product of these ranks across all samples
2. A null distribution for the rank products is calculated. This is the expected distribution if there is no differentiation between either genes or samples. Unfortunately, it is not possible to construct an analytic form for the null distribution; it is therefore constructed numerically, using a bootstrap procedure. This involves creating a random experiment by independently permuting each sample's gene expression vector, and calculating the rank product of all the genes in this random data. This is repeated many times (10,000 or 100,000 times) to build a distribution of rank products for the null hypothesis.
3. The experimentally observed rank product for each gene is then compared with the null distribution. By comparing how the actually measured value compares to chance (that is, thousands of values measured on randomized gene expression data), this allows accurate measures of the significance level and estimation of cut-off values.

As observed by Mitchell et al, it is the second of these three steps, the generation of the bootstrapped null distribution that is the computationally expensive part. The SPRINT implementation of rank product takes a task parallel approach by dividing up the requested number of bootstrap samples between available processes. This requires the input dataset to be broadcast to all processes. The bootstraps are then calculated independently, and the results collated and returned to the Master process for further analysis. Similar to the SPRINT implementation of Random Forests, the rank product implementation works well as long as the input dataset fits in the available memory of a process.

Rank product performance on ARCHER

Let's now run the SPRINT parallel implementation of rank product on the data from the study of bacterial infection in newborn babies, that is, 23,292 genes, 62 samples. Running this on a single core of an ARCHER 64 GB memory compute node for 1024 bootstrap samples (or permutations), the elapsed time is more than 2.5 hours, on 512 cores of ARCHER 64 GB compute nodes—this has been dramatically reduced to just over half a minute. This is a speed-up of close to 290, relative to the single core elapsed time. At greater core numbers, the speed-up starts to diminish. Figure 13 shows the elapsed times on 1, 2 4 8, 16, 32, 64, 128 , 256, 512, and 960 cores with Figure 14 showing the speed-up relative to the elapsed time on a single core.

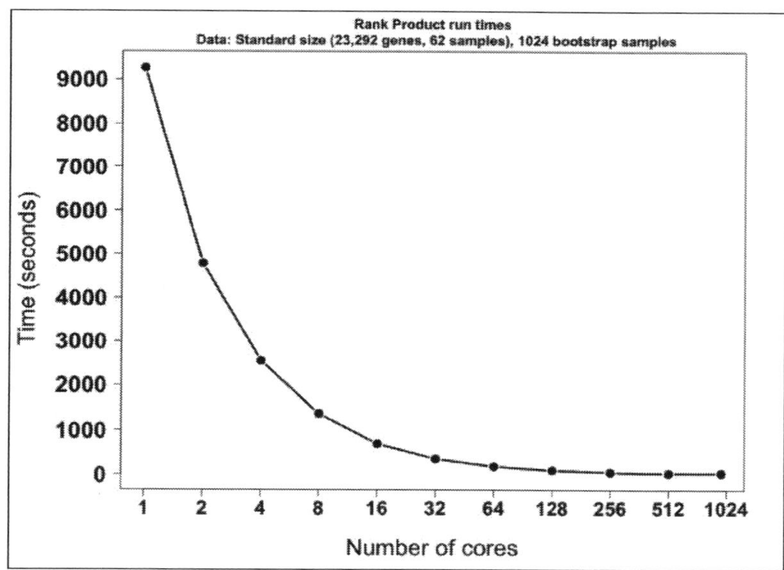

Figure 13: Elapsed (run) times for rank product with 1024 bootstrap samples (i.e. permutations) on a dataset of 23,292 genes and 62 samples. The *x*-axis is log-scaled to show the full sequence of cores used in each execution.

In Figure 14, it can be seen that the speed-up is close to optimal on smaller core numbers, but gradually tails off so that by 512 cores the speed-up is 289, and at 960 cores, the speed-up has started to decrease.

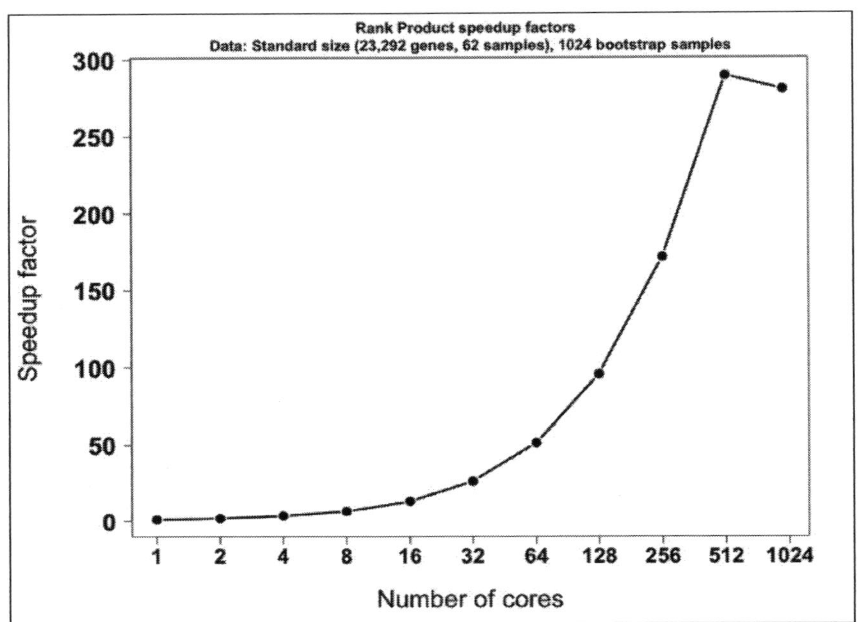

Figure 14: Speed-up of rank product relative to the elapsed time on a single core. The x-axis is log-scaled to show the full sequence of cores used in each execution.

As noted earlier in this section, in an ideal situation, somewhere between 10,000 and 100,000 permutations would be used when executing rank product. Figure 15 shows the elapsed time for this same data when 16,384 permutations are used instead of 1024. The elapsed time on a single core and two cores were not collected since these were going to be longer than 12 hours.

The elapsed time for 4 cores was over 11 hours, while on 912 cores, this has been reduced to less than 3.5 minutes.

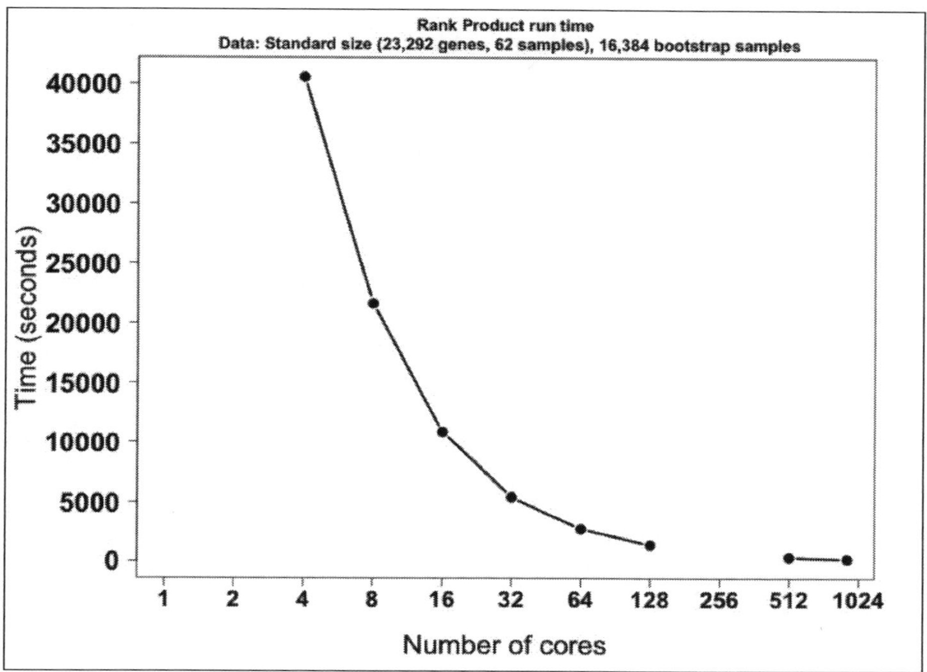

Figure 15: Elapsed time for Rank Product with 16,384 bootstrap samples (i.e. permutations) on a dataset of 23,292 genes and 62 samples. The x-axis is log-scaled to show the full sequence of cores used in each execution. A 256 core job was not executed this time hence the gap between 128 and 512 cores.

Looking at the speed-up of these latest results, relative to the elapsed time for the 4 core result, reveals more about the performance when executing rank product on the data with more bootstrap samples. Figure 16 shows that the speed-up at 912 cores is 200, which is not far off the optimal speed-up of 228, relative to the 4 core elapsed time.

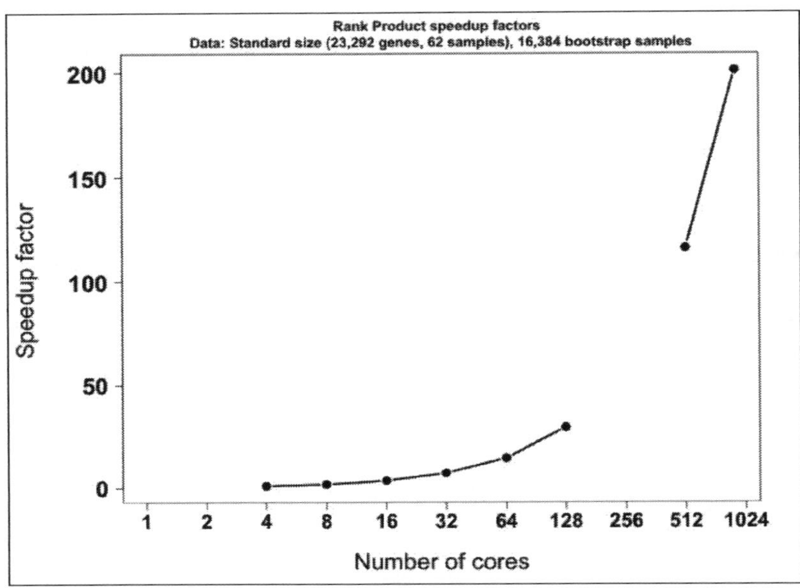

Figure 16: Speed-up relative to elapsed time for 4 cores for Rank Product with 16,384 bootstrap samples (i.e. permutations) on a dataset of 23292 genes and 62 samples. The x-axis is log-scaled to show the full sequence of cores used in each execution. A 256 core job was not executed this time hence the gap between 128 and 512 cores.

Finally, deriving from our original 23,292 genes a dataset consisting of 500,000 variables provides a size comparable to the NGS datasets. Running rank product on this with 16,384 bootstrap samples, the elapsed times are excessive for single core and small numbers of cores. In fact on ARCHER, 256 cores are needed before the elapsed time falls below 12 hours. At 912 cores, the elapsed time falls to just under 2 hours, and has a speed-up of 3.44, relative to the elapsed time at 256 cores—this is close to the optimal of 3.56. Clearly, these results demonstrate that for the larger datasets and large numbers of bootstrap samples, access to the large numbers of cores on a supercomputer can have a dramatic effect on execution times, but this is obviously algorithm-dependent.

Conclusions

It is perhaps stating the obvious, but worth repeating, that while on a supercomputer you have access to thousands of cores, whether you can actually exploit a significant number of these to any great effect depends not just on the size of your problem but also on the algorithm you wish to apply to it, and more importantly, its actual implementation.

The performance results for Random Forests and rank product provide an example of the first two of these factors, problem size and algorithm. In the Random Forests example, the quickest elapsed time for the smaller of the two datasets used was at 32 cores, while with the larger dataset, this was achieved at 128 cores. Comparing the performance of Random Forests with rank product, the latter achieved its quickest elapsed time and greatest speed-up at 512 cores on the smaller dataset with a small number of bootstrap samples. However, when first the number of bootstrap samples and then the data size were increased, dramatic reductions in elapsed time were obtained with speed-ups remaining close to optimal at high core counts.

Moreover, the reduction in elapsed times achievable on a supercomputer, such as ARCHER, are generally at their most useful when frequent reruns are necessary for parameter optimization or problem solving. For one-off analyses, the potential reduction in run-time and the size of the problem that can be tackled, needs to be weighed up against the need to create submission scripts and possible waits in a job queue. However, reusing existing, highly optimized packages such as SPRINT, that also enable a priori testing of your code on your laptop, can significantly reduce the effort needed to implement parallel code that can effectively exploit supercomputer architectures.

Summary

In this chapter, you have been shown how to write your own parallel routines and make them callable directly from R programs. You have also learnt how to create your own suite of such parallel routines, and turn them into an R package that you can then reuse in other R programs. The SPRINT package has been introduced, and its architecture examined to show how you can organize your own such package, or instead, use the SPRINT package itself and include your own parallel routines within it.

Finally, the chapter has demonstrated how you can use such an MPI-based R package on a supercomputer to exploit hundreds, and potentially thousands, of cores to dramatically increase the performance of your R programs.

In the next chapter, we switch our attention from exploiting the world's most expensive supercomputers, to the admittedly much easier-to-access supercomputer lurking in your own laptop and desktop, the **Graphics Processing Unit** (**GPU**). We will explore how to make use of the GPU's particular parallel and vector processing architecture through the portable high performance **Open Computing Language** (**OpenCL**).You will learn how to harness the thousands of much simpler processors within the GPU from R, which are normally only available for system accelerated graphics rendering, to obtain Gigaflops of performance for more general highly numerical based computation.

5
The Supercomputer in Your Laptop

In this chapter, we will unlock the parallel processing capacity of **Graphics Processing Unit (GPU)** from R, giving us access to, potentially, gigaflops and teraflops of performance for certain types of vector calculations. To do this, we need to roll up our sleeves, get technical, and step well beyond our comfort zone in R.

In this chapter, we will encounter new concepts, frameworks, and languages, including:

- OpenCL
- `ROpenCL` – The R package that provides an interface abstraction for OpenCL
- **Single Instruction Multiple Data** (SIMD) vector parallelism
- Writing code in C (C99) for execution directly from within R
- Developing an ROpenCL implementation of the distance measured as typically used in clustering algorithms

It's time to don your lab coat and your tin foil hat...

OpenCL

Open Computing Language (**OpenCL**) is an industry-standard framework for writing portable high-performance programs that are executed across heterogeneous computing platforms consisting of a mix of devices including CPU, GPU, **Digital Signal Processors** (**DSP**), and **Field-Programmable Gate Arrays** (**FPGA**). OpenCL platforms operate across laptops, desktops, supercomputers, and even mobile devices.

OpenCL was originally developed by Apple back in 2008, but has since migrated to an open standard API under the auspices of Khronos Group, of which Apple, Intel, NVIDIA, AMD, Google, Amazon, IBM, Microsoft, and many significant others in the computing industry are members.

In addition to OpenCL, Khronos oversees a set of related standards, most notably, the long-established **Open Graphics Library** (**OpenGL**), which defines a well-adopted API for high-performance 3D graphics rendering. Indeed, both OpenCL and OpenGL are designed to interoperate, enabling both efficient, generalized computation and the image rendering of the results within the same GPU device.

The latest version of OpenCL is version 2.0, publicly released towards the end of 2013, but many of the computing platforms you will encounter today may still reference earlier versions of OpenCL, typically version 1.2. It is this version that I have available on my mid-2014 Apple MacBook Pro device running OS X 10.9.4. For our purposes in this chapter, there is no material difference in API calls or feature support between version 1.2 and version 2.0 of OpenCL.

OpenCL resources

There are a number of free online resources for OpenCL that provide a useful reference and technical detail beyond what we can cover in this chapter:

- `https://www.khronos.org/registry/cl/specs/opencl-1.2.pdf`: This contains a full description of the OpenCL 1.2 API specification, including the glossary and conceptual underpinning. Other versions of the OpenCL API specification are similarly available on the Khronos website.
- `https://www.khronos.org/registry/cl/sdk/1.2/docs/man/xhtml/`: This contains an online version of the API manual with easy web navigation.
- `https://www.khronos.org/registry/cl/sdk/1.2/docs/OpenCL-1.2-refcard.pdf`: This contains a summary reference card for the API in a quick-look reminder format.
- `https://www.khronos.org/conformance/adopters/conformant-products/#opencl`: Khronos maintains a listing of devices that support OpenCL across all manufacturers.
- `http://support.apple.com/en-gb/HT5942`: Apple also provides a list of their own hardware that supports OpenCL.
- `https://developer.apple.com/library/mac/documentation/Performance/Conceptual/OpenCL_MacProgGuide/Introduction/Introduction.html#//apple_ref/doc/uid/TP40008312-CH1-SW1`: This contains an excellent exposition of how to program OpenCL and tune its performance, particularly on the OS X platform.

There are a lot of concepts to learn and low-level understanding we need to develop in order to get the best out of OpenCL and our GPU. However, we will start by first finding out exactly what we have running on our own system, and we will then peel back the various conceptual layers as we go along.

Querying the OpenCL capabilities of your system

Our interaction with OpenCL will initially be through the interface it exposes to the C programming language. This enables us to directly query the system we are running R on to determine its support for OpenCL with the minimum set of dependencies on nonstandard R packages, while also providing a gentle introduction to C before we tackle the complexities of writing OpenCL kernel functions later. In the next section, we will switch to using the dedicated `ROpenCL` package that provides us with an easy interaction with native OpenCL from R with minimum code written in C, namely, the OpenCL Kernel functions themselves.

About C

Don't worry if this is your first encounter with this low-level programming language. C has been around since the days when the Unix operating system was first created (OS X itself is a derivative of Unix), and while it may look a little alien to start with, much of its basic control structure and logical/expression syntax is similar to R (R itself is largely implemented in C). A key difference is that in C, we have to directly allocate and manage the memory for any data items or objects that we create in our program ourselves. R, by comparison, manages memory on our behalf; we don't have to be concerned with the number of bytes of memory that a numeric value requires, neither do we have to be concerned about when memory is released for reuse within our program as it is automatically garbage collected. C is also a strongly typed compiled language (ignoring C's castable memory pointers), whereas R is a polytype-interpreted language.

Simple-to-follow online tutorials for C are available at the following links:

- `http://www.learn-c.org/`
- `http://www.cprogramming.com/tutorial/c-tutorial.html`

A more in-depth free resource is *The C Book* (which is now slightly dated), which can be found at the following link: `http://publications.gbdirect.co.uk/c_book/`

Although it predates C99 and C11, which is the later development of the C standard used as the basis for OpenCL, *The C Book* is still relevant and gives you a complete grounding in syntax and how to program in C.

R is a very capable programming environment in its own right and already integrates a number of packages written in other languages, including C, C++, and Java. We will make use of a specific package, `inline`, available from CRAN (`http://cran.r-project.org/web/packages/inline/index.html`), which will allow us to directly run a snippet of C code as an R function. We will make use of this facility in the following to define a function that uses a number of the OpenCL API calls to query the configuration of the platform and devices that are available:

```
> library("inline")
> cbody <- 'cl_platform_id pfm[1]; cl_uint np;
  clGetPlatformIDs(1,pfm,&np);
  for (int p = 0; p < np; p++) {/* Outer: Loop over platforms */
   char cb1[128]; char cb2[128]; cl_device_id dev[2];
   cl_uint nd; size_t siz;
   clGetPlatformInfo(pfm[p],CL_PLATFORM_VENDOR,128,cb1,NULL);
   clGetPlatformInfo(pfm[p],CL_PLATFORM_NAME,128,cb2,NULL);
   printf("### Platforms[%d]: %s-%s\\n",p+1,cb1,cb2);
   clGetPlatformInfo(pfm[p],CL_PLATFORM_VERSION,128,cb1,NULL);
   printf("CL_PLATFORM_VERSION: %s\\n",cb1);
   clGetDeviceIDs(pfm[p],CL_DEVICE_TYPE_GPU|CL_DEVICE_TYPE_CPU,
                  2,dev,&nd);
   for (int d = 0; d < nd; d++) {/* Inner: Loop over devices */
    cl_uint uival; cl_ulong ulval; cl_device_type dt;
    size_t szs[10]; cl_device_fp_config fp;
    clGetDeviceInfo(dev[d],CL_DEVICE_VENDOR,128,cb1,NULL);
    clGetDeviceInfo(dev[d],CL_DEVICE_NAME,128,cb2,NULL);
    printf("*** Devices[%d]: %s-%s\\n",d+1,cb1,cb2);
    clGetDeviceInfo(dev[d],CL_DEVICE_TYPE,
                    sizeof(cl_device_type),&dt,NULL);
    printf("CL_DEVICE_TYPE: %s\\n",
           dt & CL_DEVICE_TYPE_GPU ? "GPU" : "CPU");
    clGetDeviceInfo(dev[d],CL_DEVICE_VERSION,128,cb1,NULL);
    printf("CL_DEVICE_VERSION: %s\\n",cb1);
    clGetDeviceInfo(dev[d],CL_DEVICE_MAX_COMPUTE_UNITS,
                    sizeof(cl_uint),&uival,NULL);
    printf("CL_DEVICE_MAX_COMPUTE_UNITS: %u\\n",uival);
```

```
    clGetDeviceInfo(dev[d],CL_DEVICE_MAX_CLOCK_FREQUENCY,
                    sizeof(cl_uint),&uival,NULL);
    printf("CL_DEVICE_MAX_CLOCK_FREQUENCY: %u MHz\\n",uival);
    clGetDeviceInfo(dev[d],CL_DEVICE_GLOBAL_MEM_SIZE,
                    sizeof(cl_ulong),&ulval,NULL);
    printf("CL_DEVICE_GLOBAL_MEM_SIZE: %llu Mb\\n",
           ulval/(1024L*1024L));
    clGetDeviceInfo(dev[d],CL_DEVICE_LOCAL_MEM_SIZE,
                    sizeof(cl_ulong),&ulval,NULL);
    printf("CL_DEVICE_LOCAL_MEM_SIZE: %llu Kb\\n",ulval/1024L);
    clGetDeviceInfo(dev[d],CL_DEVICE_DOUBLE_FP_CONFIG,
                    sizeof(cl_device_fp_config),&fp,NULL);
    printf("Supports double precision floating-point? %s\\n",
           fp != 0 ? "yes" : "no");
  }
}'
```

The C code may look a little daunting, so let's review what, exactly, it does. The code is presented as the body of a C function definition without its enclosing braces as a quoted string in R (`cbody`). The code makes calls to four OpenCL API query functions: `clGetPlatformIDs`, `clGetPlatformInfo`, `clGetDeviceIDs`, and `clGetDeviceInfo`. The outer for loop iterates over the number of OpenCL platforms defined in the system, and the inner for loop iterates over the number of OpenCL devices defined in each platform. In fact, the first loop is bound to just be one element as we limited the call to `clGetPlatformIDs()` to return a C one-dimensional array of size 1; most systems we will run on only have a single OpenCL platform defined. The second loop is also limited by a selection parameter to `clGetDeviceIDs()` to return information only for CPU- and GPU-type devices. The remaining code makes a sequence of calls to `clGetPlatformInfo` and `clGetDeviceInfo`, each call to query a specific OpenCL configuration parameter, and the returned configuration value is then printed to the console.

More about C

There are a number of observations to make about OpenCL in the preceding code presented.

Firstly, the indexing of arrays in C is from zero to *N-1*, as opposed to R, in which it is 1 to *N*. The individual pieces of code are described as follows:

`clGetPlatformIDs(1,pfm,&np)`: C enables an explicit passing of variables by reference by prefixing them with an ampersand (`&`), meaning "address of". Variables that themselves refer to arrays are always passed by reference; in this example, `pfm` is equivalent to `&pfm[0]`.

`for(int d=0; d<nd; d++)`: This is an iterative loop construct that declares an integer loop variable `d` initialized to zero on the first iteration, has a `d<nd`-terminating if-false condition that is tested at the start of each iteration, and increments `d` by 1 at the end of each iteration using the `++` operator.

`char cb1[128]`: This allocates a character buffer named `cb1` of size `128` chars. As this is a local variable, the memory is allocated from the process stack, and therefore, its unassigned contents could be any random values.

In C, we generate formatted output to the console using `printf()`, which is a little similar to `print()` and `paste()` combined to print in R. As the C code is placed inside an R string, we need to escape any control characters, such as newline (for example, "\n" becomes "\\n"), so that they are preserved by the definition and compilation process through R to C.

Take a look at the following code:

```
> clfn <- cfunction(signature(), cbody, convention=".C",
+                   includes=list("#include <stdio.h>",
+                                 "#include <OpenCL/opencl.h>"))
```

Using `cfunction()` of the `inline` packages creates the R equivalent of the function by wrapping the C body with extra boiler plate, cross-calling code and compiling it with the system's built-in C compiler. We will pass `cfunction()`, the calling signature that identifies any parameters our function expects (in our case, there are no parameters to pass in) and any header, which includes files for C library functions that the C code may call (in our case, we will make calls to `printf()` declared in `stdio.h` and the clX API calls defined in `opencl.h`).

OpenCL on other operating systems

Helpfully, OS X comes with OpenCL preinstalled. However, for other operating systems, such as Windows or Linux, you need to install OpenCL yourself. The following FAQ link from Intel provides all the pointers you need to get OpenCL set up on an Intel processor-based system: `https://software.intel.com/en-us/intel-opencl/faq`

Now that we understand what the code does, let's run it:

```
> clfn()
list()
### Platforms[1]: Apple-Apple
CL_PLATFORM_VERSION: OpenCL 1.2 (Apr 25 2014 22:04:25)
*** Devices[1]: Intel-Intel(R) Core(TM) i5-4288U CPU @ 2.60GHz
CL_DEVICE_TYPE: CPU
CL_DEVICE_VERSION: OpenCL 1.2
CL_DEVICE_MAX_COMPUTE_UNITS: 4
CL_DEVICE_MAX_CLOCK_FREQUENCY: 2600 MHz
CL_DEVICE_GLOBAL_MEM_SIZE: 16384 Mb
CL_DEVICE_LOCAL_MEM_SIZE: 32 Kb
Supports double precision floating-point? yes
*** Devices[2]: Intel-Iris
CL_DEVICE_TYPE: GPU
CL_DEVICE_VERSION: OpenCL 1.2
CL_DEVICE_MAX_COMPUTE_UNITS: 280
CL_DEVICE_MAX_CLOCK_FREQUENCY: 1200 MHz
CL_DEVICE_GLOBAL_MEM_SIZE: 1536 Mb
CL_DEVICE_LOCAL_MEM_SIZE: 64 Kb
Supports double precision floating-point? no
```

We can note from the output that my MacBook Pro laptop is an Apple OpenCL platform with one Intel i5 CPU device and one Intel Iris GPU device; obviously, your particular output may differ.

The platform and devices all support OpenCL version 1.2. The CPU has four OpenCL **Compute Units (CUs)**, which, if you recall from *Chapter 1, Simple Parallelism with R,* matches its number of independent instruction-processing threads; however, the GPU has a much larger number of CUs, namely, 280. We can determine from the manufacturer's information for the Iris GPU that there are 40 SIMD Kernel **Execution Units (EUs)** split into four subslices of 10 EUs each, where each EU is capable of running seven simultaneous threads (280 CUs=40 EUs x 7 threads).

OpenCL reports that the CPU has access to 16 GB of the main memory, while the GPU has 1.5 GB of memory from which it can directly process data. The distinctions in memory between OpenCL devices within a platform are important for both overall capability and performance. The movement of data in R between CPUs (referred to as the "host" in OpenCL), where our R session will execute, and the GPU device, which requires specific OpenCL C functions (referred to as "Kernels" in OpenCL) to perform calculations on the transferred data, are key aspects of the OpenCL programming model.

The following diagram represents the key architectural features of the OpenCL platform on my MacBook Pro device and also illustrates the basic `ROpenCL` programming model introduced in the next section:

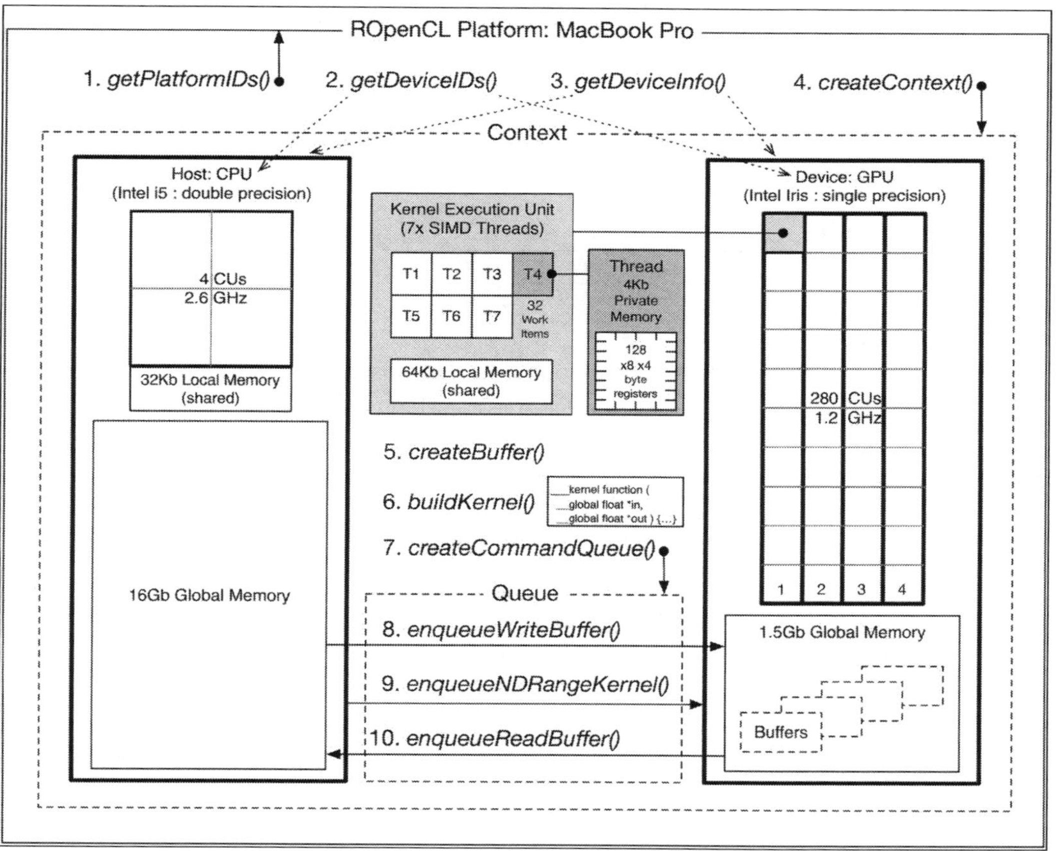

While the CPU has far fewer CUs, it can run at 2.6 GHz, whereas the GPU runs slower, at a peak of 1.2 GHz. Based on the Intel product data, the CPU has a maximum floating point performance of 166.4 GFLOPS, whereas the GPU has a significantly faster peak performance of 768 GFLOPS. These are, of course, theoretical peak GFLOPS that are not usually achieved in practice.

GFLOPS

GFLOPS refers to gigaflops or 1000s of millions of single precision "floating-point operations per second". It used to be the classic measure of performance for supercomputers, but as technology advanced in the recent years, single microprocessors became capable of GFLOPS of performance (10^{x9} FLOPS), as we can note in my own laptop. Now, supercomputers are measured in terms of PetaFLOPS (10^{x18} FLOPS). Currently at the top of the world's rankings is the Chinese Tianhe-2 supercomputer, with a measured peak performance of 33.86 PFLOPS, utilizing more than 3 million cores and requiring 24 megawatts of electricity (more than enough to power 20,000 homes!). It is also notable that the top supercomputers in the world all achieve their rankings by utilizing additional GPU coprocessors; refer to `http://www.top500.org/lists/2015/11/`.

Another distinction to highlight between the CPU and GPU is that the former has support for double-precision floating-point arithmetic (64 bits), whereas the latter only has support for single-precision floating-point (32 bits). Most current-generation consumer-level GPUs perform optimally at single-precision floating-point. However, the more expensive scientific computing-oriented GPUs will support double precision.

Double- versus single-precision floating point arithmetic

R itself stores noninteger numeric values as double-precision floating-point. Sharing floating-point data between our host-based R session and a single-precision-only-capable GPU means that we have to copy and transform floating-point data in both directions and that we also lose arithmetic precision. Depending on the numeric value domain range of our data, single-precision floating-point is typically only accurate between two and four decimal places when compared to double precision. While many forms of scientific computing may require the extra precision afforded by a 64-bit floating point, there are various approximation-based analyses for which single precision is acceptable. Later in this chapter, we will explore using the GPU to calculate the distance matrix for a large number of observations and variables as input to cluster analysis.

As already hinted at earlier, OpenCL has a large number of concepts and API calls, many of which describe capabilities beyond what we require, including multiprogram, multikernel, or multidevice scenarios and behaviors, image processing, and interaction with graphics rendering. OpenCL is a complex interface and arguably could have an entire book dedicated to it.

> **OpenCL further reading**
>
> If you wish to understand all of OpenCL's capabilities, I recommend that you look through the Khronos resources highlighted earlier. You may also like to consider the excellent—if slightly dated—book *OpenCL in Action* by Matthew Scarpino, published by Manning.

Our exploration of OpenCL will therefore focus on what we need to know in order to exploit the GPU from R. To this end, we will make use of a specific R package, `ROpenCL`, which exposes just the set of OpenCL API calls we need to perform accelerated R vector processing on the GPU.

The ROpenCL package

The `ROpenCL` package developed by Willem Ligtenberg together with this book's author, is essentially a collection of limited-scope R convenience functions that wrap the OpenCL C API and simplify many aspects of its complexity. `ROpenCL` wrappers are implemented in C++ and are dependent on the `Rcpp` package, which is available from the CRAN package repository. `ROpenCL` is not yet part of CRAN (though this may change by the time this book is published) and must be installed from source. You can do this directly from within your R session, as follows:

```
> install.packages("ROpenCL", type="source",
                   repos="http://repos.openanalytics.eu")
```

The ROpenCL programming model

The `ROpenCL` API functions we will make use of in this chapter, their supporting concepts, and how they will be used, are summarized in the following table and presented in the sequence order in which they would normally be expected to be called in a typical OpenCL program—the numbered sequence of API calls 1 to 10 is also depicted in the diagram from earlier in this chapter. If, however, you prefer to look at the real code first, then do skip forward a few pages to the following section for the simple vector addition example and refer back to this table for a detailed explanation of each of the `ROpenCL` functions used.

ROpenCL API Function	Description
`getPlatformIDs()` This returns a list of platform IDs `PlatformID` is an opaque reference that cannot be interpreted by the host.	We already encountered the CL API equivalent of this in the previous section. We require a platform ID in order to look up the available devices. Normally, this function returns a list containing only one `PlatformID`.

`getDeviceIDs(`
`PlatformID)`
This returns a list of device IDs.
`DeviceID` is an opaque reference that cannot be interpreted by the host.
	We already encountered the CL API equivalent of this in the previous section.
	We require a device ID to reference the GPU; to create an associated Context, command queue, and memory buffers; and to execute our kernels.
	The `ROpenCL` API variant of this call sorts the returned list of device IDs such that the GPU device IDs are listed first.
	`ROpenCL` also provides a convenience function to test the type of a device from its `DeviceID`; for example, `getDeviceType(DeviceID)` returns the `"GPU"` string for a GPU device and `"CPU"` for a CPU device.

<table>
<tr><th>ROpenCL API Function</th><th>Description</th></tr>
<tr><td>getDeviceInfo(

DeviceID)

This returns a list of named items.

The complete list of the available named item information about parameters is documented in the online OpenCL specification, currently at version 2.0: http://www.khronos.org/registry/cl/sdk/2.0/docs/man/xhtml/clGetDeviceInfo.html.</td><td>We already encountered the CL API equivalent of this in the previous section.

The ROpenCL variant of getDeviceInfo is a convenience function returning all the available information about the device in a single call. There are more than 70 device information parameters, and in standard OpenCL, these must each be queried separately.

You can access the specific query parameter using R's named item list syntax. The names match the equivalent OpenCL parameter constant; for example, to determine the amount of local and global memory available on a device, simply execute the following:

dinfo <- getDeviceInfo(
  gpuID
)
locMem <- dinfo$CL_DEVICE_LOCAL_MEM_SIZE
gloMem <- dinfo$CL_DEVICE_GLOBAL_MEM_SIZE</td></tr>
<tr><td>deviceSupportsDoublePrecision

deviceSupportsSinglePrecision

deviceSupportsHalfPrecision(

DeviceID,

list)

This returns either True or False.

If the function returns True and the list parameter is provided, then list will be a set of named items detailing the precision rounding, inf, NaN, and so on supported by the device.</td><td>ROpenCL provides the deviceSupportsPrecision family of functions to make it simpler to switch configuration paths appropriately in the host code.

The usual model in ROpenCL programming requires calling getDeviceInfo() to determine the capabilities of the device in order to choose an appropriate implementation of the kernel function to execute. For example, many GPU devices do not support a double-precision floating point, whereas CPUs do. Different implementations of the OpenCL kernel function are required in order to work with the single as opposed to double precision as this requires different function parameter types to be used.

An optional empty R list may be passed into this function, and if the precision is supported, it will be filled in with the precision capabilities as defined in the device information parameters, as follows: CL_DEVICE_[DOUBLE|SINGLE|HALF]_FP_CONFIG.

Half precision corresponds to the 16-bit floating-point arithmetic and is only supported by a minority of GPU devices at the current time, mainly those from NVIDIA.</td></tr>
</table>

ROpenCL API Function	**Description**

`createContext(`
`DeviceID)`
This returns context
`Context` is an opaque reference that cannot be interpreted by the host.
	This function creates an OpenCL `Context` type, a transient container, similar in some ways to an R session.
	`Context` establishes a set of selected devices from within a platform that will interoperate—in our case, the CPU that calls this function (as host) and the GPU (identified by the supplied `DeviceID`)—and through other API calls, it allows us to associate buffers to manage device memory and `CommandQueue` to pass information (data to/from buffers) and instructions (compiled kernels) between devices.

`createBuffer(`
`Context,`
`MemoryFlag,`
`GlobalWorkSize,`
`RObject)`
This returns a buffer.
The return value is an opaque reference to the device buffer that cannot be interpreted by the host.
	This function creates a specific global memory buffer on the device associated with `Context` (as opposed to on the host) to hold the `GlobalWorkSize` number of data items of C language type defined by the supplied `RObject`. If `RObject` is of the class integer, then this function will itself call `createBufferIntegerVector()` (as described here); otherwise, if `RObject` is of a class numeric, then this function will call `createBufferFloatVector()` (also described here).
	`Context` is the return value from `createContext()`.
	`MemoryFlag` defines how the buffer may be accessed by the device to read or write. The permitted values are `"CL_MEM_READ_ONLY"` or `"CL_MEM_WRITE_ONLY"`.
	`GlobalWorkSize` refers to the total number of data items within `RObject`. For example, if `RObject` is an R vector, then set `GlobalWorkSize=length(RObject)`, although as we shall discuss later, for the call to `enqueueNDRangeKernel()` itself, its `GlobalWorkSize` parameter must be an integer multiple of the `LocalWorkSize` value.

ROpenCL API Function	Description

`createBufferFloatVector(`
`Context,`
`MemoryFlag,`
`GlobalWorkSize)`
This returns a buffer.
	This function creates a specific global memory buffer on the device to hold `GlobalWorkSize` number of data items of C language type `cl_float` (the 32-bit-wide single-precision floating-point values).
	`Context`: Refer to `createBuffer()` from the previous code snippet.
	`MemoryFlag`: Refer to `createBuffer()` from the previous code snippet.
	The return value is an opaque reference to the device buffer that cannot be interpreted by the host.

`createBufferInteger`
`Vector(`
`Context,`
`MemoryFlag,`
`GlobalWorkSize)`
This returns a buffer.
	This function creates a specific global memory buffer on the device to hold `GlobalWorkSize` number of data items of C language type `cl_int` (the 32-bit-wide integer values).
	`Context`: Refer to `createBuffer()` from the previous code snippet.
	`MemoryFlag`: Refer to `createBuffer()` from the previous code snippet.
	The return value is an opaque reference to the device buffer that cannot be interpreted by the host.

ROpenCL API Function	Description

`buildKernel(`
`Context,`
`KernelSource,`
`KernelName,`
`...)`
This returns a kernel
The return value is an opaque reference to the compiled kernel that cannot be interpreted by the host.
	As a simplification, the `ROpenCL` package's `buildKernel()` function combines the behavior of `clCreateProgram`, `clBuildProgram`, `clCreateKernel`, and `clSetKernelArg`; the `program` object that is created is not exposed, only the subsequent compiled kernel is. Effectively, this means that a separate `program` object is created for each kernel. The full OpenCL API allows any number of kernels to be associated with a single `Program` container.
	`Context` is the return value from `createContext()`.
	This function takes an R string containing the OpenCL C source code (provided in `KernelSource`) that defines a specialized kernel function (the name is declared in `KernelName`) and compiles it into a form that can be executed by the compute units within an OpenCL device.
	This compilation process is similar to that invoked by `cfunction()` from the `inline` package's we used earlier in the chapter. However, the OpenCL compilation process for kernel functions is more involved as it uses a specific tailored C99 compiler and has to target the generation of code for execution on the specific device. Compiled GPU code is generally quite different to that compiled for execution on the host CPU.
	The compiled kernel is a set of instructions that can be executed by each of the CUs in the device applied to their (notionally assigned) portion of buffer data. There are specific requirements for how a kernel function should be coded, including the `cl_types` that are used to refer to data available in different areas of memory (global, local, and private) and how a kernel function determines which work items it should operate on. kernel functions are discussed in detail further on in this chapter.
	Any additional R arguments passed into `buildKernel()` will be captured and passed as additional parameters to the kernel function (in matching order) when it is executed on the device. These arguments will be mapped internally to the OpenCL C equivalents such that the integers will be mapped to `cl_int` (with `clSetKernelArgInt`), the numerics will be mapped to `cl_float` (with `clSetKernelArgFloat`), and all the other types of `Robject` will be copied and passed into the kernel function as a C memory pointer reference (with `clSetKernelArgMem`).
	The compiled kernel can subsequently be transmitted to a device for execution by adding it to the device's associated command queue using `enqueueNDRangeKernel()`.

ROpenCL API Function	Description

`createCommandQueue(`
`Context,`
`DeviceID)`
This returns `Queue`.
The return value is an opaque reference to `Queue`, which cannot be interpreted by the host.
	A command queue is the mechanism by which both data and compiled kernels are transferred between the host and device. `Queue` is associated with a specific device within a given `Context`. A device can have multiple active queues.
	In `RopenCL`, the queue is always created as "in order", meaning operations are executed in the order that they were applied to the queue, and this is fine for our purposes. In full OpenCL, a queue can be created as "out of order", meaning that the device is free to execute operations on the queue in whatever order it deems for optimal efficiency.

`enqueueWriteBuffer(`
`Queue,`
`Buffer,`
`GlobalWorkSize,`
`RObject)`
This returns `void`.
	This function operates from the host perspective and should be called prior to a kernel execution (that is, it should be queued before `enqueueNDRangeKernel`) to copy input values from the given `RObject` into the referenced device buffer.
	`GlobalWorkSize` defines the number of data items that will be copied from the R object into the device buffer which, for an R vector, for example, would normally be its length.
	In full OpenCL, this function can operate either nonblocking or blocking. In ROpenCL, the latter behavior is enforced, meaning that the device will have read the host R object into its buffer before the function call returns.

ROpenCL API Function	Description

`enqueueNDRangeKernel(`
`Queue,`
`Kernel,`
`GlobalWorkSize,`
`LocalWorkSize)`
This returns `void`.
	This function operates from the host perspective and is called to queue the execution of a kernel.
	Each execution of `Kernel` on a data item is referred to as a `WorkItem`. `Kernel` operates on the data made available in the previously created device buffers, to which host data is copied by previous `enqueueWriteBuffer` calls.
	The `GlobalWorkSize` parameter defines the number (range) of work/data items over which `Kernel` will be executed. `GlobalWorkSize` can be a scalar, in which case the work item space is simply one-dimensional; that is, the value of "`N`" in "`NDRange`" is `1`. `GlobalWorkSize` can also be a one-, two-, or three-element vector, defining the range of the work item space in terms of one, two, or three dimensions.
	`LocalWorkSize` is an optional argument, and if not set or defined as zero, it will be chosen automatically by the system. `LocalWorkSize` splits the complete global range of `WorkItems` into distinct workgroups, each of the number of `LocalWorkSize`. `WorkGroup` is executed by a single device compute unit. A compute unit can launch a large number of threads of execution to most efficiently execute the `WorkItems` locally in `WorkGroup`. The precise number of threads (or processing elements) that can execute simultaneously in a compute unit is specific to the architecture of the GPU device. Choosing the optimal number for `LocalWorkSize` is discussed further on in this chapter.
	In full OpenCL, this function can operate either in a nonblocking or blocking way. In `RopenCL`, the latter behavior is enforced (primarily because R itself is essentially single-threaded in its implementation), meaning that the device will execute `Kernel` across all work/data items before the function call returns.

ROpenCL API Function	Description

`enqueueReadBuffer(`
`Queue,`
`Buffer,`
`GlobalWorkSize,`
`RObject)`
This returns `Robject`.
	This function operates from the host perspective and should be called after a kernel is executed (that is, it is queued after `enueueNDRangeKernel`) to copy computed values from the referenced device buffer into the appropriate Host R object—for example, a presized vector.
	`GlobalWorkSize` defines the number of data items to be copied from the device buffer to the R object, which for an R vector, for example, must be at least `GlobalWorkSize` in length.
	In full OpenCL, this function can operate in either a nonblocking or blocking way. In `RopenCL`, the latter behavior is enforced, meaning that the device will copy the data from `Buffer` into the host R object before the function call returns.

`releaseResources(` ...) This returns void.	This function operates from the host perspective and should be called after all of the `ROpenCL` computation is completed in order to release all of the underlying system-allocated resources. Optional arguments may be passed to define a subset of resources to be released rather than all the allocated resources. For example, previously allocated memory buffers can be released explicitly, leaving contexts, queues, and kernels intact to be reused for further computation.

A simple vector addition example

Let's apply the `ROpenCL` programming model described in the previous table to a simple example: an element-wise addition of two vectors, $c = a + b$. To make the example slightly more interesting, the vectors will each have more than 12 million elements. Take a look at the following code:

```
# First look-up the GPU and create the OpenCL Context
platformIDs <- getPlatformIDs()
gpuID <- getDeviceIDs(platformIDs[[1]])[[1]]
dinfo <- getDeviceInfo(gpuID)
context <- createContext(gpuID)

# Initialise the input data in R on the CPU (Host)
# and pre-allocate the output result
aVector <- seq(1.0, 12345678.0, by=1.0)    # Long numeric vector
bVector <- seq(12345678.0, 1.0, by=-1.0)   # Same but in reverse
cVector <- rep(0.0, length(aVector))       # Similar result vector

LocalWorkSize = 16  # GPU/kernel dependent (explained later)
```

```
# globalWorkSize must be integer multiple of localWorkSize
GlobalWorkSize = ceiling(length(aVector) / LocalWorkSize) *
                         LocalWorkSize

# Allocate the Device's global memory Buffers: 2x input, 1x output
aBuffer <- createBuffer(context,"CL_MEM_READ_ONLY",
                        length(aVector),aVector)
bBuffer <- createBuffer(context,"CL_MEM_READ_ONLY",
                        length(bVector),bVector)
cBuffer <- createBufferFloatVector(context,"CL_MEM_WRITE_ONLY",
                        length(cVector))

# Create the OpenCL C Kernel function to add two vectors
kernelSource <- '
__kernel void vectorAdd(__global float *a, __global float *b,
                        __global float *c, int numDataItems)
{
  int gid = get_global_id(0); // WorkItem index in 1D global range
  if (gid >= numDataItems) return; // Exit fn if beyond data range
  c[gid] = a[gid] + b[gid]; // Perform addition for this WorkItem
}'
vecAddKernel <- buildKernel(context,kernelSource,'vectorAdd',
                        aBuffer,bBuffer,cBuffer,length(aVector))

# Create a device command queue
queue <- createCommandQueue(context,gpuID)
# Prime the two input Buffers
enqueueWriteBuffer(queue,aBuffer,length(aVector),aVector)
enqueueWriteBuffer(queue,bBuffer,length(bVector),bVector)
# Execute the Kernel
enqueueNDRangeKernel(queue,vecAddKernel,
                     GlobalWorkSize,LocalWorkSize)
# Retrieve the calculated result
enqueueReadBuffer(queue,cBuffer,length(cVector),cVector)

# Finish up by relinquishing all the ROpenCL objects we created
releaseResources()
```

If you run the preceding R script code, which takes less than a second on my MacBook Pro device, you should find that the resultant value of each element in vector c is set to 12345679. If so, then congratulations! You have successfully executed data-parallel code on your system's graphics processor from within R!

There are a number of aspects to the preceding code that require further explanation—in particular, `GlobalWorkSize` versus `LocalWorkSize` and the kernel function definition itself, its use of `get_global_id()`, and how it utilizes memory. These are the subject of the next section.

The kernel function

The kernel function we used in the previous vector addition example had the following definition:

```
__kernel void vectorAdd(__global float *a, __global float *b,
                        __global float *c, int numDataItems)
{
// WorkItem index in 1D global range
  1 int gid = get_global_id(0);
// Exit fn if beyond data range
  2 if (gid >= numDataItems) return;
  3 c[gid] = a[gid] + b[gid];
}
```

The first thing to note is the use of the `__kernel` qualifier to the function signature. This tells the OpenCL compiler to compile the function specifically for execution as a device kernel function.

Line 1

Inside the kernel function, the first line executed determines which of the global set of work items this function invocation is intended to process. The call to `get_global_id(0)` returns the index of this kernel invocation within the total number of global work items to process (`GlobalWorkSize`). (For single dimension, refer to the *Understanding NDRange* section of this chapter.) It helps to consider OpenCL as executing *N* separate invocations of `vectorAdd()`, one for each of the global work items. In our case, *N* is set to be the size of the vectors being added (but rounded up to be an integer multiple of `LocalWorkSize`; take a look at the following), and each work item corresponds to an addition performed on each distinct element of the input vectors: `a` and `b`. Behind-the-scenes OpenCL, in effect, executes many for loop iterations on the device, as follows:

```
# OpenCL NDRangeKernel pseudo-code device for-loop
for (id in 0:globalWorkSize-1) {
  invokeKernel(get_global_id(0)=id, vectorAdd(a,b,c,length(a)))
}
```

The key feature of OpenCL is that this notional `for` loop executes all iterations simultaneously in parallel. The reality is, of course, not quite as straightforward as this. OpenCL may need to compute subsets of the iteration space as sequences of parallel execution in order to fit the available device resources, but helpfully, OpenCL manages many such aspects of device utilization on our behalf.

`GlobalWorkSize` versus `LocalWorkSize`: There is a requirement, now thankfully largely historical, that the `GlobalWorkSize` parameter supplied to `enqueueNDRangeKernel()` for kernel invocation is an integer multiple of `LocalWorkSize`. In particular, under OpenCL version 2.0, this requirement is relaxed. However, the existing OpenCL driver implementations lag behind the latest published standard and will remain in use for some time after this book is published. Some of these driver implementations are poor at calculating the appropriate `LocalWorkSize` value when this is not provided explicitly in the call to `enqueueNDRangeKernel()`. Therefore, it may be advisable to adopt a defensive programming approach on your particular system, explicitly set `LocalWorkSize`, and ensure that `GlobalWorkSize` is an exact integer multiple.

Experimentation may be required to obtain the best performing `LocalWorkSize` value for your particular computation as this is dependent on the amount of resources consumed internally on the device by the specific function for local and private memory and internal registers. The more resources a single invocation of a kernel requires, the smaller the optimal size for its `WorkGroup` in general, because fewer resources will be available to support as many separate simultaneous threads of execution. GPUs are typically much more limited in resources for thread execution compared to a CPU, reflecting their specific design bias for accelerated graphics-related SIMD calculations.

For the Intel Iris GPU device on my MacBook Pro device, a `LocalWorkSize` value of 16 seems to work well for the `vectorAdd()` kernel function. Once you have a built kernel and prior to calling `enqueueNDRangeKernel()`, it is possible to query the preferred setting for `LocalWorkSize` using `getKernelWorkGroupInfo()`, though again, what this reveals is subject to the quality of your system's OpenCL driver implementation, for example. Take a look at the following code:

```
> kinfo <- getKernelWorkGroupInfo(vecAddKernel,deviceID)
> kinfo$CL_KERNEL_PREFERRED_WORK_GROUP_SIZE_MULTIPLE
[1] 16
```

Line 2

On the second line of `vectorAdd()`, the global index assigned to this invocation is tested to check whether it is beyond the domain of work items to process (the limit, which is less than `GlobalWorkSize`, is indicated separately by the `numDataItems` parameter), and if so, the kernel invocation exits immediately as there is no work to do. Even more importantly, we must not attempt to access memory beyond the end of the `a`, `b`, and `c` vectors as this will most likely cause the kernel function to bomb and possibly our R session too.

C memory address pointer warning

C is far less forgiving of out-of-bounds memory access errors in code, something that is much easier to miscode, given C's inherent freedom of access to memory through the address pointer calculation syntax. Such errors in kernel functions running in the context of a GPU device are quite capable of causing your entire system to crash without warning, and this can even happen on what might otherwise be considered extremely stable operating systems, including OS X!

Line 3

Finally, on the third line of `vectorAdd()`, the single vector element addition statement is executed: $c = a + b$.

Memory qualifiers

One of the four distinct qualifiers can be applied to kernel function parameters and variable declarations, as follows:

- `__global`: This indicates to the compiler that the associated address pointer refers to the memory within the device's global area (as for the `*a`, `*b`, and `*c` memory pointers in our example) and is, therefore, equally accessible to all of the device's compute units. Under certain circumstances, and if supported by the device, this qualifier may also refer to the memory within the host's global area.
- `__constant`: This indicates that the memory will be read only; that is, the corresponding OpenCL `Buffer` object was created with the `CL_MEM_READ_ONLY` memory flag (not used in our example). Such memory is apportioned from within the global memory and can confer a performance advantage on some GPU architectures.

- `__local`: This indicates that the memory referenced is held in local memory, meaning that it is only accessible to the threads of execution within the specific `WorkGroup` (not used in our example).
- `__private`: This indicates that the value is held within the private memory area accessible only to the specific CU thread that will execute a `WorkItem` with this kernel. If a qualifier is omitted (as for `numDataItems` in our example), then this is also equivalent to `__private`.

Global memory is the slowest to access, local memory is quicker, and private memory is the fastest of all to access. On some systems, private memory can be more than 100 times faster to access than global memory. However, the trade-off is that the data still has to be transferred between memory subsystems, and there is much less memory capacity available as the speed of access increases; it requires significant microchip real estate to implement fast memory, and it is more costly to produce. Faster memory should ideally be reserved for those data values that are computed and/or reused within the computation.

Understanding NDRange

The call to `enqueueNDRangeKernel()` invokes the execution of a specific kernel function across the compute resource of a device for a given set of work items. OpenCL allows us to specify how large the *range* of work items is to be processed with the `GlobalWorkSize` parameter. OpenCL also allows us to specify the work item domain in up to three dimensions reflecting the graphics processing heritage of GPUs. **ND**, therefore, refers to either **1D**, **2D**, or **3D**. OpenCL further divides the global work item space into separate local work groups in order to utilize the device's compute resources most effectively, and allows us to optionally specify how large a local work group is with the `LocalWorkSize` parameter.

Why bother with local work groups and 2D/3D?

For many situations, we need not be concerned about how OpenCL processes kernel executions within smaller localized work groups; our `vectorAdd()` example is a case in point that also operates simply in 1D. However, kernel executions within a work group can share their own local memory resource, and across a work group, local and global memory synchronization points can also be enforced (by all kernel function invocations calling the OpenCL kernel function barrier, `CLK_LOCAL_MEM_FENCE | CLK_GLOBAL_MEM_FENCE`), enabling a more efficient implementation for some types of algorithms. It can also be much more convenient to implement a matrix multiply in 2D work item space as opposed to being forced to map such indices onto 1D.

Documented in the following table are the ranges of functions that OpenCL makes available to kernels, enabling all aspects of the global/local work item space under which kernels are invoked at runtime to be queried and for kernel functions to therefore be able to dynamically adjust their behavior in response:

Kernel OpenCL Function	Description
`get_work_dim()` This returns `uint`. The value returned is an integer of the C type `uint` and is in the range 1 to 3.	This function returns the dimensionality of GlobalWorkSize—that is, the number of elements in the R vector passed to enqueueNDRangeKernel() as the GlobalWorkSize parameter for this kernel execution. As OpenCL maximally supports three-dimensional arrays, the value returned will either be 1, 2, or 3. If the GlobalWorkSize parameter value in the call to enqueueNDRangeKernel() was a scalar, then this function will return 1.
`get_global_id(uint dim)` This returns `size_t`. The value returned is an integer of the C type `size_t` and will be in the range 0 to `get_global_size(dim)`-1.	This function can be called separately to return the global work item index for the kernel execution for each of the available dimensions of the global work space domain. Each kernel invocation will therefore have a unique global index coordinate. Remember that this is a C function call accessible only to the kernel function itself, and that the valid values for the `dim` parameter are indexes based on 0 to `get_work_dim()`-1 and not on R's 1 to `get_work_dim()`.
`get_global_size(uint dim)` This returns `size_t`. The value returned is an integer of the C type `size_t` = `GlobalWorkSize[dim]`.	This function can be called separately to return the number of global work items in each of the available global work space dimensions as defined by the `GlobalWorkSize` parameter in the call to `enqueueNDRangeKernel()` for this kernel invocation. OpenCL maximally supports up to three-dimensional arrays, so valid values for the `dim` parameter are therefore 0, 1, or 2.
`get_local_id(uint dim)` This returns `size_t`. The value returned is an integer of the C type `size_t` and will be in the range 0 to `get_local_size(dim)`-1.	This function can be called separately with different values of `dim` (either 0, 1, or 2) to return the local work item index for the kernel execution for each of the available dimensions of the local work group domain. Each kernel invocation has a unique local index coordinate only within their specific work group.

Kernel OpenCL Function	Description
`get_local_size(uint dim)` This returns `size_t`. The value returned is an integer of the C type `size_t` = `LocalWorkSize[dim]`.	This function can be called separately with different values of `dim` (either 0, 1, or 2) to return the total number of work items in the corresponding dimension of the local work group. The value returned will either match the value of the `LocalWorkSize(dim+1) enqueueNDRangeKernel()` parameter, or if this was not defined, it will be selected automatically by the OpenCL framework.
`get_group_id(uint dim)` This returns `size_t`. The value returned is an integer of the C type `size_t` and will be in the range 0 to `get_num_groups(dim)`-1.	This function can be called separately with different values of `dim` (either 0, 1, or 2) to return the corresponding dimension index of the local work group in the overall set of work groups. Work group assignment is dictated by the OpenCL framework itself.
`get_num_groups(uint dim)` This returns `size_t`. The value returned is an integer of the C type `size_t` and will be ≥ 1.	This function can be called separately with different values of `dim` (either 0, 1, or 2) to return the total number of work groups in the corresponding dimension. The number of local work groups is determined by the OpenCL framework itself but does not exceed the number of global work items.

By now, you should have a firm understanding of the concepts underlying OpenCL, the `ROpenCL` programming model, how kernel functions can be written in C, and how the OpenCL framework executes kernels on devices. In the remainder of this chapter, we will explore a much more complex `ROpenCL` example that will demonstrate how to process datasets that do not fit within core GPU memory, and how to further accelerate the kernel function processing by exploiting the OpenCL device's internal support for SIMD vector instructions.

Distance matrix example

In R, we can compute a simple *Euclidean* distance measured between two observation vectors *A* and *B* of *N* variables, where the following equation applies:

$$\text{Euclidean distance} = \sqrt{\sum_{i=1}^{N} \left(A[i] - B[i] \right)^2}$$

For a matrix of [Observations] * [Variables] using the core built-in R function, `dist()`, is used.

Computing a distance matrix for a set of observations is computationally expensive with the time complexity *O(n2)*. In addition, a distance value must be computed for every combination of the observation and variable.

In the following `ROpenCL` example, we will take a look at how to code a distance matrix calculation for maximum performance utilizing the GPU. First, though, we need a reasonably large amount of interesting data.

Index of Multiple Deprivation

In the United Kingdom, a standard set of government social demographics is computed in terms of **Index of Multiple Deprivation** (**IMD**). This index is resolved to the level of geographical administration areas of between 1,000 to 2,000 people, and using a set of measures, including economic-, crime-, and health-related ones, a ranking is generated of the most to the least deprived areas. In total, there are some 32,000 such administrative areas, known as **Lower Super Output Areas** (**LSOAs**), covering the whole of England. The dataset that is used as the basis of IMD is available as Open Data from Data.Gov.UK at `http://data.gov.uk/dataset/index-of-multiple-deprivation`. We will use a reduced variant of this dataset (which is itself available for download from the associated book website) to generate a distance matrix for all LSOAs as input to a clustering analysis, which will enable us to stratify the regions of England into similar bands of social demography.

Let's have a quick glimpse at the data (note that output is trimmed for brevity):

```
> filepath <- "./chapter5_IMD_data.csv"
> data <- read.table(file = filepath, header=TRUE, sep=",", row.names=1)
> head(data)
          INCOME.SCORE EMPLOYMENT.SCORE
E01000001         0.01             0.01
E01000002         0.01             0.01
E01000003         0.07             0.05
E01000004         0.04             0.04
E01000005         0.16             0.07
E01000006         0.12             0.06
> tail(data)
          Skills.Sub.domain.Score IDACI.score IDAOPI.score
E01032477                   10.96        0.07         0.06
E01032478                   48.72        0.20         0.31
E01032479                   16.32        0.09         0.18
```

```
E01032480                    14.63         0.11          0.08
E01032481                    23.42         0.19          0.25
E01032482                     2.85         0.03          0.11
> summary(data)
 INCOME.SCORE     EMPLOYMENT.SCORE
 Min.   :0.0000   Min.   :0.0000
 Max.   :0.7700   Max.   :0.7500
 HEALTH.DEPRIVATION.AND.DISABILITY.SCORE
 Min.   :-3.100000
 Max.   : 3.790000
 EDUCATION.SKILLS.AND.TRAINING.SCORE
 Min.   : 0.01
 Max.   :99.34
 BARRIERS.TO.HOUSING.AND.SERVICES.SCORE
 Min.   : 0.34
 Max.   :70.14
 CRIME.AND.DISORDER.SCORE LIVING.ENVIRONMENT.SCORE
 Min.   :-3.280000        Min.   : 0.06
 Max.   : 3.810000        Max.   :92.99
 Indoors.Sub.domain.Score Outdoors.Sub.domain.Score
 Min.   :  0.00           Min.   :  0.00
 Max.   :100.00           Max.   :100.00
 Geographical.Barriers.Sub.domain.Score
 Min.   :  0.00
 Max.   :100.00
 Wider.Barriers.Sub.domain.Score
 Min.   :  0.00
 Max.   :100.00
 Children.Young.People.Sub.domain.Score Skills.Sub.domain.Score
 Min.   :  0.00                         Min.   :  0.00
 Max.   :100.00                         Max.   :100.00
 IDACI.score      IDAOPI.score
 Min.   :0.0000   Min.   :0.000
 Max.   :0.9900   Max.   :0.980
```

```
> length(data) # number of variables
[1] 15
> length(row.names(data)) # number of observations
[1] 32482
```

As we can note, there are `32,482` observations * `15` variables in the IMD dataset. Each observation is uniquely labeled with its LSOA identifier in the range of `E01000001` to `E01032482`. The variables cover income, employment, health, disability, education, and many more, as measured for each LSOA. (You can find out more about each of these measures at `http://data.gov.uk/dataset/index-of-multiple-deprivation`.) The summary shows that the numeric range of data values for each variable, though different, is all within a small magnitude of 100. While we could adjust all of the variables to be in the same numeric domain range, for our parallel pedagogical purposes, we will work with the data as is.

Memory requirements

As we are working with a reasonably large amount of data, we need to ensure we have sufficient memory capacity available on the GPU. We therefore need to understand the memory requirements for both the observation variables matrices as the input and the computed distance measures as the output.

On the host, the observations data requires 8 bytes per variable, because each value will be stored as a 64-bit double-precision floating-point.

The observations data (host) is *8 * 15 * 32,482 = 3.7 Mb.*

To hold this observations data on the Iris GPU requires half as much memory, as the device only supports 32-bit single-precision floating-points—that is, 1.85 MB.

The distance measures are a different story, however; we need to compute the distinct results of *(n2/2) - n*, and we only need to compute a triangular matrix as a distance measure between two observations is commutative, and we can also exclude the distance measure of an observation with itself.

The distance measures (host) are *8 * ((32,4822 / 2) − 32482) = 4 GB.*

To hold all of this data on the Iris GPU as a 32-bit single-precision floating point would require 2 GB of memory, and here is where we have a slight problem; our Iris GPU has maximally only 1.5 GB of global memory available. To resolve this issue, and for instructional purposes, we will adopt an out-of-core processing approach in conjunction with calculating the distance measure using the GPU.

GPU out-of-core memory processing

The GPU has a large amount of memory, sufficient to hold a complete copy of the observation data (the input) but not sufficient to hold a complete copy of the calculated distance measures (the output). The approach taken in the following code is to split the computation of the results into subsets of the global workspace of observations, which we will refer to as blocks of work, whereby each block performed requires a separate enqueued kernel invocation. Subsequent blocks of work will take progressively less time to execute as the number of distance measures to calculate decreases linearly. There are *N-1* distance measures to compute for the first observation in the dataset, which monotonically decreases to zero for the last observation in the dataset.

The setup

The initialization code in which we obtain the GPU `deviceID` and create the context is the same as we used previously in the vector addition example, so it is omitted here. The first block of code in the following sets up the workspace domain and creates the input and output buffers and the distance measures array indexes. The latter we can create in order to save on the extra lines of code within the kernel function itself; the GPU kernel resources are limited, so we don't want to include extra overhead such as this within the kernel function if we can avoid it. Of course, there is always a balancing act between computing a value on demand and caching a value for reuse; in this specific case, it's a marginal call:

```
# distOffset(i,N)
# Function to map an observation sequence index to its resultant
# distance matrix offset. Each observation i will have N-i
# entries, one for each of the remaining observations for which a
# distance measure must be calculated. The distance matrix is a
# triangular array realised as a compact 1D vector.
distOffset <- function(obsIndex,numObs) {
  offset <- numObs*(obsIndex-1) - obsIndex*(obsIndex-1)/2
  return(as.integer(offset))
}

maxWorkSize <- 32482 # total number of observations
LocalWorkSize <- 16
GlobalWorkSize <- 32768 # closest multiple of LocalWorkSize
blockWorkSize <- 2048 # num obs to process per kernel invocation
# distSizeBlock is max num results per invocation (=first block)
distSizeBlock <- distOffset(blockWorkSize+1,maxWorkSize)
# distSizeMax is the maximum extent of the distance results vector
```

```
distSizeMax <- distOffset(maxWorkSize,maxWorkSize)

# Precalculate distance array indices for the kernel function
outIndexes <- integer(maxWorkSize+1)
for (i in 1:maxWorkSize) outIndexes[i] = distOffset(i,maxWorkSize)
outIndexes[maxWorkSize+1] = outIndexes[maxWorkSize]

# Create a 1D vector of observations X variables from the data
dvec <- as.vector(t(data))

# Create the input, distance array offsets and output buffers
# Note that we add an extra element (uninitialised) to dvec to
# support our later use of SIMD vector processing.
inBuffer <- createBuffer(context,"CL_MEM_READ_ONLY",
                         length(dvec)+1,dvec)
indexBuffer <- createBuffer(context,"CL_MEM_READ_ONLY",
                         length(outIndexes),outIndexes)
outBuffer <- createBufferFloatVector(context,"CL_MEM_WRITE_ONLY",
                                     distSizeBlock)
```

Kernel function dist1

The kernel function to calculate the distance measure is given here. For raw speed, this implementation utilizes C's pointer arithmetic on the input data, with `sptr` marking the starting observation for this kernel invocation to calculate the distance measures for `aptr`, which is used to repeatedly iterate through the variables for the starting observation; `bptr`, which iterates through all the remaining observations and their variables; and `optr`, which iterates through the block of results being processed by the kernel invocation:

```
__kernel void dist1(/*1*/__global const float *input,
  /*2*/__global const int *indexes, /*3*/__global float *output,
  /*4*/int numObs, /*5*/int numVars,
  /*6*/int startObs, /*7*/int stopObs)
{
  // This kernel invocation is assigned the work item offset by
  // the start of the observation window for this block
  int startIndex = get_global_id(0) + startObs;
  if (startIndex >= stopObs) return;
  __global float *sptr = &input[startIndex * numVars]; // startObs
  __global float *aptr;
  __global float *bptr = sptr + numVars; // bptr is startObs+1
  int distIndex = indexes[startIndex] - indexes[startObs];
  __global float *optr = &output[distIndex];
```

```
    int obsIndex; int i;
    float sum; float diff;
    // Loop iterates through ALL observations that follow startObs
    for (obsIndex = startIndex+1; obsIndex < numObs; obsIndex++,
         optr++) // on each iter optr advances to next result slot
    {
      aptr = sptr; // aptr is reset to first variable in startObs
      sum = 0.0;
      // Loop through all variables for this pairing of observations
      for (i = 0; i < numVars; i++, aptr++, bptr++)
      {
        diff = *aptr - *bptr;
        sum += diff * diff;
      }
      *optr = sqrt(sum); // store the calculated result
    }
  }
```

Work block control loop

The final portion of the following code provides the control loop to process the observations in the data in blocked subsets. As configured, a sliding window of 2048 observations is processed on each kernel invocation, and the block of results is copied over from the GPU on each iteration for accumulation in the results vector:

```
kernelCode1 <- '__kernel void dist1(...'
kernel <- buildKernel(context,kernelCode1,'dist1',
                      inBuffer,indexBuffer,outBuffer,
                      as.integer(maxWorkSize),as.integer(15),
                      as.integer(0),as.integer(blockWorkSize))
enqueueWriteBuffer(queue,inBuffer,length(dvec),dvec)
enqueueWriteBuffer(queue,indexBuffer,
                   length(outIndexes),outIndexes)
result <- numeric(distSizeMax)

numBlocks <- GlobalWorkSize / blockWorkSize
remainingWork = maxWorkSize
obsIndex <- 1
for (b in 1:numBlocks)
{
    # On last block iteration adjust workSize to what remains
    workSize <- blockWorkSize
```

```
    if (remainingWork < workSize) workSize <- remainingWork

    # We use ROpenCL's assignKernelArg() to modify the startObs
    # and stopObs kernel arguments to move the observations
    # window on to the next block of work
    kernelStartObs <- obsIndex-1  # R:1..n maps to C:0..n-1
    kernelStopObs <- kernelStartObs + workSize
    assignKernelArg(kernel,6,as.integer(kernelStartObs))
    assignKernelArg(kernel,7,as.integer(kernelStopObs))

    # block/GlobalWorkSize must be a multiple of LocalWorkSize
    enqueueNDRangeKernel(queue,kernel,blockWorkSize,LocalWorkSize)

    # Copy the block of results computed into the host's distance
    # measures array +offset for the observations window processed
    distOffset <- outIndexes[obsIndex]
    distSize <- outIndexes[obsIndex + workSize] - distOffset
    enqueueReadBuffer(queue,outBuffer,distSize,result,distOffset)

    # Update observations window and remainingWork for next iter
    obsIndex <- obsIndex + workSize
    remainingWork <- remainingWork - workSize
}
```

In the preceding code, it is important to highlight the use of the R `as.integer()` type converter to pass numeric values that the kernel function will interpret as the C type `int`. It is all too easy to attempt to pass a numeric integer constant to a kernel function from R only to have R quietly convert it to a double-precision floating-point numeric behind the scenes, with unpredictable and difficult-to-debug side effects. It is also worth noting the use of the `ROpenCL` package's `assignKernelArg()` function to change the value of the compiled kernel's `startObs` and `stopObs` parameters prior to calling `enqueueNDRangeKernel` for each block iteration.

Running this GPU-enhanced `dist1()` function on my MacBook Pro device takes around seven seconds. By comparison, R's built-in `dist()` function running on my laptop utilizing just the CPU takes around 25 seconds to process the same observations dataset. In summary, we achieved a performance improvement using the GPU, but it is not quite such a dramatic result as we might have hoped for. Part of the issue is the extra copying and transferring of data required between the host and GPU, but there is one aspect of GPU programming that we have not yet exploited, which should help accelerate the kernel function, namely, SIMD vector processing.

The kernel function dist2

Presented in the following is a second variant of the GPU `dist` kernel function that is rewritten to utilize OpenCL SIMD vector operations:

```
__kernel void dist2(/*1*/__global const float *input,
  /*2*/__global const int *indexes, /*3*/__global float *output,
  /*4*/int numObs,   /*5*/int numVars,
  /*6*/int startObs, /*7*/int stopObs)
{
  int startIndex = get_global_id(0) + startObs;
  if (startIndex >= stopObs) return;
  __global float *sptr = &input[startIndex * numVars];
  __global float *bptr = sptr + numVars;
  int distIndex = indexes[startIndex] - indexes[startObs];
  __global float *optr = &output[distIndex];
  int obsIndex; float sum;
  float16 a, b, d, d2;   // Allocate private SIMD vector registers
  a = vload16(0,sptr);   // Load start obs into SIMD vector16
  for (obsIndex = startIndex+1; obsIndex < numObs;
       obsIndex++, optr++, bptr += numVars)
  {
    b = vload16(0,bptr); // Load next obs into SIMD vector16
    d = a - b;    // fast vector element wise subtraction
    d2 = d * d;   // fast vector element wise multiplication
    // Use vector element accessors to sum first 15 elements only
    sum = d2.s0 + d2.s1 + d2.s2 + d2.s3 + d2.s4 +
          d2.s5 + d2.s6 + d2.s7 + d2.s8 + d2.s9 +
          d2.sA + d2.sB + d2.sC + d2.sD + d2.sE;
    *optr = sqrt(sum);
  }
}
```

To support SIMD vector processing, OpenCL compilers accept a wider range of C syntax, as highlighted in the preceding code. I think it's worth noting how much simpler and easier to read the resultant C code is (tending towards R!); we have been able to remove the inner loop entirely and unroll the summation.

OpenCL can support single vectors of 2, 3, 4, 8, and maximally, 16 elements, which are simply defined by specifying the C type, such as float, with the numeric vector width, for example. The float4 type defines a vector of four floats. The OpenCL compiler will convert simple mathematical expressions applied to vectors into SIMD instructions that can operate on multiple values within a single processor cycle, depending on the capability of the underlying compute unit.

OpenCL provides special functions to load SIMD vectors from and to store SIMD vectors in global or local memory. Our `dist2` kernel function makes use of OpenCL's `vload()` function to bring an entire observation (16 floats of data) from the global memory into one of the compute unit's private vector registers. The final summation of the first 15 elements of the differences in vector illustrates the use of the OpenCL vector element accessor "`.hexadecimal_digit`" syntax. Recall that we added an extra unused element to the input buffer, and this allows us to safely execute 16 element vector-wise operations without overrunning the memory bounds on the last observation.

The capacity of a device to execute SIMD vector instructions can be queried with `getDeviceInfo()`. For the Iris GPU in my MacBook Pro device, the following is returned:

```
> dinfo$CL_DEVICE_PREFERRED_VECTOR_WIDTH_FLOAT
[1] 1
> dinfo$CL_DEVICE_NATIVE_VECTOR_WIDTH_FLOAT
[1] 1
```

On the face of it, a supported vector width of `1` implies that SIMD vector processing will not yield us any benefit on this device. However, in practice, running the out-of-core GPU processing code with the `dist2` kernel achieves a sub three second performance, so at the very least, by virtue of the compiler being smarter at optimizing the declared vector code, we now have an 8x performance advantage over R's standard core `dist()` implementation running on the host.

As the last word on the subject, one of the many neat features of OpenCL is its support for heterogeneous computing. We can trivially change the device we are targeting to that of the host CPU and compare the runtime of our optimized `dist2()` example between GPU and CPU. On my MacBook Pro 4xCU host CPU, I can achieve a runtime of around five seconds. Arguably, then, I have not just one supercomputer lurking in my laptop but two: my GPU and CPU!

Summary

In this chapter, we looked in detail at how to exploit the capability of the GPU in your laptop to perform computation on behalf of R programs through the use of the `ROpenCL` package. Along the way, you also learned a little about programming highly efficient kernel function code in the C programming language, with loop unrolling and a careful use of high speed memory.

As we noted, while the goal for OpenCL is one of heterogeneous portability, in which the same code can run on a variety of devices (including the CPU itself), the reality is that with GPUs in particular, there is room for code optimization that is tailored to the characteristics of the underlying device hardware to extract the maximum possible performance. Obtaining the best performance for a kernel function is about balancing memory access and exploiting vector processing, and ultimately requires your own experimentation.

In the next and final chapter, we will distill the essential lessons from the various different approaches to successful parallel programming that we explored throughout this book. We will also take a more scientific approach to evaluating and achieving maximum parallel efficiency. We will end the book with a glimpse into the future at the up-and-coming technology developments that are set to massively increase the amount of compute available for us to exploit, including directly from the palm of your hand.

6
The Art of Parallel Programming

This chapter has the somewhat grandiose and unusual title "*The Art of Parallel Programming*" as adding the word "art" to the engineering discipline of "programming" may seem odd. While good programming is reflected in good design and good design is often an expression of beauty that exhibits some elemental symmetry—and in the world of the abstract, a recognition of regained inherent simplicity—my intention is to also capture the Harry Potter notion of "Dark Arts": those areas where danger lies. Perhaps an alternate title for this chapter may therefore be "Here, there be dragons!"....

There are many pitfalls that can catch the unwary in the world of parallel programming, and this chapter will alert you to these:

- Deadlock - How message passing, in particular, can result in unpredictable program behavior
- Numerical instability - The variation in results that can arise when computing in parallel
- Random numbers - Ensuring that each processor has its own unique random sequence when running in parallel

In this chapter, we will also discuss the concept of SpeedUp, the limitations of *Amdahl's law,* and how to achieve parallel efficiency in different situations, including task farm, grid, and MapReduce contexts. We will finish by distilling the lessons you learned along our journey from the previous chapters, lessons that will hopefully enable you to become a true practitioner of the art of parallel programming. Finally, we will take a look into "Delores' Crystal Ball" at what the future holds for massively parallel computation that will likely have a significant impact on the world of R programming, particularly when applied to big data.

Understanding parallel efficiency

Let's first go right back to the very beginning and consider why we might choose to write a parallel program in the first place.

The simple answer, of course, is that we want to speed up our algorithm and want to compute the answer much faster than we can do simply by running in serial, in which only a single thread of program execution can be utilized.

In this day and age of big data, we will extend this view to cover the otherwise incomputable, where the resources of a single machine architecture make it intractable to compute a complex algorithm across a massive scale of data; therefore, we have to employ thousands upon thousands of computational cores, terabytes of memory, petabytes of storage, and a supporting management infrastructure that can cope with the inevitable runtime failure of individual components during the aggregate lifetime of the computation of potentially millions of hours.

Another approach to utilizing parallelization, and arguably its simplest exposition, is to improve overall throughput. Perhaps you are running a simulation and want to evaluate a wide spectrum of variance on the inputs; in this case, with a large cluster of N machines, you can simultaneously evaluate N different simulations. Each simulation is completely independent of one another, so there is no additional overhead or management of the shared state for each simulation run. This form of the *embarrassingly parallel* problem is often referred to as *naïve parallelism*, where the workload is simple to apportion among a group of fully independent acting agents.

SpeedUp

It is important to examine the efficiency of a parallel implementation compared to an equivalent serial implementation of an algorithm. The simplest measure we use for this is *SpeedUp*, the ratio of time taken in serial to the time taken in parallel for the execution of the algorithm applied to a specific input, as follows:

$$SpeedUp = \frac{T_{serial}}{T_{parallel}}$$

As we increase the amount of parallelism applied, the time taken for parallel execution $T_{parallel}$ should reduce, and so it follows that *SpeedUp* will increase. Assuming that optimal serial implementation is equivalent to a parallel implementation executing on a single processor with no overheads as it scales—that is, exhibiting perfect parallelism—, one can define $T_{parallel}$ as the equivalent of T_{serial} divided by however much parallelism is being used (N), as follows:

$$\text{Perfect parallelism: } T_{parallel\_N} = \frac{T_{parallel\_1}}{N}$$

It is often the case that we start from the basis of a serial computation and seek to improve its performance incrementally through progressive parallelization. Acknowledging that this is a gross simplification for now, consider that for a given algorithm execution for a specific input, there is a nonparallel component and a parallel component, as in the following equation:

$$\text{Total time: } T_{overall\_N} = T_{non-parallel} + T_{parallel\_N}$$

The overall time for algorithm execution is the sum of the time taken for the serial (nonparallel) component plus the time taken to execute the parallel component. We can reduce the time taken for the parallel component by adding more processing elements—that is, by increasing *N*. Eventually, though, no matter how many more parallel processing elements we may be able to add, the overall time will be dominated by $T_{non-parallel}$.

Any measureable $T_{non-parallel}$ component fundamentally limits the scalability of the overall algorithm. For example, imagine you were to start out with the $T_{non-parallel}$ component being 10% of overall execution time compared to $T_{parallel}$ when both the components are run on a single-processor machine. Assuming a perfect implementation for the $T_{parallel}$ component and then rerunning this component with 10 processors will immediately make $T_{non-parallel}$ the dominant runtime component, rising to 53%. Increasing the $T_{parallel}$ component to 100 processsors may speed its aspect up a further tenfold. However, because of the relative dominance of $T_{non-parallel}$, the overall runtime will be in the order of only twice as fast and unable to show any further meaningful improvement even with a thousand processors or beyond.

Amdahl's law

We can recast the preceding formula in terms of *SpeedUp* with *Amdahl's law*, which states the maximum achievable *SpeedUp* for *N* processors, where the proportion of the algorithm that can be made parallel is designated as *P* (0.0 to 1.0).

Amdahl's law is represented as follows:

$$SpeedUp(N) = \frac{1}{(1-P)+\frac{P}{N}}$$

For our example where 90% of the runtime can be parallelized, it will be:

SpeedUp(10) = 1 / (1 – 0.9) + 0.9/10 = 5.26

SpeedUp(1000) = 1/(1-0.9) + 0.9/1000 = 9.91

SpeedUp(100) = 9.17

SpeedUp(10000) = 9.99

The following figure depicts a graph of *SpeedUp*, in which we parallelized 90% of the algorithm:

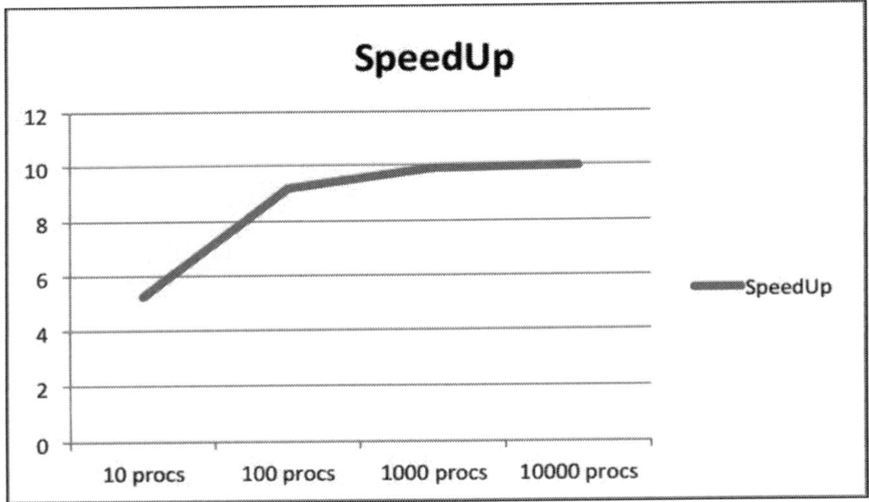

Figure 1: *SpeedUp* graph where parallelizable component of algorithm is 90%.

As we can see our maximum achievable *SpeedUp* tails off very quickly at just 10, despite employing thousands of processors.

Estimating P

Interestingly, a recasting of *Amdahl's law* can be applied to estimate the proportion of the algorithm that is parallel (*P*) based on a single parallel runtime measurement, as follows:

$$P_{estimated} = \frac{\frac{1}{SpeedUp} - 1}{\frac{1}{N} - 1}$$

If we apply this to our example, in which we had 10 processors and a *SpeedUp* value of 5.26, our estimate of *P* is calculated as 0.898 ≈ 0.9. Thus, from a single parallel runtime and comparison with the serial runtime, we can determine what the maximum scalability will be without having to make further (potentially costly) runs with more parallelism in order to evaluate the effectiveness of our implementation.

To parallelize or not to parallelize

What is important to recognize is that we need to minimize the serial component associated with any parallel algorithm in order to achieve high scalability. Even if just 5% of the program is nonparallel *Amdahl's LAW* shows we can achieve a maximum *SpeedUp* of only 20. It is certainly not worth incurring the cost of maintaining a cluster of hundreds of processors on standby if we can only effectively utilize a small proportion of them in our parallel algorithm implementation.

Algorithm overhead is therefore a critical consideration. More complex parallelization implies a level of overhead, either in setting up separate input configurations for each independent computation and collecting and combining the generated results or in terms of the computation itself, in which the intermediate shared state among independent processing elements must be maintained. Both of these overhead costs may also combine for a specific algorithm implementation.

Its not all doom and gloom, though; *Amdahl's law* is tied to a fixed specification of input and is based on the premise that the parallel component has no other advantage than *N* threads of simultaneous execution to confer to the algorithm for a given nonparallel overhead. In practice, there are many applications where this is not true.

The nonparallel overhead may be constant or increase marginally for a range of problem sizes being solved. Certain parallel algorithms may be able to achieve a greater level of detailed analysis of data or operate on a larger dataset within the same time window. The parallel system being used may scale not just in terms of compute but also, importantly, in terms of the core memory and other aspects of system resources, such as communications bandwidth or local disk storage, massively increasing the capacity for the caching of large datasets for accelerated access when compared to the equivalent single processor serial execution. This can lead to *superlinear SpeedUp*, where N-way parallelism achieves more than *N* times factor of comparable serial performance.

Parallelism can be incredibly effective when applied to the kind of problem that is *embarrassingly parallel*. In general, though, most types of computational problem can gain some level of benefit from parallelism. Some applications may be uniquely time-critical; consider an analysis of bio-imagery in a critical patient care context, for example. Absolute efficiency may give way to any level of accelerated performance that can be gained.

Chapple's law

However, one further word of caution. One must always make due consideration of the time and effort required to construct a parallel implementation of an algorithm. Here's Chapple's law (tongue firmly in cheek) that highlights that it's only worth putting effort into parallelizing code if you will execute your new parallel code a sufficient number of times (*N*) to offset the time you spent developing it, as demonstrated by this formula:

$$\textbf{Chapple's Law:}\ (T_{parallel} \times N) + T_{parallel\_algorithm\_development} \ll T_{serial} \times N$$

There are many things that can impact you when building a parallel implementation of an algorithm, and therefore, parallelization may require a substantially greater effort on your part compared to developing a serial implementation.

For a start, scaling immediately adds an extra dimension to your test matrix. Further, if you seek to use direct message passing in your implementation, then this lower level of programming is subject to more opportunity for errors and, in particular, ones that are timing-dependent and may not manifest themselves until they operate at specific levels of parallelism.

You also need to take into account the potential for the results generated by a parallel implementation to be marginally different to serial execution or numerically less repeatable; we will explore some examples of these later in this chapter.

It should be particularly noted that you may find differences in behavior where serial execution uses a machine environment entirely separate from that of the parallel execution platform due to variation in the versions of system libraries or the arithmetic behavior of the different underlying computational FPU hardware.

Of course, if you plan to share the fruits of your labor with others who can benefit from using your parallelized algorithm then great, go for it—just be aware that technology continues to advance at an accelerating pace with increases in core processor speed, cache, memory capacity, and data transfer bandwidth. The architecture you implement and test for "today" may well change considerably by "tomorrow". Parallel code, therefore, comes with an ongoing maintenance overhead to at least ensure that it is tuned for optimum efficiency.

Numerical approximation

Let's have a little fun!

Question: What do you get in R if you sum 1 with successive fractions 1/2, 1/3, 1/4, and so on all the way up to 1/500000th? Well, let's take a look....

Here's some simple code that sets up the vector of fractions:

```
v <- 1:500000
for (i in 1:length(v))
{
    v[i] = 1/i
}
> v[1]
[1] 1
> v[2]
[1] 0.5
> v[3]
[1] 0.3333333
> v[500000]
[1] 2e-06
```

And now, let's explicitly sum all the elements in the vector:

```
suma <- 0.0
for (i in 1:length(v))
{
    suma = suma + v[i]
```

```
}
> suma
[1] 13.69958
```

This seems fine. So, let's take a look at what happens if we add the numbers up in reverse:

```
sumz <- 0.0
for (i in length(v):1)
{
    sumz = sumz + v[i]
}
> sumz
[1] 13.69958
```

Great, the same answer; it's all good, move along, nothing to see here....

Um, yeah, actually; let's take a closer look:

```
> print(suma,digits=15)
[1] 13.6995800423056
> print(sumz,digits=15)
[1] 13.6995800423055
```

Err- Houston...?

What happens if we try with fractions up to 1/5 millionth? Take a look:

```
> print(suma,digits=15)
[1] 16.0021642352986
> print(sumz,digits=15)
[1] 16.0021642353001
```

Yikes! Now we have difference in the results from the tenth decimal place!

So, the answer to our question is: it depends on the order in which you add up the numbers. Hmm, perhaps this is not what you were expecting?

What gives? Something must be wrong, surely; how come the results are different and keep getting worse?

Well, it all comes down to the numerical precision of floating-point numbers and the cumulative error carried over between mathematical operations. For example, one-third of course cannot be represented precisely with any form of floating-point precision and neither can many other fractions; the computer has a finite amount of memory in which to represent such numbers and therefore has to make an approximation. Resultant arithmetic on such numbers is also, therefore, approximate, and the approximation varies depending on which numbers are being combined. So, even though we combine the same set of numbers, the different orders in which we apply our approximate arithmetic means we carry a different pattern of error and end up with slightly different approximate results.

This observation has important implications to comparing parallel with serial execution for correctness and, indeed, parallel execution on *N* processors with parallel execution on N+1 processors. If such numerical data is presented and processed in a different order—and parallelism typically leads to exactly this happening—then the results may differ. As we increase the amount of numerical data involved so it is likely that the compound error will increase, and the difference in results will drift further apart.

Integers are fallible too

It's not just the approximately represented noninteger numbers that we have to be concerned about; we have issues with the exact representational integers too. When running in parallel and at scale on datasets larger than we are able to achieve running in serial, we need to be even more aware of the bounds of value representation. A 32-bit signed integer—R's native integer type is a 32-bit signed integer—can represent a value ceiling of 2,147,483,647. Let's say the algorithm keeps track of the total number of data items it processes. When running in serial, the number of data items may never be expected to reach the limits of such an integer, but when running a parallel version of the algorithm, such assumptions may no longer apply. While R can automatically carry out the promotion of value representation from an integer to double, where double usually employs 64-bit representation, when utilizing R packages built using C/C++ or Fortran, such value representation is much more hardwired; therefore, you need to be aware of how values may be truncated or NA-ed when passed back and forth through the package's functional interface.

Even when utilizing 64-bit double precision, arithmetic overflow can cause unusual behavior in a program with the side effect of generating nonsensical output and yet be difficult to determine and resolve; worse, it may even go unnoticed.

Of course, for some applications such as simulation or near optimal solution search, everything is approximate in any case, so this may be less of an issue. On the flip side, the most extreme algorithms may choose to sort the data or use more accurate number representations and explicit non-FPU arithmetic, although both these approaches will introduce significant overhead and arguably may negate some of the rationale for parallelization.

Ultimately, what we have to realize is that our numerical results are only ever accurate within the constraints of the machine representation for numbers we choose to employ. When running serial code, people often overlook this aspect as such code invariably generates the same result for a given input. However, running parallel code brings issues such as this fully to the front and square; even a repeated execution of the same parallel code on the same input with the same amount of parallelism could produce a slightly different result from a previous execution, particularly where the code may involve time-variant communication for message exchange. These effects are difficult to predict and are, in essence, random. And that, dear reader, is the perfect segue into our next topic, random numbers.

Random numbers

Random numbers take on a new significance in parallel programs, given that usually, you want to have different random number sequences in use across a set of cooperating parallel processes; simulation and optimum search type workloads being prime examples.

The default random number generator in R is **Mersenne Twister** and is generally recognized to be a good quality pseudorandom number generator, though it's not cryptographically very secure.

Mersenne Twister

To find out more about the properties of the Mersenne Twister **random number generator** (**RNG**) you can refer to:

`https://en.wikipedia.org/wiki/Mersenne_Twister`

`http://www.math.sci.hiroshima-u.ac.jp/~m-mat/MT/emt.html`

You can, of course, select alternate generators from the set of built-ins as well as supply your own using the base R `random` package function `RNGKind()`.

R in itself has always been a single-threaded implementation and is not designed to exploit parallelism within its own language primitives; it relies on specifically implemented external package libraries to achieve this for certain accelerated functions and to enable the use of parallel processing frameworks. As we discussed, the general implementation for these parallel frameworks is based on **Single Program Multiple Data (SPMD)**, meaning that one program executable or a sequence of computational instructions is replicated across a number of parallel processes, but each maintains its own individual state—that is, has independent memory for its R objects and variables.

If we were to blithely ask for a random number on each parallel process, then all the processes will return the same random number sequence. What we need to do is set the seed explicitly to a different value for each parallel process.

Depending on the type of parallelism being used, we could choose to generate a sequence of unique seeds from a master process and hand out the next unused seed, as part of the parallel task description, to the next free worker to execute a task. Here's an example:

```
# master process initializes a set of ten random numbers
# between 1 and 10 to distribute to workers
x_real <- runif(10,1.0,10.0)    # 1.0 < x < 10.0
x_integer <- sample(1:10,10)    # 1 <= x <= 10
```

Alternatively, we could use the unique identifier of the process or, where tasks outnumber parallel processes, the unique task number as part of the seed. One can also use the current time in milliseconds to help manufacture a unique seed and combine this with all of the previously listed options to generate a well-differentiated seed value that is suitable for your chosen RNG:

```
# worker processes each set their own unique seed based
# on their process id and seconds time in milliseconds accuracy
# and (if applicable) the unique id for the task itself
task <- getNextTask()     # illustrative pseudocode call
seed <- Sys.getpid() * as.numeric(format(Sys.time(),"%OS6"))
set.seed(seed * getTaskId(task))
```

The key requirement is that it must be the parallel process itself that makes the call to `set.seed()` with its unique seed value and that this be done for each parallel task to be executed because you should never assume that each process will be given the same set of tasks to process in sequence, as could happen with an adaptive load-balancing task farm, for example.

MPI random numbers

If you use the pdbR MPI, then you are in luck as this package provides a simple mechanism to create separate streams of random numbers across the parallel processes with the following:

```
library(pbdMPI, quiet = TRUE)
init()
comm.set.seed(diff=TRUE)
x_real <- runif(1,1.0,10.0)
```

This function can also be used to create an identical stream of random numbers across all parallel processes should you so wish by calling it with the `diff=FALSE` parameter.

The `pdbR` multistream random number generation utilizes the `rlecuyer` package internally at `https://cran.r-project.org/web/packages/rlecuyer/index.html`.

Whatever scheme you use to set random seeds, it is important to record what `seed` value each parallel process uses. Without this, you will not be able to set the `seed` again to the same explicit value when you want to reproduce the results generated or to trigger identical computational behavior in order to track down a bug. It is also important to consider that you may be using functions in your code from other R packages, which themselves, internally make use of the standard random number stream.

Deadlock

Deadlock is a classic problem that affects parallel code built on explicit message passing. It arises when a process or thread of execution waits to receive a message that is never sent or to send a message but the intended recipient isn't listening and never will be.

In computing, deadlock as a concept arose from the context where a number of agents compete for mutually exclusive access to a shared resource—for example, a portion of memory representing a value that is to be updated via a locking mechanism that singularizes access to the resource; think simultaneous ATM transactions applied to a shared bank account. In this case, if the lock is not freed by the previous agent, then no other agent can gain access to the lock and may be queued indefinitely.

A classic deadlock scenario is where Agent A has gained access to resource 1, Agent B has gained access to resource 2, Agent A is waiting to gain access to resource 2 (which B now exclusively holds), and likewise, Agent B is waiting to gain access to resource 1 (which A now exclusively holds). Neither agent can proceed and have therefore reached deadlock.

It is simple to construct a deadlock example using blocking communications between MPI processes; `init()` and `finalize()` are omitted from the following `pbdR` example, which simply passes the MPI process' rank identity to its next numerically higher ranked neighbor—that is, from the predecessor to successor with wraparound from the last process to the first process. Take a look at the following code:

```
r <- .comm.rank
succ <- (r + 1) %% .comm.size
pred <- (r - 1) %% .comm.size
v <- 1:1000    # dimension vector v
v[1] <- r      # set first element to my MPI communicator rank
w <- 1:1000    # receive into vector w
send(v,rank.dest=succ)     # Send v to my next in rank
recv(w,rank.source=pred)   # Recv w from my previous in rank
comm.print(sprintf("%d received message from
%d",r,w[1]),all.rank=TRUE)
```

You can run this example with two, or however many processes you like, and it will deadlock; all the processes will be stuck in their send calls… or not!

Exactly what happens in this case depends on the behavior of your MPI implementation. We utilized blocking sends and receives in this example, and you might therefore be wondering how it is possible to send data when there is no prior matching receive for it. Well, MPI has some subtleties that are designed to improve performance.

In MPI, the blocking send can be implemented to dispatch a message to the designated receiver and be held within the MPI communications subsystem at either the sender or intended receiver until a matching receive is executed to complete it. In fact, this mode of behavior is very much part of the MPI standard. A blocking send is only defined to be blocking in the sense that the system will not return control from a blocking send until it is free to enable the program to reuse the send buffer or R object; that is, the program is free to change its contents or state. In this sense, the data may be considered sent but not yet received. However, this behavior is of course dependent on there being sufficient memory resources to temporarily cache a copy of the sent message (pending a matching receive), thereby freeing up the R program-level send buffer.

On my own laptop, if I now increase the size of the vectors being sent to 10,000—your own cutoff point may vary—then the MPI subsystem's internal cache is exceeded, and it will be unable to maintain a separate cached copy of the sent data; the MPI send call will subsequently block indefinitely as it needs a matching receive call to be invoked, along with adequate assigned buffer memory, to enable the larger-than cache transfer of data to take place. As all the processes execute sends without matching receives, a deadlock will result.

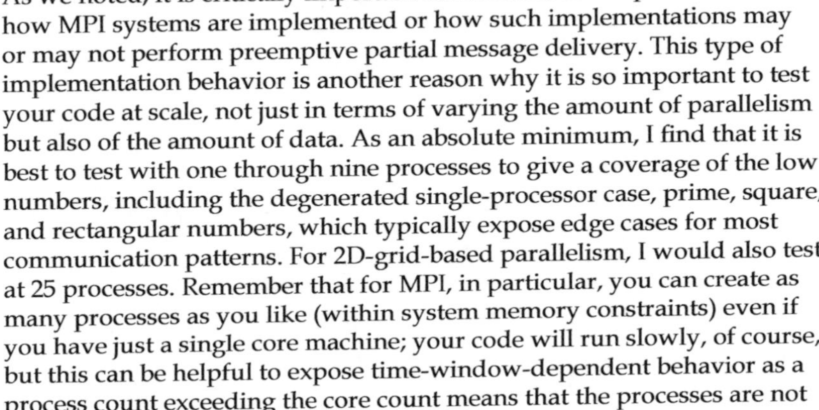

Testing, testing, testing!

As we noted, it is critically important not to make assumptions about how MPI systems are implemented or how such implementations may or may not perform preemptive partial message delivery. This type of implementation behavior is another reason why it is so important to test your code at scale, not just in terms of varying the amount of parallelism but also of the amount of data. As an absolute minimum, I find that it is best to test with one through nine processes to give a coverage of the low numbers, including the degenerated single-processor case, prime, square, and rectangular numbers, which typically expose edge cases for most communication patterns. For 2D-grid-based parallelism, I would also test at 25 processes. Remember that for MPI, in particular, you can create as many processes as you like (within system memory constraints) even if you have just a single core machine; your code will run slowly, of course, but this can be helpful to expose time-window-dependent behavior as a process count exceeding the core count means that the processes are not able to execute all simultaneously in real time.

Avoiding deadlock

There are three simple alternate ways to recode the deadlock example to ensure that a deadlock will not result regardless of how much data is exchanged. Firstly, we can ensure that only some of the processes send while the others receive. The following code snippet ensures that even ranked processes send while odd ranked processes receive and then flips to odd sending and even receiving:

```
if (r %% 2 == 0) { # even
  send(v,rank.dest=succ)
  w <- recv(w,rank.source = pred)
} else { # odd
  w <- recv(w,rank.source = pred)
  send(v,rank.dest = succ)
}
```

Alternately, we can utilize the `pbdR` MPI's nonblocking `iSend` method so that all processes progress directly into their receive rather than wait to send. Note that for completeness and good practice, we also wait on the send request (the number `1`) after the receive to ensure the send is finished, but in this example, it's not strictly necessary. Take a look at the following:

```
isend(v,rank,dest=succ,request=1)# Send non-blocking
w <- recv(w,rank,source=pred)     # Recv blocks
wait(request=1)# Wait for nb-send to complete (it must have)
```

Finally, we can also use MPI's higher-level combined `SendRecv` function thus:

```
sendrecv(v, x.buffer=w, rank.dest=succ, rank.source=pred)
```

Exactly which alternate form you choose depends on the nature of your algorithm. When each process executes the same program sequence in the near-lock step, then `SendRecv` is a good choice, or even `SendRecvReplace` if you want to receive new content in the same object as you send. When each process is loosely coupled with variable work to process, then the nonblocking mode of communication may be more efficient but with the additional overhead of extra code to manage the outstanding comms. When you need to carry out a more complex but regularized pattern of communication and the processing load is evenly distributed, then you might choose the first alternative with a rank-specific sequencing of `send` and matching `recv` functions

Reducing the parallel overhead

Each parallel algorithm comes with its own overhead, particularly in terms of setup, in apportioning the work among a set of processors and tear-down in compiling the aggregated results from the set of processors.

To get a handle on how we can approach reducing these overheads, let's first examine the process of result aggregation.

The following figure shows a very typical master-worker task farm-style approach utilizing 15 independent worker nodes. In this case, each separate task undertaken by the workers contributes to an overall result.

Each worker transmits the partial result it generates back to the master, and the master then processes all the partial results to generate the final accumulated result.

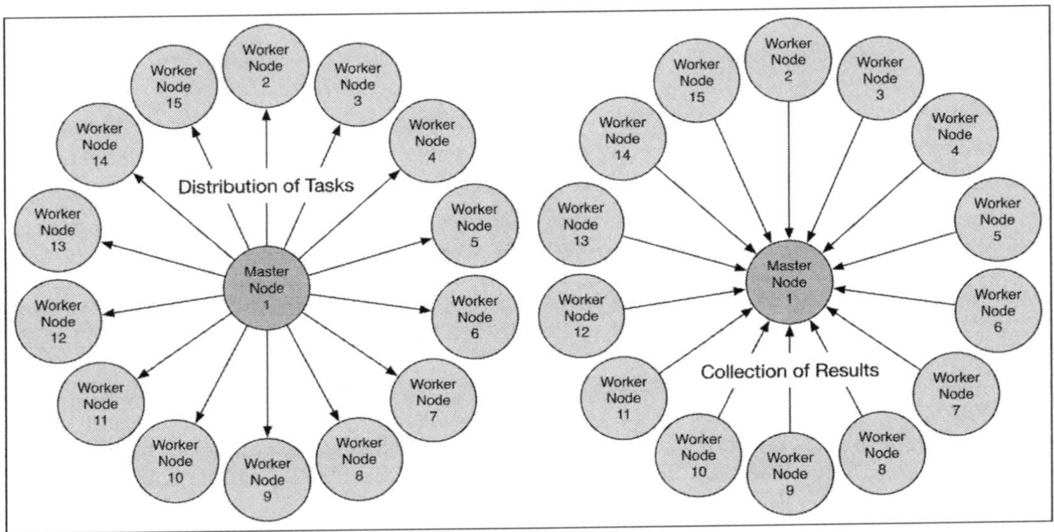

Figure 2: Master-Worker flower style arrangement.

Let's also consider that each worker task takes the same amount of computational effort, and thus, each worker finishes its task at approximately the same moment in time.

It's not difficult to see from the flower arrangement in the figure that such a circumstance generates maximum communication contention for the master to service simultaneous result messages from every worker. The master will also have to process *N* partial results to generate the final combined result. For certain algorithms, this final step may in itself require significant computation.

If the tasks being undertaken by the workers are fully independent—that is, the workers do not need to communicate with one another while undertaking their task—and there is a sufficiently large number of tasks or a constant stream of tasks to be undertaken—that is, several factors more tasks than workers—then the overhead of setup and tear-down can effectively be amortized by the master ensuring that it sends out a new task to a worker immediately, and that the worker returns the previous task's result. It may then be possible to adjust the task sizes and numbers of workers such that the system can settle into an efficient state, whereby there are few, if any, waiting periods and all processors achieve near-100% utilization.

However, for those problems not amenable to such treatment, such as those in which all processors are involved either synchronously or asynchronously in each other's tasks, a different approach is required.

The following figure shows the master and worker result communications rearranged as a binary tree structure. Here, we are able to spread the computation of the partial results among the workers rather than relying on the master to perform all result aggregation.

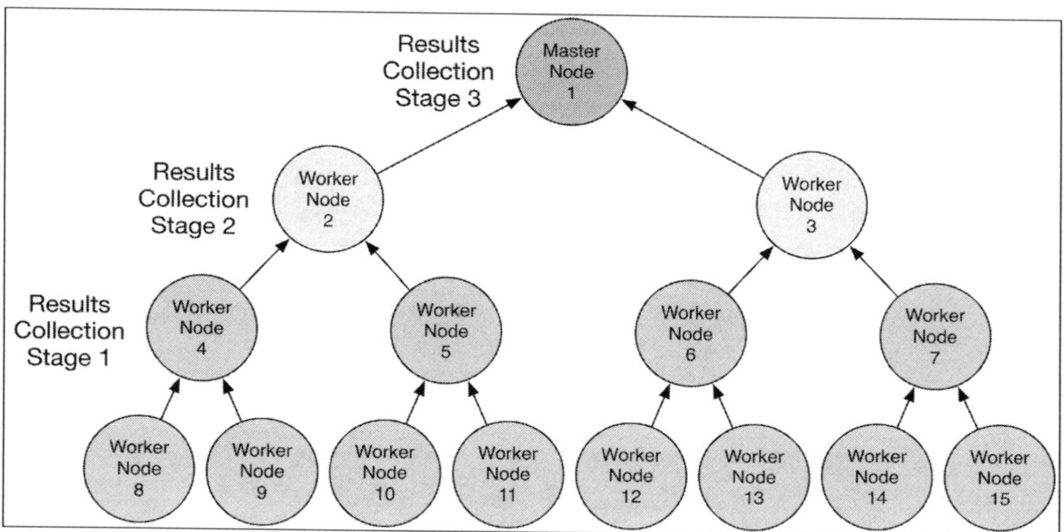

Figure 3: Master-Worker tree style arrangement.

The process of result aggregation starts with the bottom layer of pairs of workers, such as 8 and 9, 10 and 11, and so on, sending their partial results to their single designated parent—for example, workers 4 to 7. Workers 4 to 7 (blue) then aggregate the results they received in stage 1. They feed their partial aggregated results to workers 2 and 3 for stage 2 (yellow), and then finally, the master node (orange) receives the further partial aggregated results in stage 3. In this tree arrangement, the master only has two sets of results to process, rather than all fifteen as in the previous flower arrangement.

If we assume that all the other aspects of result processing are equal, then we have reduced the result aggregation overhead from the flower arrangement of *O(N)*, where *N* is the number of processors, to *O(log2 N)* for the tree arrangement.

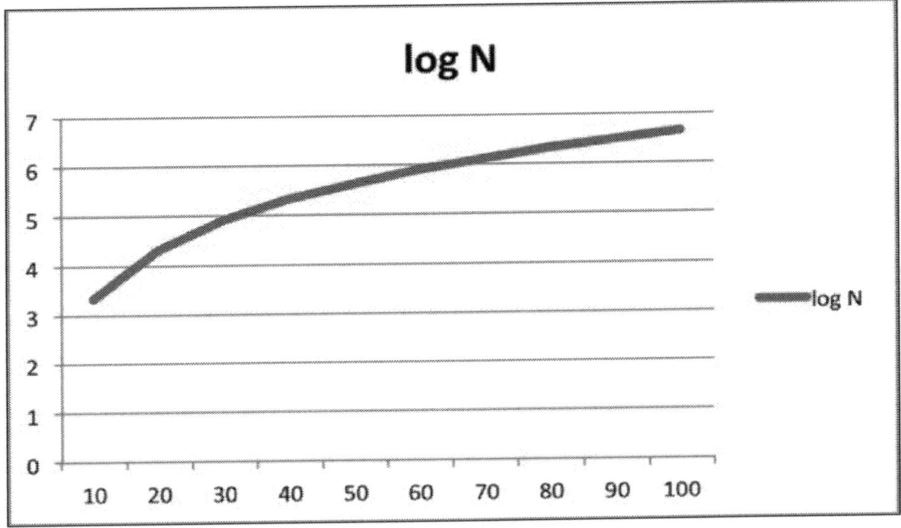

Figure 4: Time complexity of *log N* for tree based result aggregation.

What we did is parallelize the result processing by constructing a more sophisticated multistage implementation applicable to generalized task farms as well as Map/ Reduce contexts. While we should not forget *Chapple's law*, this is a significant improvement, with this particular *O(log2 N)* approach becoming even more effective and minimizing the overhead cost as we utilize higher orders of parallelism.

The tree approach can also be applied to the initial task assignment process. Input data may require preprocessing to segment it into smaller tasks (*Map*). This effort can be spread across a tree arrangement in reverse flow compared to the aggregation operation (*Reduce*).

Of course, the frequency and size of communication impacts on parallel overhead too. Data transfer costs can be minimized, where input data can be localized at the point of its consumption. It may even be worth holding some level of duplicate or overlapping data within the local storage of processing nodes in order to reduce the number of communications required during the execution of the parallel algorithm. In most forms of communication, both end points are tied up for the duration of the data exchange. In certain cases, it may even be worth exchanging compressed data and using processor cycles to compress/decompress messages in order to minimize the duration of transfer.

Adaptive load balancing

Previously, we noted how important it is to create balanced workloads, where the compute time for each task is equal.

The task farm

When the nature of the problem is such that there are many more tasks available than workers and each task is truly independent, then a task farm is a simple parallel processing scheme that ensures 100% utilization of workers by the master feeding the next available task to the next free worker, as depicted in the following diagram:

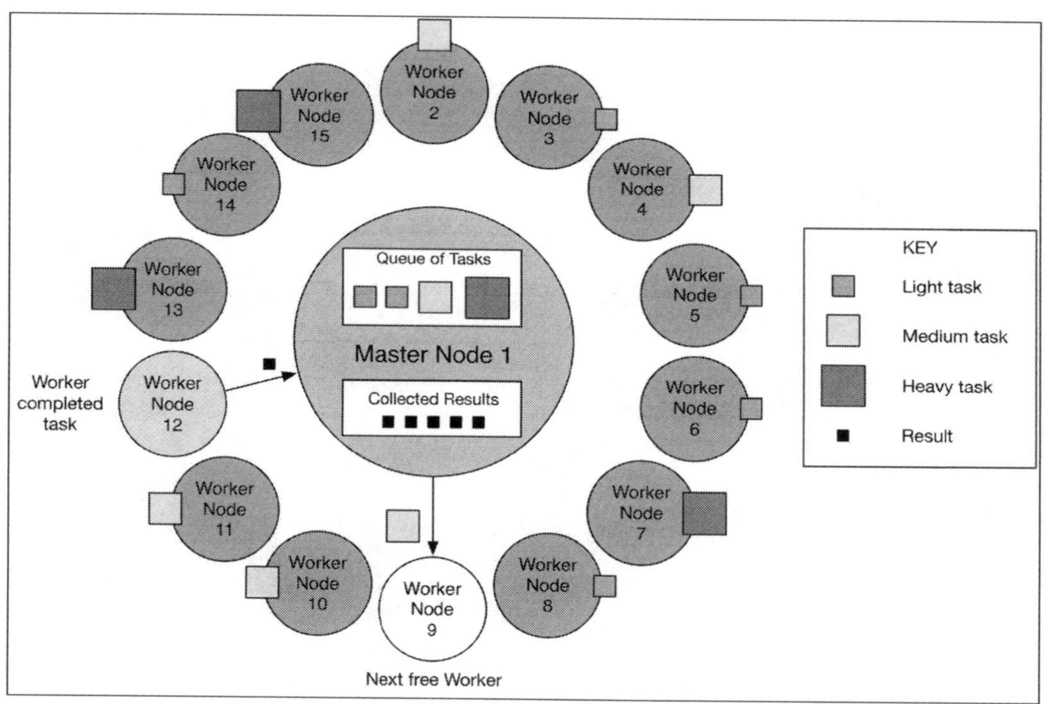

Figure 5: Task farm operating with mixed independent variable compute tasks.

In this case, it does not matter that each task varies as to the amount of compute it requires as there is no intertask dependency during the compute phase (at least).

Efficient grid processing

When the nature of the problem is such that the workers must cooperate during the execution of their tasks, then workload variance across the workers can lead to poor utilization, with some workers having to wait for the others to complete intermediate processing steps within their tasks.

Let's take image processing, specifically edge detection, as an example. We have a grid of 5x5 processors that each work on a separate subregion of a single large 10k x 10k pixel image, and each of the 25 processors handles a 2k x 2k pixel tile. The nature of the edge detection algorithm is such that its time complexity is a function of the number of edges present within the image. The parallel edge detection algorithm also requires periodic boundary exchange of derived data between each processing node's eight spatial neighbors. Let's consider that the types of images being processed have a nonuniform density of edges across their area, and in fact, the density can vary substantially across small subregions of the image. Take a look at the following example of a generated fractal image where edge complexity varies enormously across different zones within the image:

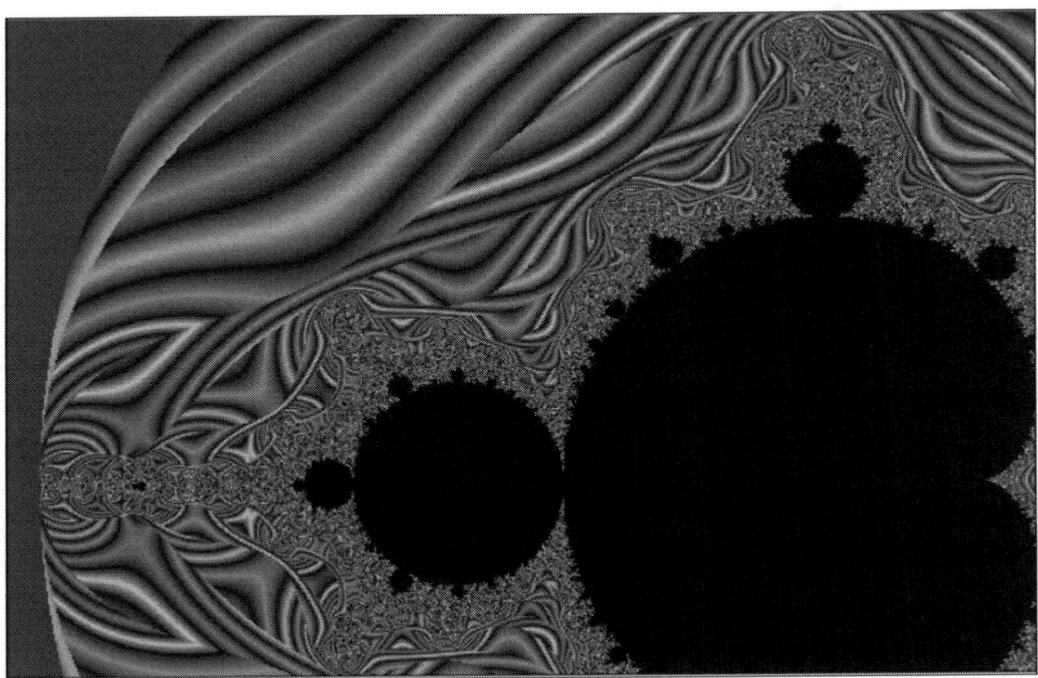

Figure 6: Fractal image exhibiting dense and sparse edge regions.

Let's also assume that the first phase of edge detection performs a pixel-by-pixel analysis, has the same time complexity regardless of tile edge density, and is able to estimate the number of edge transitions. From this, we can create a cost profile map of subsequent processing for the collection of individual tiles, as in the following diagram:

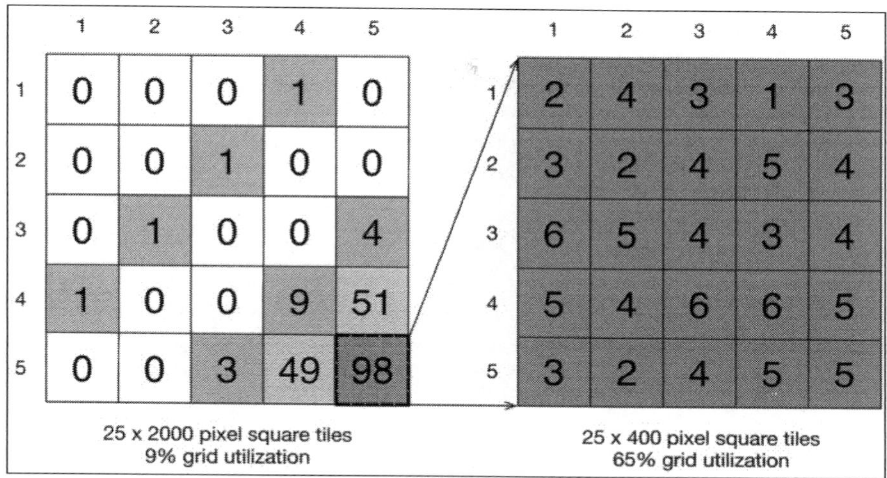

Figure 7: Example cost profile for edge processing of image tiles.

We can use the cost profile to determine the level of utilization that will be achieved across the processor grid and critically whether it is more optimal to take an individual tile (or tiles) and interject an additional task to process it using the entire grid, such that each processor would now handle a 400 x 400 pixel subtile before going on to complete the processing of the larger-scale image as full-sized 2k x 2k tiles.

In the example given in the preceding figure, the full image cost profile is shown (to the left) and expanded for the bottom corner tile (to the right). A separate processing of the dense corner tile (red) by the whole processor grid leads to a much better overall utilization and efficient use of parallelism.

Three steps to successful parallelization

The following three-step distilled guidance is intended to help you decide what form of parallelism might be best suited for your particular algorithm/problem and summarizes what you learned throughout this book. Necessarily, it applies a level of generalization, so approach these guidelines with due consideration:

1. Determine the type of parallelism that may best apply to your algorithm.

   Is the problem you are solving more computationally bound or data bound? If the former, your problem may be amenable to GPUs (refer to *Chapter 5, The Supercomputer in your Laptop*, on OpenCL). If the latter, then your problem may be more amenable to cluster-based computing (refer to *Chapter 1, Simple Parallelism with R*), and if your problem requires a complex processing chain, then consider using the Spark framework (described in the bonus chapter).

   Can you divide the problem data/space to achieve a balanced workload across all processes, or do you need to employ an adaptive load-balancing scheme—for example, a task farm-based approach?

   Does your problem/algorithm naturally divide spatially? If so, consider whether a Grid-based parallel approach can be used (refer to *Chapter 3, Advanced Message Passing*, on MPI).

   Perhaps your problem is on an epic scale? If so, maybe develop your message-passing-based code and run it on a supercomputer (refer to *Chapter 4, Developing SPRINT, an MPI-Based R Package for Supercomputers*).

   Is there an implied sequential dependency between tasks? Do processes need to cooperate and share data during their computation or can each separate divided task be executed entirely independently from one another?

   A large proportion of parallel algorithms will typically have a work distribution phase, a parallel computation phase, and a result aggregation phase. To reduce the overhead of the startup and close down phases, consider whether a Tree-based approach to work distribution and result aggregation may be appropriate in your case.

2. Ensure the basis of the compute in your algorithm has optimal implementation.

   Profile your code in serial to determine whether there are any bottlenecks, and target these for improvement.

   Is there an existing parallel implementation similar to your algorithm that you can use directly or adopt?

Review *CRAN Task View: High-Performance and Parallel Computing with R* at `https://cran.r-project.org/web/views/HighPerformanceComputing.html`; in particular, take a look at the subsection entitled *Parallel Computing: Applications*, a snapshot of which at the time of writing can be seen in the following figure:

Parallel computing: Applications

- The caret package by Kuhn can use various frameworks (MPI, NWS etc) to parallelized cross-validation and bootstrap characterizations of predictive models.
- The maanova package on Bioconductor by Wu can use snow and Rmpi for the analysis of micro-array experiments.
- The pvclust package by Suzuki and Shimodaira can use snow and Rmpi for hierarchical clustering via multiscale bootstraps.
- The tm package by Feinerer can use snow and Rmpi for parallelized text mining.
- The varSelRF package by Diaz-Uriarte can use snow and Rmpi for parallelized use of variable selection via random forests.
- The bcp package by Erdman and Emerson for the Bayesian analysis of change points can use foreach for parallelized operations.
- The multtest package by Pollard et al. on Bioconductor can use snow, Rmpi or rpvm for resampling-based testing of multiple hypothesis.
- The GAMBoost package by Binder for `glm` and `gam` model fitting via boosting using b-splines, the Geneland package by Estoup, Guillot and Santos for structure detection from multilocus genetic data, the Matching package by Sekhon for multivariate and propensity score matching, the STAR package by Pouzat for spike train analysis, the bnlearn package by Scutari for bayesian network structure learning, the latentnet package by Krivitsky and Handcock for latent position and cluster models, the lga package by Harrington for linear grouping analysis, the peperr package by Porzelius and Binder for parallised estimation of prediction error, the orloca package by Fernandez-Palacin and Munoz-Marquez for operations research locational analysis, the rgenoud package by Mebane and Sekhon for genetic optimization using derivatives the affyPara package by Schmidberger, Vicedo and Mansmann for parallel normalization of Affymetrix microarrays, and the puma package by Pearson et al. which propagates uncertainty into standard microarray analyses such as differential expression all can use snow for parallelized operations using either one of the MPI, PVM, NWS or socket protocols supported by snow.
- The bugsparallel package uses Rmpi for distributed computing of multiple MCMC chains using WinBUGS.
- The partDSA package uses nws for generating a piecewise constant estimation list of increasingly complex predictors based on an intensive and comprehensive search over the entire covariate space.
- The dclone package provides a global optimization approach and a variant of simulated annealing which exploits Bayesian MCMC tools to get MLE point estimates and standard errors using low level functions for implementing maximum likelihood estimating procedures for complex models using data cloning and Bayesian Markov chain Monte Carlo methods with support for JAGS, WinBUGS and OpenBUGS; parallel computing is supported via the snow package.
- The pmclust package utilizes unsupervised model-based clustering for high dimensional (ultra) large data. The package uses pbdMPI to perform a parallel version of the EM algorithm for finite mixture Gaussian models.
- The harvestr package provides helper functions for (reproducible) simulations.
- Nowadays, many packages can use the facilities offered by the **parallel** package. One example is pls, another is PGICA which can run ICA analysis in parallel on SGE or multicore platforms.

Figure 8: CRAN provides various parallelized packages you can use in your own program.

3. Test and evaluate the parallel efficiency of your implementation.

   Use the $P_{estimated}$ form of *Amdahl's law* presented earlier in this chapter to predict the level of scalability you can achieve.

   Test your algorithm at varying amounts of parallelism, particularly odd numbers that trigger edge-case behaviors. Don't forget to run with just a single process. Running with more processes than processors will trigger lurking deadlock/race conditions (this is most applicable to message-passing-based implementations).

   Where possible, to reduce overhead, ensure that your method of deployment/initialization places the data being consumed locally to each parallel process.

What does the future hold?

Obviously, this final section is at a considerable risk of "crystal ball gazing" and getting it wrong. However, there is a number of clear directions in which we can see how both hardware and software will develop that make it clear that parallel programming will play an ever more important and increasing role in our computational future. Besides, it has now become critical for us to be able to process vast amounts of information within a short window of time in order to ensure our own individual and collective safety. For example, we are experiencing an increased momentum toward significant climate change and extreme weather events and will, therefore, require increasingly accurate weather prediction to help us deal with this; this will only be possible with highly efficient parallel algorithms.

In order to gaze into the future, we need to look back at the past. The hardware technology available to parallel computing has evolved at a phenomenal pace through the years. The levels of performance that can be achieved today by single-chip designs are truly staggering in terms of recent history.

The history of HPC

For an excellent infographic review of the development of computing performance, I would urge you to visit the following web page:

`http://pages.experts-exchange.com/processing-power-compared/`

This beautifully illustrates how, for example, iPhone 4 released in 2010 has near-equivalent performance to the Cray 2 supercomputer from 1985 of around 1.5 gigaflops, and the Apple Watch released in 2015 has around twice the performance of iPhone 4 and Cray 2!

While chip manufacturers have managed to maintain the famous *Moore's law* that predicts transistor count doubling every two years, we are now at 14 nanometers (nm) in chip production, giving us around 100 complex processing cores in a single chip. In July 2015, IBM announced a prototype chip at 7 nm (1/10,000th the width of a human hair). Some scientists suggest that quantum tunneling effects will start to impact at 5 nm (which Intel expects to bring to market by 2020), although a number of research groups have shown individual transistor construction as small as 1 nm in the lab using materials such as graphene. What all of this suggests is that the placement of 1,000 independent high-performance computational cores, together with sufficient amounts of high-speed cache memory, inside a single chip package comparable to the size of today's chips could potentially be possible within the next 10 years.

NIVIDA and Intel are arguably at the forefront of dedicated HPC chip development with their respective offerings used in the world's fastest supercomputers, which can also be embedded in your desktop computer. NVIDIA produces Tesla, the K80 GPU-based accelerator available now that peaks at 1.87 teraflops double precision and 5.6 teraflops single precision utilizing 4,992 cores (dual processor) and 24 GB of on-board RAM. Intel produces Xeon Phi, the collective family brand name for its **Many Integrated Core** (**MIC**) architecture; Knights Landing, which is new, is expected to peak at 3 teraflops double precision and 6 teraflops single precision, utilizing 72 cores (single processor) and 16 GB of highly integrated on-chip fast memory when it is released, in 2016.

The successors to these chips, namely Volta by NVIDIA and Knights Hill by Intel, will be the foundation for the next generation of American $200-million-dollar supercomputers in 2018, delivering around 150 to 300 petaflops peak performance (around 150 million iPhone 4s) as compared to China's *TIANHE-2*, ranked as the fastest supercomputer in the world in 2015, with peak performance of around 50 Petaflops from 3.1 million cores.

At the other extreme, within the somewhat smaller and less expensive world of mobile devices, most currently use between two and four cores, though mixed multicore capability such as ARM's *big.LITTLE* octacore makes eight cores available. However, this is already on the increase with, for example, MediaTek's new MT6797, which has 10 main processing cores split into a pair and two groups of four cores with different clock speeds and power requirements to serve as the basis for next-generation mobile phones. Top-end mobile devices, therefore, exhibit a rich heterogeneous architecture with mixed power cores, separate sensor chips, GPUs, and **Digital Signal Processors** (**DSP**) to direct different aspects of workload to the most power-efficient component. Mobile phones increasingly act as the communication hubs and signal processing gateways for a plethora of additional devices, such as biometric wearables and the rapidly expanding number of ultra-low power **Internet of Things** (**IoT**) sensing devices, smartening all aspects of our local environment.

While we are a little bit away from running R itself natively on mobile devices, the time will come when we seek to harness the distributed computing power of all our mobile devices. In 2014 alone, around 1.25 billion smartphones were sold. That's a lot of crowd-sourced compute power and potentially far outstrips any dedicated supercomputer on the planet either existing or planned.

The software that enables us to utilize parallel systems, which as we noted are increasingly heterogeneous, continues to evolve. In this book, we examined how you can utilize OpenCL from R to gain access to both the GPU and CPU, making it possible to perform mixed computation across both components and exploiting the particular strengths of each for certain types of processing. Indeed, another related initiative, **Heterogeneous System Architecture** (**HSA**), that enables even lower-level access to the spectrum of processor capabilities may well gain traction over the coming years and help promote the uptake of OpenCL and its counterparts.

HSA Foundation

HSA Foundation was founded by a cross-industry group led by AMD, ARM, Imagination, MediaTek, Qualcomm, Samsung, and Texas Instruments. Its stated goal is to help support the creation of applications that seamlessly blend scalar processing on the CPU, parallel processing on the GPU, and optimized processing on the DSP via high bandwidth shared memory access, enabling greater application performance at low power consumption. To enable this, HSA Foundation is defining key interfaces for parallel computation utilizing CPUs, GPUs, DSPs, and other programmable and fixed-function devices, thus supporting a diverse set of high-level programming languages and creating the next generation in general-purpose computing. You can find the recently released version 1.0 of the HSA specification at the following link:

`http://www.hsafoundation.com/html/HSA_Library.htm`

Hybrid parallelism

As a final wrapping up, I thought I would show how you can overcome some of the inherent single-threaded nature of R even further and demonstrate a hybrid approach to parallelism that combines two of the different techniques we covered previously within a single R program. We also discussed how heterogeneous computing is potentially the way of the future.

This example refers back to the code we developed in *Chapter 5, The Supercomputer in your Laptop*, and will utilize MPI through `pbdMPI` together with `ROpenCL` to enable us to exploit both the CPU and GPU simultaneously. While this is a slightly contrived example and both devices compute the same `dist()` function, the intention is to show you just how far you can take things with R to get the most out of all your available compute resource.

Basically, all we need to do is to top and tail our implementation of the `dist()` function in OpenCL with the appropriate `pbdMPI` initialization and termination and run the script with `mpiexec` on two processes (for example, `mpiexec -np 2 Rscript chapter6_hybrid.R`). Take a look at the following code:

```
# Initialise both ROpenCL and pdbMPI
require(ROpenCL)
library(pbdMPI, quietly = TRUE)
init()
# Select device based on my MPI rank
r <- comm.rank()
if (r == 0) { # use gpu
 device <- 1
} else { # use cpu
 device <- 2
}
# Main body of OpenCL code from chapter 6
...
# Execute the OpenCL dist() function on my assigned device
comm.print(sprintf("%d executing on device %s", r,
getDeviceType(deviceID)), all.rank = TRUE)
res <- teval(openclDist(kernel))
comm.print(sprintf("%d done in %f secs",r,res$Duration), all.rank = TRUE)
finalize()
```

This is simple and very effective!

Summary

In this book, we covered many different aspects of parallelism, including R's built-in multicore capabilities with its `parallel` package, message passing using the MPI standard, and parallelism based on **General Purpose GPU (GPGPU)** with OpenCL. We also explored different framework approaches to parallelism from load balancing, through task farming to spatial processing with grid layout and more general purpose batch data processing in the cloud using Hadoop through the `segue` package as well as the hot new tech in cluster computing, Apache Spark, that is much better suited for real-time data processing at scale.

You should now have a broad coverage and understanding of these different approaches to parallelism, their particular suitability for different types of workload, how to deal with both balanced and unbalanced workloads to ensure maximum efficiency, and how to use the technologies that underpin them from R to exploit multiple cores on your PC/GPU using SPMD and SIMD vector processing.

We also looked into the Crystal Ball and saw the prospects for the combination of heterogeneous compute hardware that is here today and will expand in capability even further in the future both in our supercomputers and laptops but also our personal devices. Parallelism is the only way these systems can be utilized effectively.

As the volume of new, quantified, self- and environmentally-derived data increases, and the number of cores in our compute architectures continues to rise so does the importance of being able to write parallel programs to make use of it all; job security for parallel programmers looks good for many years to come!

Well, that's almost the last word. We hope this book has helped you begin a very fruitful journey on bringing parallelism to bear on your tackling of the most difficult problems in data science with R—go forth and distribute your computation!

Index

T

Made in the USA
Lexington, KY
26 October 2016